Exploring Historic Dean

Fourteen scenic walks in and around an ancient forest

John Sheraton and Rod Goodman

Exploring Historic Dean

Fourteen scenic walks
in and around an ancient forest

by

John Sheraton and Rod Goodman

Fineleaf Editions, 2009
www.fineleaf.co.uk

First edition © 2009 John Sheraton & Rod Goodman
ISBN 978 0 9557577 5 4

Design: Philip Gray
Text: Warnock Pro
Print: SS Media
FSC   Forest Stewardship Council certified paper

Published by Fineleaf Editions, 2009
Moss Cottage, Pontshill, Ross-on-Wye HR9 5TB
www.fineleaf.co.uk
books@fineleaf.co.uk

British Library Cataloguing in Publication Data
A catalogue record for this book is available from the British Library

Contents

Foreword

Tucked between the Rivers Severn and Wye, the Forest of Dean is undoubtedly one of Britain's most beautiful areas. It includes some of the most attractive woodland in the country, as well as providing superb views over the Welsh hills, Malverns, and Cotswolds. Such a landscape offers almost unlimited opportunities for walking. Today it is a peaceful place, so it may come as a surprise to learn that the area was once a busy industrial centre, with mines, quarries, ironworks, and others. However, if you know where to look, there is still plenty of evidence, not only of its industrial past, but also of a fascinating history going back several thousand years.

This book, which describes 14 walks covering the whole Forest area, will show you where some of the most interesting historic sites are to be found, and also gives you a taste of the varied landscapes which it offers. It includes descriptions of the sites and other places of interest, as well as details of the natural history and geology. It should therefore appeal to walkers and non-walkers alike, both locals and visitors, indeed anyone who would like to know more about the countryside they are exploring. An excellent way to find out more about the area you live in would be to join your local Ramblers Group. The Forest of Dean Group has a varied programme of walks throughout the year.

Floella Benjamin OBE DL, Ramblers President

Ramblers is a national organisation for all those interested in preserving public footpaths. It aims to protect rights of way, encourage walking, campaign for access to open country, and defend the beauty of the countryside. It has more than 400 local groups, of which the Forest of Dean Group is one.

For details of membership, please contact:
Ramblers
2nd floor, 87–89 Albert Embankment, London SE1 7TW
Phone: 020 7339 8500
www.ramblers.org.uk
ramblers@london.ramblers.org.uk

ramblers
at the heart of walking

Introduction

This book is intended as a follow-up to two earlier walk books published by the Forest of Dean Group of the Ramblers' Association in 1988 and 1993. The authors have participated in, and sometimes led, many walks with the Group over the years, and one of us has also spent many pleasant hours exploring the nooks and crannies of the Forest, searching for the locations of old mines and other historic sites. Hence, this book not only describes 14 new walks in this lovely area, but is designed to encourage people to look at the many natural and historic features which they pass on the walks. The area has a long and fascinating history, including some unique traditions. It has long been a working forest, and an important centre of coal and iron mining and stone quarrying. Indeed it played a significant part in the industrial revolution. Because much of the area is still forest and has not been built on or converted to other uses, evidence of many of the old industrial sites can still be seen. It is surprising what can be seen as you walk through the woods, although you do need to keep your eyes open. In these walks, we have tried to cover as many aspects of the history of Dean as possible, from prehistory to recent times, as well as taking in some beautiful areas of woodland, attractive villages, and spectacular viewpoints. The Forest is probably at its best in spring and autumn, but can be enjoyed at any time of year. We hope that visitors will be encouraged to come back and explore more of this beautiful area. Maybe local people will learn something new about the area they live in. However, we would be pleased if anyone can add any interesting information about the places we have described.

All the walks are located on the Ordnance Survey Explorer sheet OL14: Wye Valley & Forest of Dean (1:25 000 scale). We have included some basic information for each walk: a brief description of the terrain (including the number of stiles), highlights, parking, refreshment facilities (if any), public transport, and total distance. We have not attempted to 'grade' the walks or to indicate times, as these depend so much on individual ability. Most involve some climbs and descents, but should still be suitable for people of reasonable fitness. Some parts of Walks 5 and 7 include sections of relatively flat former railway lines, now used as cycle tracks, and these can generally be accessed by wheelchair users.

A few words of caution: much of the area is a working forest, so, although the details were correct at the time of writing, some things will inevitably change. Some forest tracks are gradually becoming overgrown, whereas others may be widened or new ones constructed, particularly when areas of woodland are being harvested (please obey warning signs). Note particularly that old mines and quarries are dangerous, so keep well clear of any old shafts or quarry faces, whether fenced or not, especially if you leave the designated walk routes. Never venture underground unless guided by an experienced mine explorer with local knowledge. Some parts of the forest can be muddy at any time of the year, notably during the famous 'non-summer' of 2008, so do wear appropriate footwear, preferably boots. Waterproof clothing is also advisable, and we recommend taking a compass and copy of the OL14 map. The number of stiles given is only approximate, as some can be by-passed by using an adjacent gate, and others may have been replaced by kissing gates.

We have tried to use footpaths which are reasonably clear and well-used, but a few may tend to become rather overgrown during the summer months. Any problems, such as blocked footpaths or broken stiles, on public rights of way (shown in green on the OL14 map) should be reported to the Public Rights of Way Team at the Gloucestershire County Council offices (see 'Useful Contacts'). Most of the walks can be reached by bus, although not necessarily to the starting point given. Information on local bus services is available from the bus companies (again, see 'Useful Contacts'). The nearest main-line railway stations are at Gloucester, Lydney, and Chepstow. Refreshment facilities should only be taken as a guide, so please check opening times first if you plan to use them on a walk. Unfortunately, quite a number of pubs have closed recently. Many of the points of interest mentioned are on private land, so please only view from a public place and do not trespass.

Acknowledgements

Most of the walks in this book are based, to some extent, on routes covered by various leaders on FoD Ramblers' Group outings, which we gratefully acknowledge. However, only one (Walk 14) is directly 'borrowed' from other leaders: thanks to Sheila and Fred Gray. We thank the following for their help, either with putting walks together or acting as 'guinea pigs' to check out the route descriptions and maps: Christine and Brian Bamber, John Bevan, Chris Bracey, Henry Burden, Rosemary Callow, Les Caton, Pete Ellis, Barbara and Alan Fisher, David Fisher, Sandy and Dougie Gentles, Fred Gray, Olive Jeanes, Paul McMahon, Phil Rawlings, Derek Sheppard, Jean Sheraton, Alec Waldie, Ronnie Walker, and Susan and Robin Warren. Martin Hillier kindly loaned some old postcards for scanning, and Peter Crow provided the LIDAR image of Welshbury Hillfort. Ian Pope allowed us to use some of his historic images, and John Norman allowed us to use photos from the Hallam Collection. Finally, we thank our wives, Jean and Marian, for their patience and support.

The Forest of Dean, situated between the Wye and the Severn, has long been a somewhat isolated, mysterious place. To an extent it still is, which only adds to its attraction. It is impossible to summarise the history (both natural and human) of this beautiful area adequately in only a few pages, so we will just try to provide a brief outline in order to put the walks into some sort of context.

Geology

The Forest of Dean may be a largely upland area, but the underlying rocks are in the form of a large basin or syncline. This consists of sandstones and mudstones of the Devonian Old Red Sandstone around the edge of the Forest, overlain by Carboniferous Limestone and Upper Carboniferous Coal Measures in the middle (*see section and map below*). The Carboniferous rocks have been economically important since Roman times, yielding iron ore, coal, and building stone, as well as limestone for burning. Much of the area to the west and north of the Forest consists of Lower Old Red Sandstone, although there are older (Silurian) sandstones, shales, and limestones around May Hill and Woolhope, and the Malvern Hills are made up of even older Precambrian igneous rocks (mainly granite and diorite). To the east, the wide floodplain of the River Severn is formed in Triassic mudstones belonging to the Mercia Mudstone Group (Keuper Marl). These are overlain by the clays and thin limestones of the Lower Jurassic Lias Group, which, in turn, is overlain by the Middle Jurassic Inferior and Great Oolite Groups, the cream-coloured limestones so characteristic of the Cotswold Hills. However, much of the Severn Vale is covered by deposits of sand, gravel and clay deposited during repeated glaciations over the last 2 million years of the Ice Age or Quaternary.

Apart from the Silurian rocks of the Longhope–May Hill area, the oldest rocks in Dean are the Raglan Mudstone and St Maughan's Groups and the Brownstones, all belonging to the Lower Old Red Sandstone (Upper Silurian and Lower Devonian), which form the rim of the basin. These are overlain by the Upper Devonian Quartz Conglomerate, which contains large numbers of pebbles, mainly quartz, and was widely used for making millstones, and the Tintern Sandstone Group. The Devonian rocks represent continental deposits laid down on a wide, arid coastal plain over which large rivers meandered. In early Carboniferous times, the sea spread over the whole area, and the Lower Limestone Shale was deposited relatively close to land. As the sea became deeper, purer limestones were formed: the Lower Dolomite and Crease

Quartz Conglomerate.

Forest of Dean Geology

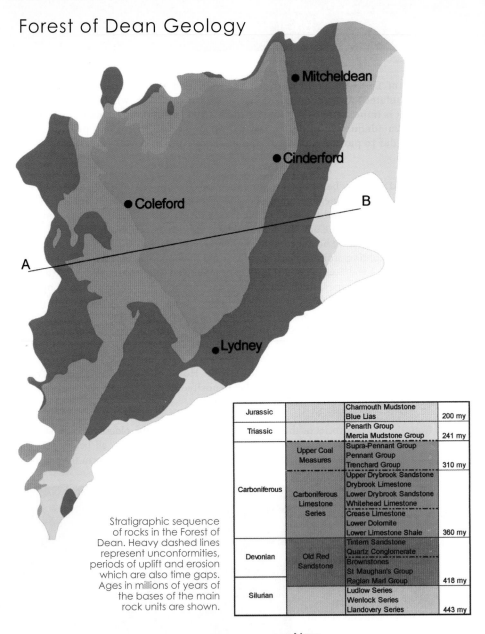

Stratigraphic sequence of rocks in the Forest of Dean. Heavy dashed lines represent unconformities, periods of uplift and erosion which are also time gaps. Ages in millions of years of the bases of the main rock units are shown.

Jurassic		Charmouth Mudstone Blue Lias	200 my
Triassic		Penarth Group Mercia Mudstone Group	241 my
Carboniferous	Upper Coal Measures	Supra-Pennant Group Pennant Group Trenchard Group	310 my
	Carboniferous Limestone Series	Upper Drybrook Sandstone Drybrook Limestone Lower Drybrook Sandstone Whitehead Limestone	
		Crease Limestone Lower Dolomite Lower Limestone Shale	360 my
Devonian	Old Red Sandstone	Tintern Sandstone Quartz Conglomerate	
		Brownstones St Maughan's Group Raglan Marl Group	418 my
Silurian		Ludlow Series Wenlock Series Llandovery Series	443 my

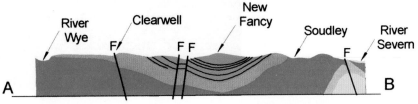

Limestone (which contains most of the iron ore), and, after an intervening period of uplift and erosion, the Whitehead Limestone. The sea then became shallower, and the sandstones and grits of the Drybrook Sandstone Group were deposited. A long period of uplift and erosion followed and a shallow nearshore–intertidal basin was formed, into which rivers discharged from higher ground to the north. Extensive swamp forests grew up, and rotting vegetation formed thick beds of peat, now compressed into coal seams. The Upper Carboniferous Coal Measures consist of the Trenchard and Pennant Groups (sandstones and minor mudstones), separated by the important Coleford High Delf Seam, and the Supra-Pennant Group (mainly mudstones, with some sandstones). There are around 15 workable coal seams. The end of the Carboniferous was another period of uplift and folding during the Variscan orogeny (an episode of mountain building caused by compression of the crust). The Forest of Dean basin was formed at this time. The Triassic Mercia Mudstone Group (mudstones, sandstones, and thin layers of gypsum and rock salt), which occurs in a down-faulted basin just to the east of the Forest (e.g., around Newnham), reflects a return to arid conditions. It probably represents wind-blown dust, deposited in shallow salt-lakes and sun-baked mudflats. However, the overlying shales, sandstones, and limestones of the Penarth Group (seen near Westbury) record the inundation of the Triassic desert by a shallow sea. Finally, the Jurassic Liassic shales and limestones, world-famous for their fossils, were formed under marine conditions. Something of the geology of the area is seen on most of the walks, but particularly *Walks 1, 3, and 10–13.* The formation of the Lower Wye Gorge is explained on *Walks 1 and 6.* The 'Geomap' at New Fancy picnic site is a large-scale stone geological map of Dean, which shows the relationships between the mining and quarrying industries and the underlying rocks. A visit is highly recommended.

This large stone geological map shows the main stone quarries, iron mines, and collieries, as well as coal seams (black) and railways (white).

Prehistory

Dean does not have anything like the number of known prehistoric sites of places like the Wiltshire Downs, but this is hardly surprising in view of the largely forested nature of

The Longstone near Staunton.

the area. Nevertheless, concentrations of Mesolithic (Middle Stone Age, c. 8000–4000 BC) flint tools in much of the more open country are probably the sites of hunters' camps. Many are on relatively high ground (e.g., near St Briavels and English Bicknor), but others (Taynton and Newent) are low-lying. Finds of Neolithic stone and flint axes and other tools have a generally similar distribution. This is thought to be a time when hunter-gatherer communities began to give way to farming settlements, although there is little direct evidence for this in Dean. One of the most important archaeological sites in Dean is King Arthur's Cave *(Walk 1)*, where a variety of Upper Palaeolithic to Neolithic flint implements, as well as coarse pottery of Neolithic type, have been recovered. During the Bronze Age (c.2000–7th century BC), concentrations of artefacts, including copper and bronze, suggest the sites of settlements, probably of circular thatched timber huts. A number of round barrows (burial mounds) are known, but only one (on Tidenham Chase) has been excavated *(Walk 14)*. Several large standing stones probably date from about this time, the best known being the Longstone, by the main road about ½ mile southeast of Staunton.

During the Iron Age which followed, iron-smelting techniques were introduced, so that the iron-ore deposits of Dean would have become a valuable resource. This was also the time when impressive hill forts were built. Three of these are seen on walks, Little Doward *(Walk 1)*, Welshbury *(Walk 10)*, and Soudley *(Walk 3)*, and there are others at Symonds Yat and Lydney Park. Their purpose is uncertain, but they may well have been tribal and/or religious centres, and could have been used for storage of produce and defence in time of war; some (Lydney Park, Symonds Yat) seem to have been used for iron working. Associated settlements are difficult to find, but the newly developed LIDAR aerial survey technique may help to discover any that do exist *(Walk 10)*. Excavations have yielded a variety of pottery, metalwork (brooches, weapons, etc.). A late Iron Age ('Celtic') warrior burial, found near Coleford in 1987, included an iron sword and shield boss, and three bronze rings.

History

British recorded history begins with the Romans, but most of the evidence for Roman activity in Dean is archaeological. Dean was probably the most important iron-mining centre in Britain between the mid-3rd and mid-4th centuries, and coal was also mined here, e.g., north of Coleford. There were major iron-smelting settlements at Ariconium, near Ross-on-Wye, and Monmouth (Blestium), and smaller ones elsewhere. A Roman road ran from Ariconium to the Severn, near Lydney *(Walk 2)*. A large temple complex dedicated to Nodens was built near Lydney, where it clearly post-dates iron workings, in the 4th century, and there is a temple to Sabrina at Dean Hall *(Walk 12)*. Unfortunately, neither is generally open to the public, but that at Lydney Park can be seen when the gardens are open for a limited season in the spring. Roman villas are more modest than those of the Cotswolds, many being involved with iron making. There are examples at Clearwell, St Briavels, Lydney Park, Boughspring and Chesters, near Woolaston, the last being close to a contemporary port. The most important early medieval earthwork is Offa's Dyke, built by King Offa of Mercia in the late 8th century as a boundary marker, which stretches for about 80 miles near the present English–Welsh border *(Walks 6 and 14)*. The circular churchyard at Hewelsfield suggests a Saxon origin *(Walk 14)*, and St Dubricius may have founded a church at Welsh Bicknor in the 5th or 6th century *(Walk 8)*. Some of the ridge and furrow field-strips still evident in places near the Severn may date from Saxon times.

Roman temple of Nodens in Lydney Park. Underneath are Roman iron mines.

Soon after the Norman conquest of 1066, stone castles were built at Chepstow and Monmouth, followed in the next few decades by those at Goodrich and St Briavels. There were other fortifications at English Bicknor, Littledean, Stowe, and Lydney Park. St Briavels Castle was the administrative and judicial centre of the Forest of Dean, which became a Royal hunting forest. It was the official residence of the Constable of St Briavels and Warden of the Forest, who looked after the King's interests *(Walk 6)*. For centuries it was used for sittings of the Verderers' and Miners' Courts; verderers are responsible for preserving the vert (trees) and venison of the Forest, and gavellers are responsible for leasing 'gales' (areas of ground) to 'Free Miners' to work for iron, coal, or stone, on behalf of the Crown *(Walks 5 and 7)*. The Cistercian Flaxley and Tintern Abbeys were both founded in the mid-12th century, and made fortunes from sheep farming. After the Dissolution of the Monasteries under Henry VIII in 1536–40, part of Flaxley became a (much modified) private house *(Walk 10)* and Tintern fell into ruin *(Walk 14)*. Many of the churches in villages outside the Forest boundaries (English Bicknor, Littledean, Mitcheldean, Newland, Ruardean, St Briavels, Staunton, etc.) were founded in, or soon after, Norman times, and are surrounded by a core of ancient (mostly late medieval) buildings *(Walks 6, 9, and 13)*.
A number of large 16th century houses, some originally manor houses, can be seen *(Walks 2 and 4)*, but the oldest and most interesting survival is Dean Hall (unfortunately not open to the public), which, although partly early 17th century, includes substantial remains of a Saxon or early Norman hall and later medieval additions *(Walk 12)*. Mansions built for the landed gentry or newly-rich industrialists, mainly in the

Dean Hall

The 17th century former New Inn is in the oldest part of the large village of Bream.

18th and 19th centuries, include Flaxley Abbey, Clearwell Castle, Bigsweir House, The Haie, Lydney Park, and Oaklands Park *(Walks 6, 9, 10, and 12)*.

Many villages and towns on the boundary of, or within, the Forest (Bream, Cinderford, Coleford, Drybrook, Lydbrook, Parkend, etc.) were little more than hamlets until after the expansion of the mining and related industries which began in the 17th century and peaked in the 19th and early 20th centuries (see below) *(Walks 7–9 and 11)*. The Civil War saw only a few skirmishes in Dean *(Walk 9)*, although, as a Royalist in a largely Parliamentarian area, Sir John Wintour, who owned timber and mineral rights to much of the Forest, was forced to flee to France. After the restoration he re-established control of much of the Forest, but due to his excessive tree clearance he was forced to relinquish his rights. The resultant Dean Forest (Reafforestation) Act of 1668 allowed the enclosure of 11 000 acres, divided into six Walks, each with a lodge and keeper. The first of these was King's Lodge or Speech House *(Walk 5)*. Further problems throughout the 18th century led to a new Enclosure Act in 1808, which allowed construction of 24 more lodges *(Walks 3, 7 and 13)*. The 17th to the early 20th centuries was the 'industrial period' when iron and later coal mining reached their peaks, only to fall into decline and virtual extinction (see below). Other heavy industries have also come and gone, but stone is still being quarried, and forestry is still of major importance. Today, tourism is a major industry, the Forest woodlands and Wye Valley AONB attracting visitors for a range of outdoor pursuits, such as walking, cycling, horse riding, and canoeing. The towns and villages now provide the services needed by visitors and locals alike. The Forest still has its unique customs and traditions. A few Free Miners still mine for coal or iron *(Walks 7 and 9)*, 'sheep badgers' allow their flocks to roam freely (pigs were also allowed to forage in the Forest, termed pannage), and wood can still be collected from the Hudnalls by residents of St Briavels, which includes one of the authors *(Walk 6)*.

Industry and Transport

The Forest of Dean has been an industrial centre for centuries, and the extractive industries (iron, coal, and stone) have been particularly important. Unsurprisingly, timber has also long been, and still is, a major product, for building, firewood, and, in particular, for naval ships until iron replaced wood. Related industries included charcoal production *(Walk 6)* and tanning, which used oak bark *(Walk 9)*. The area played a significant, if little-recognised, part in the Industrial Revolution. David and Robert Mushet's experimental work led to methods for producing high-quality iron and steel products *(Walks 7 and 9)*. An early 19th century tramroad here included one of longest tunnels in the world at that time *(Walk 3)*, and a very early attempt to build a major subaqueous tunnel (under the River Severn) was well advanced before being defeated by water ingress *(Walk 12)*. Several local families made their fortunes as coal owners, iron masters, or other industrialists during this period. One example is the Teague family of Ruardean, who rose from being humble miners to powerful businessmen (coal, iron, railways, etc.) in a single generation *(Walks 4, 7, 8, and 11)*. Another prominent industrialist was Edward Protheroe (died 1856), a West Indies merchant and Whig MP for Bristol, who acquired interests in many collieries, iron mines and ironworks, and became chairman of both the Severn and Wye Railway *(Walk 7)* and the Forest of Dean Railway *(Walk 3)*. The area was in some respects at the forefront of technology. For example, Trafalgar Colliery *(Walk 5)* was unique in Dean in being lit by gas, and electric pumps were installed underground in 1882, the first recorded use of electric power in a mine.

Iron mining dates back to Iron Age/Roman times. The earliest, near-surface, workings, known as 'scowles', closely follow the outcrop of the Crease Limestone, the main host to the iron-ore deposits *(see Walks 1, 3, and 9)*. The presence of iron ore at the surface would have attracted the first miners to the area. For many centuries iron was produced in small bloomery furnaces, the resultant impure iron bloom requiring hammering by a blacksmith before it could be used. Iron mining only really began to expand after the introduction of charcoal blast furnaces in the early 17th century, and, more particularly, with the development of coke blast furnaces at the end of the 18th century. The Dean Forest (Mines) Act of 1838 formally defined the rights of miners (of iron, coal, and stone), and the 1841 Awards of Mines and Quarries listed those persons entitled to work 'gales' (mining licence areas). The latter give an invaluable snapshot of the industries at that time. Iron mining peaked in the second half of the 19th century, but increasing difficulty of extraction and cheap imports of Spanish ore led to a rapid decline *(Walks 3 and 9–11)*.

Scowles near Bream.

Coal has been mined in Dean since Roman times, initially largely for heating and lime burning. The earliest workings were shallow pits close to where the seams reach the surface (outcrop workings). Areas of more-or-less circular depressions, known as 'delves', can still be seen (e.g., near Brierley), but are not easy to spot. Mines then became deeper, working the seams via tunnels (drifts or adits) and shafts *(Walks 2, 3, 5, 7, and 8)*. Demand only began to increase significantly after coke blast furnaces, and later steam railways, were introduced. Output peaked towards the middle of the 20th century, 1.35 million tons being produced in 1938, but output steadily declined until closure of the last deep mine (Northern United) on Christmas Eve 1965. Six major collieries (Arthur & Edward, Cannop, Eastern United,

Morses Level, near Mallards Pike, dates from about 1832.

Remains of New Bowson Colliery, near Cinderford.

Capped shaft at New Fancy Colliery, now a picnic area and site of the Geomap.

Lightmoor Colliery Engine House, one of the few to survive in Dean.

Norchard, Northern United, and Princess Royal) had survived to be taken over by the National Coal Board on 1 January 1947. The difficulties in working relatively thin seams, combined with the expense of pumping water from the workings (the Forest pits were notoriously wet, if relatively free of gas), were major factors in the decline of the coalfield, which was one of the first to virtually cease production in Britain. Some opencast mining took place during the 1970s *(Walk 5)*, but only a handful of 'Free Miners' now maintains the coal-mining tradition *(Walk 7)*. Three small mines, all working the Yorkley Seam, were still operating at the time of writing. There are more than 2500 known mine entrances (most now blocked) in Dean.

Stone quarrying has been carried out for many centuries, and there are said to be thousands of old quarries in Dean. In 1860 there were 360 working quarries in Parkend and Worcester Walks alone. Many quarries were small, typically 40 x 60 ft, and probably had only short working lives as a source of stone for local buildings or walls. Others worked limestone, which was burnt to produce lime for agricultural use. The remains of old lime kilns can be found near many of these *(Walks 1, 9, 10, and 14)*. There was a great demand for Forest stone in the 19th and early 20th centuries, and it was exported for use in Avonmouth Docks and Cardiff Castle, among many other places. Several major quarries have worked, or still work, the Carboniferous Limestone Series, mainly for aggregate *(Walks 3, 9, 10, and 14)*. Quartz conglomerate was once in demand for the manufacture of millstones, and was quarried along much of its outcrop *(Walks 6 and 13)*. Sandstone quarries in Coal Measures *(Walk 7)* and Old Red Sandstone rocks continue to produce building and decorative stone, with 15 small free-miner quarries still operating today.

Many other industries in Dean developed along the tributary streams of the Severn and Wye, where a ready supply of water power was available. Hence, there were once many water-powered corn mills, whereas windmills were rare. Early charcoal blast furnaces were also powered by water wheels, and the valleys of Lydbrook, the Lyd (Lydney), Redbrook, and Westbury Brook all had their furnaces and forges by the 17th century *(Walks 1, 8, 10, and 13)*. In contrast, later coke furnaces commonly used steam engines to provide the blast *(Walks 3, 7, and 9)*. Many of the valleys were associated with other metal industries, such as copper smelting at Redbrook, tinplate works at Lydbrook, Lydney, and Redbrook, and wire making at Tintern *(Walks 2, 8, 13, and 14)*. Other mills produced paper *(Walks 3 and 10)*. Many towns and even villages once had their own breweries *(Walks 10 and 13)*. There was a glassworks at Newnham in the 17th century

(Walk 12). Since World War Two a diverse range of light industries has replaced most of the extractive and 'heavy' industries of earlier centuries, although the decline of the latter caused considerable unemployment. Nevertheless, stoneworks *(Walk 7)*, brickworks, and sawmills still operate. Many of the works are now concentrated on industrial estates around the main towns of Coleford, Cinderford, Lydney and Mitcheldean. However, many people must commute to places like Gloucester, Bristol, and Cardiff.

The oldest 'highways' were the Rivers Severn and Wye, which were certainly used by Roman vessels and most likely by prehistoric peoples. Fishing has long been important, but the traditional fisheries are now virtually extinct, due to the dramatic decline in stocks of salmon and other fish *(Walk 4)*. There are records of a river trade on the Severn by the 13th century, the 'pills' (small inlets) at Newnham, Bullo, Gatcombe, Purton, and Lydney being used as ports. Many also had shipbuilding yards. Once the first tramroads were built in the early 19th century, most of the river traffic was concentrated on Bullo and Lydney, with the latter, which had the better facilities, surviving as a port into the 1970s *(Walks 4 and 12)*. Coal, pig iron, bark, timber, and stone were all important exports, with most trade being around the Bristol Channel and to Ireland. The Wye was once navigable up to Hereford and beyond, although goods had to be transferred between sea-going and river craft at places like Brockweir and Llandogo. These villages were once thriving ports, and many shallow-draught sailing vessels (including the famous trows) were built there until the mid-19th century *(Walks 6 and*

Abandoned millstones by the River Wye, south of Redbrook.

Parkend Ironworks engine house, now a field studies centre.

14). The canal-building mania of the 18th and early 19th centuries had little effect in Dean, only the short Piddock's Canal being built at Lydney *(Walk 4)*. However, the Gloucester and Sharpness Canal provided better access to Gloucester than the difficult voyage up the Severn *(Walk 4)*. Ancient roads or trackways have also been used since prehistoric times. One probable route

Unloading grain at Brockweir Wharf.
Brockweir Local History Group/Hallam Collection.

goes from the Severn, near Stroat, to Brockweir *(Walk 14)*. The Romans built their own network of roads, including one from the iron-working centre of Ariconium, near Ross, to the Severn near Lydney *(Walk 2)*. In medieval times, roads were little better than muddy tracks. Many of the old holloways (sunken tracks) are very old, although not easy to date. Part of the burial path near Newland is a typical example *(Walk 9)*. It was only with the coming of the turnpike trusts in the 18th and 19th centuries that things began to improve. A good example is the route between Monmouth and Chepstow, via Redbrook, St Briavels, and Tidenham Chase, first turnpiked in 1755. In part, it followed Duffield's Lane *(Walk 13)* and Coxbury and Wyegate Lane *(Walk 6)*. A much better route along the Wye Valley was opened in 1828 when Bigsweir Bridge, complete with toll house, was built *(Walk 6)*. Today we have a vastly

'Roman' road near Blackpool Bridge. The bridge in the background was built by the Forest of Dean Central Railway.

improved (and vastly busier!) road network, which includes the first Severn road bridge, itself now a listed historic monument.

Railways, in the form of horse-drawn tramroads, came early to the Forest of Dean, and indeed were instrumental in allowing the expansion of the mining and quarrying industries during the early 19th century. The first major tramroads (there were others), the Severn & Wye, Bullo Pill (later Forest of Dean), and Monmouth Railways, all provided outlets for the mineral and other products of Dean to wharves on the Severn or the Wye, although only the first two companies enjoyed much success *(Walks 2, 3, 5, 7, 9, 12, and 13)*. A tramroad, incidentally, differs from the railways we know today in that the wagon wheels were flangeless and ran on L-section iron rails or plates, usually mounted on stone blocks. All these lines were converted to standard-gauge (some initially to broad-gauge) lines in the mid-1800s, although some branch tramroads survived in use into the 20th century *(Walk 7)*. Two other standard-gauge railways, the Forest of Dean Central and Mitcheldean Road & Forest of Dean Junction Railways *(Walks 4 and 11)*, were built in the Forest at about this time, but neither was successful, and the latter was never operated throughout. Four lines were built near the periphery of the Forest in the same period (1850–80): the Wye Valley, Ross & Monmouth, Hereford, Ross & Gloucester, and South Wales Railways *(Walks 1, 4, 6, 12, and 13)*, all of which later became part of the Great Western Railway. Connections were made to the previously-mentioned lines from the Forest. Most of the lines had closed by the 1960s, only the former South Wales Railway surviving today as the busy main line between Gloucester and South Wales.

Natural History

The area covered by this book includes part of the Wye Valley AONB, the high ground of the Forest of Dean proper, together with the mainly limestone plateau to the south (St Briavels Common, Tidenham Chase, etc.), and the lower country of the Severn Vale. It includes a wide variety of landscape and vegetation types, including large areas of woodland and farmland (both arable and pasture), together with smaller areas of permanent grassland, heathland, field boundaries (hedges, ditches, and walls), and wetland (rivers, streams, bogs, ponds, and small lakes). Each of these has its own distinctive flora and fauna. The Forest itself covers 35 square miles. The introduction of commercial conifer plantations during the 20th century means there is now a mosaic of mature deciduous trees (especially oak and beech) and younger conifers (spruce, larch, Douglas fir, Scots pine, etc.), divided by forest roads and rides. There are also extensive woods along the Lower Wye Gorge, much being ancient semi-natural woodland, historically managed through coppicing and timber growing. They are dominated

Tunnel on tramroad branch from Point sandstone quarry under the trackbed of the standard-gauge railway which replaced it (the Coleford Branch of the Severn & Wye Railway).

Blackpool Brook in Wenchford picnic area.

by beech, oak, and ash, together with lime, yew, birch, chestnut, whitebeam, alder, and others. Shrubs include hazel, dogwood, spindle, hawthorn, privet, and holly. There is also a wide variety of ground plants, including rare species. Much of the forest floor is carpeted with flowers, notably snowdrops, bluebells, wild garlic, wood anemones, primroses, and, in some places, wild daffodils, in the spring; orchids may be found. Heavily shaded rock exposures, like old quarry faces, are habitats for ivy and shade-loving ferns. Dean has many veteran trees, unusually large examples of native or long-established species, which are important for wildlife and for their cultural and landscape value. They harbour a unique array of wildlife, including rare fungi, lichens, mosses, liverworts, and invertebrates, and provide habitats for woodpeckers, owls, and bats. Most of the walks include woods, but *Walks 1, 3, 6, and 13* include some particularly attractive sections, perhaps at their best in the spring and autumn. *Walk 3* passes through what must be some of the best bluebell woods in the country if you time it right. Local people have started a project in the Wye Valley to encourage the restoration of grassland as flower meadows *(Walk 14)*. Heathland habitats can be seen on *Walks 11 and 14*.

Mandarin ducks.

Cannop Ponds in winter.

If you are lucky you might see deer in the woods, particularly in the early morning or evening. There are currently about 300 in the Forest, mostly fallow deer, but including a few red deer and, increasingly, roe deer and muntjac. There is also a breeding population of boar, descended from dumped and escaped animals. Badgers are common, but rarely seen in daylight. The area is particularly important for bats, notably greater and lesser horseshoe bats, which hibernate in the many caves and old mines and railway tunnels. Otter and polecat numbers have been increasing in recent decades, and the dormouse population is of national significance. Many bird species have been recorded, far too many to list here. However, Dean is an important area for bird conservation, with the RSPB having a nature reserve at Nagshead *(Walk 7)*. Some of the more significant species from a conservation point of view include birds of farmland (grey partridge, linnet, tree sparrow, barn owl, and lapwing), deciduous woodland (hawfinch, nightingale, redstart, pied flycatcher, wood warbler, and lesser spotted woodpecker), coniferous woodland (firecrest, crossbill, and siskin), heathland and other open areas (nightjar, tree pipit, and woodlark), and rivers and streams (cormorant, goosander, kingfisher, sand martin, grey wagtail, and dipper). Birds of prey include kestrel, buzzard, sparrowhawk, and goshawk. Limestone cliffs along the Lower Wye are important breeding sites for peregrine and raven; the RSPB has a viewing post at Symonds Yat Rock. Waterbirds can be seen on the many ponds and lakes in the Forest, which are also important habitats for newts, frogs, and invertebrates, such as dragonflies *(Walks 3, 7, and 11)*. All three British snakes (adder, grass, and slow worm) and several species of lizard live in the area. More than 30 species of fish, including the rare allis and twaite shad (members of the herring family), have been recorded in the Wye, making it one of the most important river systems in northern Europe.

Walk Location Map

Little Doward, Symonds Yat, and the Wye Gorge

The Wye Gorge, Symonds Yat, superb woodland, an Iron Age hill fort, and King Arthur's Cave. A straightforward walk on good tracks and paths, with one steady descent and ascent; 2 stiles.

START at forest car park above King Arthur's Cave, Doward. This can be reached by turning off the A40 to Crocker's Ash and taking the road through Little Doward. About 1 mile from Crocker's Ash, where the road bends sharply left, turn right past Doward Park Campsite entrance (also signed Biblins Campsite). The parking area is 200 yds along on the right: GR SO 548156. **Refreshments:** none on walk route, but pub in Symonds Yat East (accessible via ferry).

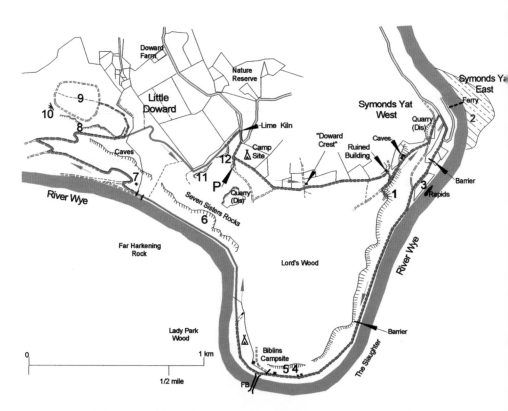

TURN LEFT OUT OF THE CAR PARK (back towards the road) for about 40 yds, then turn right onto a lane, which goes downhill at first and passes several houses.

Keep straight ahead at a track junction on the left near 'Doward Crest'. Continue along the dirt track, narrower in parts, ignoring a waymarked footpath to the right, after which the track bends left. Turn right at the next waymarked (yellow arrow) footpath, near a ruined stone building. The path bears right and descends for about 100 yds past old iron mines to a junction with a wider rocky track. Turn right here and then bear left, following a fence to a view of more iron-ore workings *(1)*. Retrace your steps back up to the path junction, keeping the fence on your right. Bear right here and follow the track downhill past caves on the left. Turn left at the next junction, where the Highmeadow Trail (yellow arrow) goes right. Fork right just past an old quarry, ignoring a yellow arrow to the left, and descend steeply to a tarmac road, where there are good views of the River Wye and Symonds Yat East, with its pub, hotel, and rock *(2)*.

Turn right down the road to a sharp left-hand bend, where you keep ahead onto a waymarked track, signed The Biblins. *Going left down the road here takes you to the ferry across to the Saracen's Head for refreshments, if required. Wave frantically towards the pub and, unless it is the off season or the river is in spate, someone should come to fetch you.* The track passes houses and a barrier, descending, with the river, former weir, and the site of a forge *(3)* on the left, and eventually becomes a footpath. It then widens again before entering Biblins Camp site (for youth groups). Just after the toilet block, on the right, are the 'Dropping Wells' (tufa deposits, *4*) and a mine entrance *(5)*. Continue through the camp site past Biblins Bridge, with good views of the river and Seven Sisters Rocks *(6)*. Follow the track and then a footpath to the far end of the camp site, continuing on a waymarked path (Wye Valley Walk and, initially, Highmeadow Trail) into the woods just above the river. Follow this path, passing old quarries on the right, for about ½ mile (ignoring the Highmeadow Trail path on the right) to an old metal gate. 100 yds ahead is a second gate and a ruined building. Go through a kissing gate here and follow an uphill track, signed 'Little Doward', to a junction, where you turn right. After about 100 yds, where the track bends sharp left,

there are some nicely restored limekilns *(7)* on the right. Keep on the track as it bends left and right, and then continue for about 400 yds to the next junction (with a wooden marker post), where you turn sharp right uphill. Follow this track round to the left, ignoring the first track on the right (after 60yds), but turning sharp right at the next junction after another 100 yds or so. The track climbs steadily, passing outcrops of thinly-bedded Lower Limestone Shale. Just after where it bends sharply left and then right, the top of the Lower Limestone Shale can be seen below massive Lower Dolomite. The track continues through magnificent woodland *(8)* to a rock cutting (in Crease Limestone), just after which is a stile on the right where the walk continues.

However, for an optional walk to Little Doward hill fort *(9)*, continue along the track to a junction immediately past the hill fort ramparts (more obvious on the right). You can then keep ahead (on an indistinct path) across the open hilltop to the far end of the fort, turning left on a path along the top of the upper rampart (with good views to Monmouth and beyond, *10*) to return to the track junction. Alternatively, turn right and follow the rampart all the way round to return to the junction. Retrace your steps from here to the stile, now on the left. Climb this, and a second (ladder) stile below, following the path which winds downhill through attractive woods into a small valley, with open fields on the left. At a junction, follow the path to the left, keeping a wire fence on your left. Continue uphill for a short distance to King Arthur's Cave *(11)*, ignoring a waymarked path (Highmeadow Trail again) to the right. After looking at the cave, continue alongside the fence, which bears left just below the cave, following an uphill path past more caves and a natural arch. Keep left near an old quarry *(12)*, going past the remains of quarry buildings to emerge at a tarmac road (with a ruined limekiln opposite). Turn right and right again past the camp site entrance and back to the car park.

Iron Mines (1)

Old workings represented by shafts, pits, and spoil heaps, as well as natural caves, can be seen near the top of the cliffs, in or near outcrops of Crease Limestone. They include a mixture of natural (cave) and artificial (mining) features, typical of 'scowles' *(see Walk 9)*. These mines seem to have been active before the 18th century, but are difficult to date. However, it has been suggested that, together with those at Wigpool, they provided ore for the important Roman iron-working settlement of Ariconium, about 7 miles to the northeast.

Symonds Yat and the Wye Tour (2)

A 17th century Sheriff of Herefordshire, Robert Symonds, gave his name to the 'Yat', a local name for gate or pass. Most of the far side of the river, south of Symonds Yat East, is in Gloucestershire, whereas the whole of this walk is in Herefordshire. The two parts of the village are connected by an ancient ferry operated by a ferryman who pulls the boat across the river using an overhead rope. The ferry can be used to visit the 16th century Saracen's Head Inn. There is a similar ferry by the Olde Ferrie Inn, about 500 yds upstream. The 16th century Old Court Hotel, near the A40 in Symonds Yat West, was the ancestral home of the Gwillim family. Colonel Thomas Gwillim fought with General Wolfe at the Battle of Quebec in 1759. Elizabeth Gwillim married John Graves Simcoe, who became the first Lieutenant Governor of Upper Canada in 1791. The Royal Lodge, just below the Saracen's Head, was originally built in 1876 as a Royal hunting lodge and was converted to a hotel in the 1920s. It stands near the site of Symonds Yat Station on the former Ross and Monmouth Railway. This opened on 3 August 1873 and remained independent until its absorption into the Great Western Railway on 1 January 1922. Closure to passenger services occurred on 5 January 1959, and to goods in January 1964. Part of the trackbed is now a walking and cycle path. Other popular activities in the area include canoeing and kayaking down the rapids and boat trips.

Ferry over the Wye near the Saracen's Head at Symonds Yat.

Symonds Yat Rock (on top of the hill, directly opposite) is a well-known scenic viewpoint towering about 500 ft above the Wye, with lovely views of the river's horseshoe bend, Goodrich, Ross-on-Wye, and beyond. From here, between April and August, it is possible to see peregrine falcons nesting on the limestone cliffs of Coldwell Rocks. Other birds of prey, such as goshawks and buzzards, may also be seen. Just south (right) of the rock is the Iron Age Symonds Yat Hill Fort, a triangular promontory fort of about 6 acres. The south side is protected by a series of five banks and ditches. The discovery of iron slag and early Roman pottery suggests that iron-smelting was carried out there.

Symonds Yat Rock was one of the many scenic attractions of the Wye Tour, popular amongst the gentry in the late 18th and 19th centuries. This originated in 1745, when Dr John Egerton started taking friends on boat trips down the river from the rectory at Ross-on-Wye. However, it was the Reverend William Gilpin who really popularised the Wye Tour when his "Observations on the River Wye", arguably the first tour guide to be published in Britain, appeared in 1782. Gilpin was the pioneer of the 'picturesque', who saw the landscape as "expressive of that peculiar beauty which is agreeable in a picture". Demand grew so much that by 1808 there were eight boats in use on the Wye. Many famous poets, writers, and artists took the tour, including Pope, Coleridge, Wordsworth, Thackeray, Turner, and Thomas Gray. As well as observing the natural beauties of the river, hills, gorges, and viewpoints (Yat Rock, the Kymin, Piercefield Cliffs, etc.), they would visit the castles of Wilton, Goodrich, and Chepstow, and the romantic ruins of Tintern Abbey.

New Weir Forge (3)

Most water-powered mills were on tributaries of the Wye (as at Lydbrook and Redbrook), because construction of weirs on the river itself was both expensive and hindered navigation. The only weir allowed to remain on the Wye below Hay under an Act of Parliament of 1695–6 was New Weir, and an efficient lock had to be maintained here. New Weir Forge (on the near bank) appears to have been built in 1684 by George White and Thomas Fletcher of Monmouth for the fining of pig iron. A leat supplied water to power a wheel. A lease was granted to John Partridge of Ross in 1753,

A rather imaginative sketch of the Forge at New Weir in about 1810, by J. Powell.

and the works were sold to George Griffin in 1798. The forge was advertised for lease in 1811–5, when it included two hammers, three fineries, and a rolling mill, but by then it was out of use and was soon abandoned. The slag was dumped in the river and now forms the island ('Cinder Island') in the centre of the rapids. Fragments of walls and an arch are all that remain of the forge buildings.

Dropping Wells (4)

The Dropping Wells are a series of tufa deposits formed where lime-rich water emerges from springs in the limestone cliffs. Tufa (a soft, porous type of limestone) is gradually deposited on moss, grass, leaves, and other vegetation, eventually forming quite thick masses, boulders of which lie below the cliff. The lime-loving moss, *Gymnostomum calcareum*, can be seen growing here. A well-known example of such a 'petrifying spring' is Mother Shipton's Cave at Knaresborough in Yorkshire, where, for centuries, people have placed various objects to be 'turned to stone'.

Dropping Wells Mine (5)

A single entrance leads to two horizontal adits, 5 ft high and 5–6 ft wide and 100 yds and 75 yds long. They appear to have been driven in an unsuccessful search for iron-ore deposits.

Seven Sisters Rocks (6)

Biblins Bridge is a good place to look at the geology of the Lower Wye Gorge. The steep sides of the gorge, including the prominent Seven Sisters Rocks, consist of Lower Dolomite, part of the Carboniferous Limestone Series. This is overlain by the Crease Limestone, host to the iron-ore deposits, as seen earlier in the walk. A short distance downstream, the river has cut down into the underlying Devonian rocks of the Old Red Sandstone (Tintern Sandstone Group, Quartz Conglomerate, and Brownstones), and the valley becomes less steep-sided. The Wye Gorge is unusual because the river meanders into and out of the more resistant Carboniferous rocks on the edge of the Forest of Dean, rather than following a course around them as might be expected. During Tertiary times, more than 20 million years ago, the Wye meandered through a gently-rolling landscape of Mesozoic (Jurassic–Cretaceous) rocks. Falling sea level, uplift of the land, or both then resulted in the removal by erosion of these younger rocks, and the original meander pattern of the river was preserved as it started to cut down into the more resistant rocks beneath. During the Ice Age, further down-cutting at times of low sea level resulted in formation of the present Wye Gorge.

Wye Gorge below Symonds Yat.

Across the bridge, on the slopes beyond the old railway trackbed, is Lady Park Wood National Nature Reserve. The reserve (not open to the public) is an example of unmanaged woodland, considered to be one of Britain's most important areas for woodland conservation. The main tree species here (and elsewhere along the valley) are beech, oak, ash, small- and large-leaved lime, wych elm, and birch. Other trees include maple, aspen, cherry, yew, whitebeam, alder, and sallow. The most abundant and widespread shrub is hazel, but dogwood, spindle, hawthorn, privet, and holly are also present. Ground plants are dominated by dog's mercury and bramble, but plants of interest include wood barley, fingered sedge, wild madder, bird's-nest orchid, toothwort, and lily-of-the-valley. There is a rich breeding bird community, which includes all three woodpecker species, redstart, wood warbler, tawny owl, pied flycatcher, tree creeper, blackcap, chiffchaff, and marsh tit.

There are several caves and old iron mines, one of which (The Stalactite Cave) was a show cave from 1880 to 1910, in the woods, and a variety of rare bats have been recorded, notably greater and lesser horseshoe bats. Animals include fallow deer, most likely to be seen in the early morning or at dusk, badgers, and foxes. Otters have been sighted on nearby stretches of the River Wye. Grass snakes and adders can occasionally be seen basking in the sunlit clearings. There is also a rich assemblage of invertebrates, including the uncommon wood white, pearl bordered fritillary, and white admiral butterflies. A short distance upstream on the opposite bank is an area known as The Slaughter, said to be the site of an ancient battle, although who was involved and when it took place are unclear. Nearby is a major resergence, where water from a large area of the limestone to the east emerges. Using dye tests, cavers have shown a connection with Slaughter Stream Cave, which can be entered through Wet Sink near Joyford, about 2 miles away. Here, they have discovered over 8 miles of passages, as well as the skeleton of an unfortunate dog which had become trapped.

There was a short-lived tramroad from Highmeadow Colliery about here in the late 19th century, and apparently another which brought iron ore from Staunton down the Whippington Brook valley to the river.

Lime Kilns (7)

Much of the valley side here has been quarried for limestone (the Lower Limestone Shale and Lower Dolomite of Lower Carboniferous age). The old quarries are now favourable habitats for ferns and other flora. These nicely restored stone limekilns were loaded from the top and the burnt lime raked out of the draw-holes at the base *(see Walk 9)*.

Woodland (8)

The Little Doward supports a wide range of woodland and habitat types. Historical management was as pasture woodland, first as common land and then partly as a deer park, when Richard Blakemore, a South Wales industrialist, built the mansion at Wyastone Leys in 1824. This resulted in the development of an open woodland structure on the

southern slopes, with the retention of many magnificent ancient trees (notably beech) which represent a continuity of habitat extending back through centuries. Parts of the woodland have been replanted with conifer blocks and non-native broadleaves, but much is ancient and semi-natural. Areas of calcareous grassland are associated with some of the limestone outcrops. Beech, oak, ash, and lime are prominent in the woodlands, together with field maple, whitebeam, and guelder rose. Secondary woodland of ash and silver birch has developed through regeneration over formerly cleared areas (e.g., near King Arthur's Cave). The positions of old stone walls and former carriage drives are now marked by lines of beech trees. Bluebells, primroses, and wood anemones carpet the ground in spring, and orchids may be found. Heavily shaded rock exposures, including some of the old quarry faces, have been colonised by ivy and shade-loving ferns, such as hart's tongue, common spleenwort, and, locally, maidenhair fern. Both greater and lesser horseshoe bats roost in limestone caves in the area.

Little Doward Hill Fort (9)

The Iron Age hill fort above Ganarew overlooks the Wye and consists of an oval enclosure of about 12 acres, surrounded by a double bank with a medial ditch. There is a rectangular annex on the southeastern side, defended by natural rock outcrops on three sides. The site includes possible round barrows and a 'well' (probably an iron-ore pit). The fort has recently been cleared by the Woodland Trust, revealing evidence for rabbit warrening, charcoal burning, iron-ore extraction, and the remnants of a 19th century designed landscape constructed after the area was converted into a deer park by the owner of Wyastone Leys. This included carriage drives, follies, and an iron look-out tower, some of which were built on the hill-fort ramparts. The hill fort is one of several candidates for 'Caer Guorthigirn' (City or Fortress of Vortigern). Vortigern seems to have been High King of Britain in the mid-5th century, and it was he who invited Saxon mercenaries under Hengist into Britain to help fight the invading Scots and Picts. His authority eventually waned, however, and power was assumed by Ambrosius Aurelianus, who pursued Vortigern into Wales. Legend has it that he died when a wooden castle on the old hill fort of Caer Guorthigirn was struck by lightning.

View of Monmouth (10)

The view from here takes in the River Wye flowing towards Monmouth, with the A40 trunk road on its right bank, and the trackbed of the Ross and Monmouth Railway on its left. Monmouth's Wye Bridge dates from 1617, but was widened in 1879. It is still the main link between the town and the Forest of Dean. Monmouth is an important market town, and one of the main shopping and trading centres in the area. More details are given in **Walk 13**. The large house with prominent chimneys across the fields on the left of the river is Hadnock Court, and the wooded hill beyond is the site of the Kymin *(see Walk 13)*.

King Arthur's Cave (11)

The cave is situated at the foot of a low cliff of Crease Limestone at the northwestern end of Lord's Wood. It consists of a broad entrance platform, a double interconnected entrance, and two main chambers. A skeleton, said to be of gigantic proportions and since lost, was discovered in 1695 and was thought by some to be the bones of King Arthur, hence the cave's name. There is a possible, if tenuous, connection with Arthur's predecessors, Vortigern and Ambrosius Aurelianus, at nearby Little Doward Hill Fort *(9)*. The cave was partly excavated in 1871 by the Revd W.S. Symonds, and by others in the 1920s. The remains of mammoth, hyena, woolly rhino, cave lion, cave and brown bear, wild ox, reindeer, Irish Elk, horse, hare, and lemming, a typical Late Pleistocene fauna, were found. Many of the bones had been gnawed by hyenas. A variety of flint implements, ranging from Upper Palaeolithic (Aurignacian) to Neolithic in age, as well as coarse pottery of Neolithic type, was also recovered. The cave was one of the richest and most clearly stratified sites in Britain, but unfortunately the haphazard nature of the early excavations resulted in much valuable information being lost forever.

The small cave openings and rock overhangs in the low cliff by the path up to the road have produced little of archaeological interest, other than a small scatter of medieval pottery. They are, however, of considerable geological interest. They show evidence for smoothing by water over a considerable period of time, and seem to be older than the formation of the Wye Gorge in late Tertiary times (*see 6 above*). The caves appear to follow the base of the gently-dipping Crease Limestone, rather than some essentially horizontal shoreline or river bank, consistent with them pre-dating the folding of the rocks. This point is significant, because the iron-ores of Dean are thought to have been deposited in such ancient cave systems in Permo–Triassic times *(see Walk 9)*.

Quarry (12)

Rocks of the Carboniferous Limestone Series (Lower Dolomite, Crease Limestone, and Whitehead Limestone) have been extensively quarried around the Doward. By the early 20th century, this area was essentially an industrial site. A large limestone crusher stood by the side of the track up to the road, and two nearby buildings, probably dating from the 1920–30s, housed the engine that powered the crushers before electricity was installed, together with a manager's office and workers' canteen. The crusher took limestone from the quarry just down the track, and also from Lord's Wood Quarry nearby. When quarrying ceased, the machinery was dismantled, but the foundations for the crusher still remain, together with the office building. There is also a thick bank of crushed lime on the west side of the track. Many of these old quarries are now nature reserves.

A Roman road, extensive views, old mill sites, and a working steam railway. Mostly on lanes and forest paths or tracks, this walk is initially uphill, but then levels out with good views to the Cotswolds; 7 stiles.

Limited parking is available at the beginning of a track off the B4234 road between Lydney and Parkend, just opposite the main entrance to the Dean Forest Railway (not the entrance to DFR car park): GR SO 630044. Please do not obstruct access to the house. If using the DFR car park, please check in their shop first to ensure you will be back before it is locked. **Refreshments:** Nag's Head pub, Yorkley Slade; Dean Forest Railway café (open on operating days); other pubs in Yorkley, Pillowell, and Whitecroft. **Bus:** 727 (Lydney–Parkend) to Norchard or Yorkley Slade.

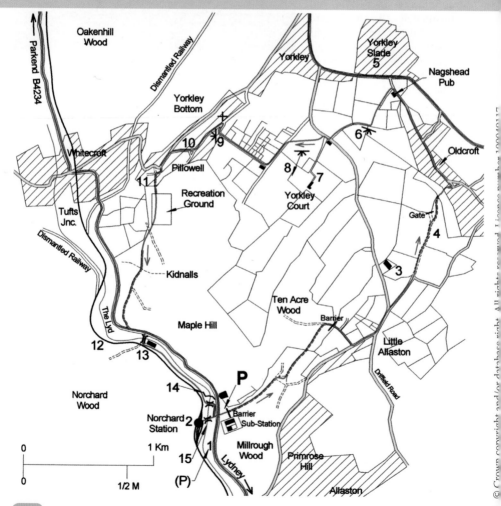

THE DEAN FOREST RAILWAY car park site was originally occupied by the waste tips of Norchard Colliery *(1)*, and, from 1923, by Lydney Power Station. The colliery was situated just across the River Lyd, on land which is now the headquarters of the Dean Forest Railway *(2)*. A visit to the latter, which has a cafeteria (open on operating days), shop and museum (both open most days), is a must, and combining this walk with a train ride to Lydney and/ or Parkend would make a good day out (but do check the train times first). The walk starts from the parking area (just across the main road from the DRF main entrance) by going past a barrier and along the track to the left of a substation. The track, which for a short distance narrows to a footpath, goes steadily uphill to the right of a stream. It then bears right at a junction for a few yards to emerge onto a small clearing. Bear left onto a wide gravel track and continue to a T-junction, where you turn right. Pass a wooden barrier, keeping ahead onto a tarmac lane at the first junction, but turning left at the T-junction onto the main road in Little Allaston.

Follow this road (which can be quite busy, so take care) around a left-hand bend and, after another 200 yds, fork right onto a tarmac lane. The large house across the field to the left is Soilwell *(3)*. Keep ahead where the lane turns sharp right, and then go through a gate onto a stony track. Note the kerbstones at intervals: this was once a Roman road *(4)*. At a fork, about 50 yds before the main track reaches a gate into a field, bear slightly right down a sunken path which descends between hedges. Backtrack if you miss this and reach the gate. At the end of this path, go through a kissing gate, over a small stream, and up the middle of the field beyond to a stile near some pylons. Turn right on a tarmac road, take the next sharp left and then bear left onto the road through Oldcroft. Pass Cut And Fry Road (!), the former Bethesda Chapel (1876), and the Nag's Head pub at Yorkley Slade *(5)*. Just past

the latter, turn left over a stile. Follow the hedge on your left to a stile, then continue in the same direction across the next field to another stile in the far fence. Do not cross this, but turn right and follow the fence and then a hedge to yet another stile. There are good views of the Severn Vale and Cotswolds from here *(6)*. Follow the left-hand side of the next field to a stile leading onto a road.

Turn right for a few yards, passing a driveway, and cross a stile on the left just beyond it. Bear right across the field. To the left is Yorkley Court *(7)*, and the Severn Road Bridges *(8)* can be seen on a clear day. Climb a stile a little way to the left of a house, and turn left to follow the tarmac road as it bends right after 200 yds and goes downhill. When you come to a T-junction, stop and admire the view of the Forest, with Bream and Whitecroft across to the left, and Sling, Ellwood, and Coalway on the skyline ahead *(9)*. Turn right down to another junction, and then sharp left just before the Primitive Methodist Church (1885). Follow the road through Pillowell *(10)*, noting the array of models in the garden of Glenoak just before the road bears right downhill. Continue down to a main road, turn left for 200 yds, and then left again into Corner Road where the main road bends right. After 150 yds, opposite Underwood Cottage, turn left onto a gravel track. Near this point, but hidden on private land, is Pillowell Level *(11)*.

The track leads past a barrier onto playing fields, with a seat which would make a pleasant picnic spot. Keep right of the playing fields to enter the woods in the far right-hand corner. Bear right on a footpath leading downhill and after 50 yards cross a muddy forest track. The footpath (which may be indistinct) bears left just inside the woodland and soon becomes a broader track, which then bears slightly left away from the fence-line. Keep right on reaching a gravel track at a sharp bend, and follow this down to a main road. Cross with care, turn left and walk along the verge for about 60 yds to a footpath (which may be rather overgrown in summer) on your right. Cross a bridge over the River Lyd and turn left down some steps just before reaching a metal gate beside the railway line, part of the former Severn and Wye Railway *(12)*. The ruined buildings were part of Upper Forge *(13)*. The path follows the railway line for a while and passes a large stone 'abutment' of unknown purpose before bending left to recross the river near the site of New Mills *(14)*. Follow the gravel drive past a house to the DFR entrance gate. Norchard Drain *(15)*, which empties into the Lyd, can be seen on the left as you enter the DFR facilities. The parking area is just across the main road from here.

Norchard Colliery (1)

Coal has been worked in this area since at least 1282, and a level existed in 1810, when it formed part of an ironworks complex leased by the Pidocks. By 1842 coal was probably being worked through the nearby Norchard Pit. The colliery was unique in Dean as it was situated under the Lydney Park Estate, rather than Crown land. It worked coal seams in the Pennant and Trenchard Groups, the Trenchard Seam averaging 4 ft 6 in. thick. Sidings connected to the Severn and Wye Railway were constructed in 1873 and 1879, and a loop and screens were added in 1906. The West Gloucestershire Power Company built a power station alongside the colliery in 1923, coal being supplied direct by overhead conveyer belt. The Park Colliery Co., formed in 1912, owned several other gales, including Pillowell United, and coal from the latter area was being worked through Norchard by 1924. However, pump failures in this area led to water bursting into Princess Royal Colliery in 1925, and in 1930, after a lengthy legal battle, a controlling interest was obtained in Norchard by the Princess Royal Co. By 1936 most coal production was concentrated in the Pillowell section, and a new slanting heading (New Norchard) was therefore opened to the surface at Pillowell the following year. New sidings and screens were built there and coal taken to Norchard via the S&WR's mineral loop. At its peak the colliery produced 1800–2000 tons of coal per week, but up to 38 tons of water had to be pumped for each ton of coal won. By 1957 the workings east of Norchard had reached thin coals and the decision was taken to close the pit. The power station closed in 1968, but there is still a substation on the site.

GWR 0-6-0PT leaving Lydney Junction Station.

Dean Forest Railway (2)

The Dean Forest Railway Society, which acts as a support organisation for the railway, was formed in 1970 to preserve the former Severn and Wye Railway's Lydney to Parkend line *(see 12)*. Operations at that time were centred on Parkend as British Rail had not set a date for closure. The first steam open day took place in October 1971, with Peckett locomotive *Uskmouth* hauling brake van rides over 200 feet of siding, earning the Society the reputation of running the "World's Shortest Passenger Railway!" Restricted space at Parkend led to the acquisition in

1974 of the former Norchard Colliery site, together with land vacated by West Gloucestershire Power Station. The first open day at Norchard was staged in 1978, when there were 150 yds of running line. British Rail finally announced closure of the line to traffic in the early 1980s and this decision enabled DFR to complete the purchase of most of the track and land in 1985. It later bought part of the redundant Lydney Junction site, situated adjacent to the station on the main Gloucester–South Wales line. Train services finally crossed the A48 road in 1991 to terminate at St. Mary's Halt (then known as Lydney Lakeside). Lydney Junction Station was opened to DFR trains in 1995, Lydney Town Station in 2001, and in 2006 Parkend Station was re-opened to the first regular passenger trains since 1929; the DFR had returned to its birthplace. Today it is possible to sample travel behind genuine Great Western Railway tank locomotives, as well as industrial, visiting, and diesel locomotives.

Soilwell (3)

Soilwell Farmhouse (or Manor) dates from 1661. It has two storeys, a basement, and an attic, and there are 3 brick chimney stacks. Although much modified, Soilwell is one of the most historic buildings in the parish. Nearby Driffield Farm, near Little Allaston, is another 17th-century farmhouse, which was altered in the 19th century.

Roman Road (4)

The route here follows the line of an important Roman road (known locally as the "Dean Road") between Ariconium and the Severn at Lydney. Ariconium, east of Ross, was an important Roman iron-working centre from about 50 AD, when it was taken over, until the early third century. Indeed, by the second century, the Dean area was possibly the most important iron-producing region in Britain. Considerable remains of kerbstones and paving survive on this stretch of road near Soilwell. Another exposed length can be seen by Blackpool Bridge, near the Wenchford Picnic Area on the Blakeney–Parkend Road, although the actual surface here is probably medieval.

Yorkley (5)

Yorkley is a large Forest village, which comprises Yorkley Slade, Yorkley proper, and Yorkley Bottom, the latter down the hill towards Pillowell. The Nag's Head dates from the late 18th century, but was extended in the mid-19th. Cut and Fry Green, incidentally, is the name given to the old sports field, now a cricket pitch. The name may have originated because the wind was said to cut across the green in winter, whilst the sun fried you in summer. Another suggestion is that in a nearby inn called The Loyal Forester they used to cut and fry bacon for the miners. In nearby Cockshoot Wood is Danby Lodge, one of the original six Forest lodges authorised by the Dean Forest (Reafforestation) Act of 1668, which allowed the enclosure of 11 000 acres of woodland, divided into six walks. The lodges were built to house the keepers who would protect each of these walks. The Gloucestershire poet F. W (Will) Harvey (1888–1957) was living in Yorkley at the time of his death, and a lane near the Bailey Inn is named after him. Born in Hartpury, he served in France during the First World War, and many of his early poems were written in German prisoner-of-war camps after he was captured. His *In Pillowell Woods* was published in 1926.

View of Severn Vale and Cotswolds (6)

The view takes in the River Severn, with the Vale of Berkeley and Cotswold Escarpment beyond. Prominent just across the river are the warehouses of Sharpness Docks, at the entrance to the Gloucester and Sharpness Canal, and a short way downstream (to the right) the large angular buildings of the now-closed Berkeley Nuclear Power Station *(Walk 4)*. Between these two is the town of Berkeley, famous for its medieval castle and birthplace of Edward Jenner, the originator of vaccination. To the left of Sharpness is Slimbridge (note the church spire), home of the Wildfowl & Wetlands Trust. On the hill (Knibley Knoll) directly beyond Sharpness Docks is the 111ft-high Tyndale Monument, erected in 1866 to commemorate William Tyndale (c. 1494–1536), who translated the Bible into the English of his day. Below the escarpment just to the north (left) of the monument are the towns of Dursley and Cam, with Stonehouse and Stroud a few miles further north.

Yorkley Court (7)

Yorkley Court dates from the late 17th and early 18th centuries. The older section is partly domestic and partly agricultural, with a raised doorway which may have been for a granary. It is now a farmhouse.

Severn Road Bridge (8)

The first Severn Bridge was built in 1961–6 by Freeman Fox and Partners in association with Mott, Hay & Anderson to carry the new M4 (now M48) motorway; the consulting architect was Sir Percy Thomas. It replaced a ferry service from Aust Cliff to Beachley Peninsula, and was opened by HM the Queen on the 8th September 1966. The bridge has steel cables, deck, and towers, with concrete substructures and foundations (cable anchorages and piers for the towers), and was the first bridge in the world to use the revolutionary concept of a streamlined deck and inclined hangers. The suspension bridge spans are 1000ft, 3240ft, and 1000ft, making it by far the longest span in England when it was built. The bridge was strengthened and refurbished in 1985–91 and has been repainted white to reduce thermal stress. It is currently (2008) again undergoing repairs. The crossing from England to Wales actually comprises five bridges: Aust Viaduct (514ft long; three spans consisting of two steel box girders with a concrete deck slab), Severn Bridge, Beachley Viaduct (2024 ft long; 10 spans; streamlined all-welded steel deck supported on concrete piers), Wye Bridge (1340 ft cable-stayed bridge; steel deck, pylons, and cables; concrete piers and foundations; two pylons in central reservation with two (originally one) cables on each side of each pylon), and Chepstow Viaduct (420 ft; two spans). For comparison, the second Severn Crossing (built 1992–6) is 3.19 miles long, with a central suspension span of 1496 ft. One of the original ferries, the *Severn Princess*, has been recovered from Ireland and is being restored.

View of Bream, etc. (9)

The view encompasses Bream, up the hill to the left, with Whitecroft in the valley below; Sling and Ellwood can be seen ahead on the skyline, beyond the woods of Parkend Walk, with Coalway a little to the right, beyond Nagshead Plantation *(Walk 7)*. Bream is said to be the largest village in Gloucestershire, and possibly even in England, with an estimated population of 3060 in 2006. The oldest part of the village is near the junction between the High Street and the Lydney to Coleford road. The former New Inn here has a 1637 date, and nearby Bream Court Farmhouse is also early 17th century. However, St James Church is relatively modern, dating from 1823, although it was rebuilt to a design by William White in 1860–1. The main areas of employment were iron and coal mining, farming, and forestry, but closure of the mines has meant that most people need to commute to work. However, the engine house of Flour Mill Colliery (closed 1928) is still used for repair and restoration of steam locomotives. Unlike many smaller villages, Bream is large enough to support a good range of shops and other services, including two pubs. It has a Male Voice Choir, a Silver Band, and several sports teams.

Whitecroft was the location of Princess Royal Colliery, one of six deep mines taken over by the National Coal Board on 1 January 1947. The Princess Royal Colliery Co. Ltd was formed in 1891 to work both Princess Royal (Park Gutter) and Flour Mill, although raising of coal did not begin until 1897. Under the Forest of Dean (Mines) Act of 1904 several gales were amalgamated to be worked by the company. In 1914–15 the Park Gutter shaft was deepened to allow working of the Coleford High Delf Seam (reached at 617 ft). An underground connection was made to Flour Mill in 1916, although coal continued to be wound there until 1928. In 1925 water from Norchard burst into Princess Royal and in 1930, after a lengthy legal battle, a controlling interest was obtained in that colliery. In 1938 the steam winding engine was replaced by an electric one, and the electric pumps were removing about 2700 gallons water per minute. Annual output of coal in the 1930s was around 300000 tons, with a peak employment of 1300 men. Underground developments in the 1950s were not successful, and the colliery closed on 30 March 1962. The brick colliery buildings, including the baths, can be seen from here. Their future is uncertain, but it is hoped that they will be

Princess Royal Colliery baths.

preserved. The S&WR opened a mineral loop line from Tufts Junction, near Whitecroft, to Drybrook Road in 1872 *(see 12 below)*, and there was also a short branch to Princess Royal. Sling was an important centre for iron mining, but this rapidly declined after the late 19th century. Sling Pit, near the Miners Arms, was one of the last to operate, until the 1920s. However, the British Colour & Mining Co. was formed in 1927 to extract ochre from mines in the nearby Clearwell–Milkwall area, and survived until about 1975. Ellwood Lodge is one of the many Forest lodges used by keepers to control the woods. It was built in several stages, from the late 16th to the 19th century, although most dates from the 17th century.

Pillowell (10)

Settlement at Pillowell began before 1742, most dwellings being at the lower end, near the well which gave the village its name. However, the village only began to expand significantly in the mid-19th century as coal miners located themselves as near to the pits as possible. Most houses were built between then and the early 20th century. Quarrying and forestry also provided employment, but collieries were by far the most important. Norchard *(see 1 above)* was a major employer, but, until the New Norchard heading was opened in 1937, involved a walk of 2 miles from Pillowell to the shaft and another 2 miles to the face below Yorkley! Like much of the Forest, the area was badly hit when the last mines closed down. Now there is only one pub, the Swan.

Pillowell Level (11)

Pillowell Level was in existence by 1832, and was being worked by James and Robert Morrell in 1841. It exploited coal seams in the Pennant Group, including the Yorkley, Whittington and Coleford High Delf, the latter being worked by means of cross levels. It also acted as a drainage adit and access point for collieries in nearby gales. A tramroad connection with the Severn and Wye Railway was built in 1856, replaced by a broad-gauge line in 1869, and the colliery was served by sidings when the standard-gauge S&WR mineral loop opened in 1872. The remains of a viaduct on the latter can still be seen in the valley down towards Whitecroft. In June 1898 the colliery and its equipment was put up for auction, and it was in the hands of the Wallsend Colliery Co. by 1907. In 1937 Norchard Colliery *(see 1 above)* opened a new slanting heading to the surface at Pillowell, and this closed in 1957. The playing fields were constructed on the site of the waste tip.

Severn and Wye Railway (12)

The Severn and Wye Railway and Canal Co. opened a 3 ft 6 in. gauge horse tramroad from Lydney to Lydbrook via Serridge Junction in 1810. The main line, together with a number of branches, was built to serve collieries and stone quarries in the area. The southern part of the main tramroad was converted to broad gauge in 1869, and steam locomotives were introduced. A mineral loop line from Tufts Junction, near Whitecroft, to Drybrook Road *(see Walk 5)* was opened in 1872. The broad-gauge lines were soon converted to standard gauge, and the first passenger train ran from Lydney to Lydbrook on 23 September 1875; a branch from Parkend to Coleford opened to passengers soon after. An extension to Cinderford opened in 1900. Regular passenger services north of Lydney ceased on 6 July 1929, but the service from Berkeley Road to Lydney Town was only terminated in 1960 by the collapse of the Severn Bridge. Goods services lasted longer: stone from Whitecliff Quarry was transported over the Coleford Branch until 1967, and the final Parkend to Lydney section closed in 1976. *(For more details of the S&WR see Walk 7)*

Ruins of Upper Forge, beside the former S&WR's main line.

Upper Forge (13)

Middle and Upper Forges were built in the early 1600s by Sir Edward Wynter to make and work iron. By 1640 Upper Forge was in use as a slitting mill, making flat bars for use in sail making, but by 1673 it was being use as a forge again. The works was sold to Benjamin Bathurst in 1719, and the family then leased it to various people: by 1800 it was held by the Pidcocks, who had built a 1.5 mile canal from Middle Forge (between Norchard and Lydney) to Lydney Pill on the River Severn in about 1779. John James took over the lease in 1814 and sidings off the S&WR's tramroad were laid. In 1866, about 1000 boxes of tinplate were being produced each week. The lease was transferred to R. Thomas & Co. in 1875, but the works was dismantled in 1890.

New Mills (14)

New Mills was built in 1824 to produce flat sheet for tinplate manufacture. It was part of the complex which also included Upper, Middle, and Lower Forges, and a tramroad connection was retained even after the S&WR's main line had been converted to standard gauge. New Mills was dismantled in 1891.

Norchard Drain (15)

This drains around 5000 gallons of water per minute from the old colliery workings between Norchard and Pillowell.

Coal and iron mine remains, geology, attractive woodland (particularly in the bluebell season), and a heritage museum. The walk is mostly on forest tracks and old railway trackbeds, with two fairly gentle ascents, but steeper descents; 1 stile.

START at the Dean Heritage Centre car park at Lower Soudley on the Blakeney to Cinderford Road (small charge for those not visiting the museum or café): GR SO 664106. **Refreshments:** Café at Dean Heritage Centre; White Horse pub, Soudley. **Bus:** 717 (Lydney–Cinderford) to Soudley.

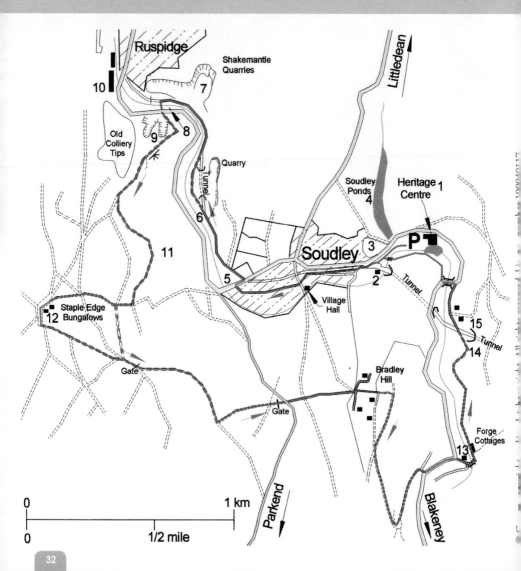

THE DEAN HERITAGE CENTRE is housed in the former Camp Mill (1) and is well worth a visit. Leave the far end of the parking area, near the childrens' playground and woodworking area, over the plank bridge, and bear right to climb steps leading to a footpath. Turn left and then bear right after about 100 yds, noting the small stone bridge over the stream and the railway embankment on your left. Continue to a tarmac lane, with the Bradley Hill Tunnel and crossing keeper's cottage of the former Great Western Railway's Forest of Dean Branch (2) on the left. Soudley Camp (an ancient earthwork, 3) and Soudley Ponds (4) are a short distance to the right along the main road. Turn left along the lane, but soon bear right on the second (less overgrown) of two grass tracks, which soon rejoins the lane near some houses. The lane becomes a footpath (with the site of Upper Soudley Halt on the right), then a lane again, bearing left downhill. Continue ahead at the crossroads, eventually curving right to a T-junction at the main road. Turn right here, then go left after 30 yds onto a track past a barrier.

This is the old railway trackbed, which is now part of the Soudley Valley Geology Trail (5). After some 500 yds (just before Blue Rock Tunnel, with Blue Rock Quarry up steps on the right), down on the left is a sculpture (The Hod Boy, 6), which commemorates the use of child labour in the collieries; there is also a memorial to the sheep culled in the foot-and-mouth epidemic of 2001. Continue past the far (northern) end of the tunnel (on your right), and keep left at a fork. The right-hand track was originally a short railway branch into Shakemantle Iron Mine and Limestone Quarry (7); note the remains of sleepers and the stone bridge over the stream. About 60 yds before a metal barrier and footbridge, turn left up a steep, narrow path onto a road. In the undergrowth below the road about 100 yds to the left is the covered-in shaft of Perseverance Iron Mine (8).

Cross the road with care, and bear left up the track opposite, past a metal barrier. This track gradually bends right uphill, with old sandstone quarries (9) on the right and views of Shakemantle Quarry on the left. After a while, where the track goes under power lines, views of the Soudley Valley and part of the Geology Trail, with the Cotswolds in the distance, can be seen on the left. The track now bends left past the old waste tips of Eastern United Colliery (10) on the right. Just after the track bends right, take the first of two grassy tracks on the left. After about 300 yds (as the track starts to bend right), look out for a stone chimney some 60 yds away in the woods on the left. This is a ventilation chimney for Findall Iron Mine (11). It is worth a short detour to look at the old iron workings or 'scowles' beneath the chimney, which can best be viewed by following the fence a few yards downhill to the left, before retracing your steps to the main track. Continue for another 300 yds to a cross track, and turn right. After 100 yds another cross track, at a marker post, is reached. *The walk may be shortened at this point by turning left, then left again after 250 yds.* Otherwise, continue ahead uphill, soon entering pine forest, over a forest road, and past an open area on the left to emerge onto a gravel road near some buildings (Staple Edge Lodge, 12), here keeping left. Continue bearing left, ignoring stiles on the right, to reach a straight length of the forest road. *After about 400 yds the short cut comes in from the left.* Keep generally ahead through a gate (with a stile on its right) across the road, and immediately bear left onto a grass track. This eventually curves right downhill (more views of the Cotswolds), turns sharp left following a fence, and continues to a gate (and adjacent stile) just before a tarmac road.

Cross the road and follow the lane opposite, signposted Bradley Hill. The woods here have a stunning display of bluebells in the spring. At a crossroads, continue generally ahead up a rough track to the left of a house. Where this track turns right, keep ahead up a track for 60 yds to a T-junction. Turn right here, then fork left after about 350 yds onto a crossing track which soon heads downhill. On reaching a small clearing, turn sharp left onto a broader track, still heading downhill. Turn right at the bottom, then left onto a main road. Follow the road (with care) for 200 yds to a left-hand bend, where you go right down a lane past Bradley House *(13)*. Turn left at the bottom of the hill onto a bridleway (signed), which follows the valley past Forge Cottages. This was originally a tramroad. It soon becomes a footpath, then a gravel track again. The site of Soudley Ironworks *(14)* is passed, followed by Haie Hill Tunnel (on the right, *15*) and Bradley Hill Tunnel (on the left, the other end was seen near the start of the walk) on the Forest of Dean Branch. Turn left at the main road, then after 100 yds take the second track on the right, heading uphill on a grass track. Keep the boundary fence of the Dean Heritage Centre on your right until you come to the stone bridge seen at the start of the walk. Cross this, turn right, then right again down the steps to return to the car park.

Camp Mill (1)

The first recorded use of the site on the Soudley Brook (in 1823) was an iron foundry, which was later run by Samuel Hewlett of Bradley; however, the site is probably much older. The present building, first used as a corn mill, dates from 1876. It soon became a wood turnery, and the Dulcote Leatherboard Co. used it from 1902–11. James Joiner ran a sawmill here between 1920 and 1952, after which it became a piggery and then a scrapyard. In 1981, Stanley Joiner purchased the site to house the Dean Heritage Museum. This describes the history of the Forest from the Ice Age to the present day, and should not be missed. There are displays describing the geology, prehistoric and Roman periods, the medieval hunting forest, industries (notably coal and iron mining), and cottage crafts. A pre-1830s beam engine from Lightmoor Colliery, built by Hewlett's Iron Foundry at Camp Mill, is now preserved here. Outdoor exhibits include a Forester's Cottage, woodworking area, charcoal burner's camp, and a replica of a free mine. There is also a blacksmith, library, café, picnic area, and adventure playground.

Forest of Dean Branch (2)

The Bullo Pill Railway Co. Act of 10 June 1809 authorised construction of a horse tramroad from Bullo Pill to Cinderford Bridge and Churchway, with several short branches. The first section opened in about 1810, and the tramroad was used to transport coal, iron ore, stone, timber, and bricks down to the Severn at Bullo. By 1826 the tramroad was almost at a standstill, and it was bought by Edward Protheroe, a prominent coal owner and chairman of the Severn & Wye Railway *(Walk 7)*. A new company, the Forest of Dean Railway Co. was formed with Protheroe as chairman. This was taken over by the South Wales Railway (SWR, *see Walk 4*) in 1851 and the tramroad was replaced by a broad-gauge locomotive railway to Churchway, which opened to goods traffic on 24 July 1854. The SWR became part of the Great Western Railway in 1863, and the line (by then the FoD Branch of the GWR) was converted to standard gauge in 1872. Passenger services, using steam railmotors, from Newnham, on the SWR main line, to Steam Mills (soon extended to Drybrook) began on 3 August 1907, and a loop to enable branch trains to reach Cinderford station (opened by the Severn and Wye Railway in 1900) was opened in April 1908. There were intermediate halts at Ruddle Road (short-lived), Bullo Cross, Upper Soudley, Staple Edge, Ruspidge, and Bilson. Passenger services to Drybrook ended on 7 July 1930, and to Cinderford on 1 November 1958, but goods traffic lasted until 1967. In 1953 there were three daily services each way between Newnham and Cinderford, with more on Saturdays.

Soudley Camp (3)
The origins of this small earthwork on the end of the ridge near the southern end of Soudley Ponds are uncertain. It may have been used in Iron Age, Roman, and medieval times, as it is situated near an ancient trackway that was certainly in use by the Roman period.

Soudley Ponds (4)
The ponds were built as a water supply for the ironworks a little way down the Soudley Valley. They are now a haven for wildlife, including birds, beetles, and dragonflies. The surrounding woods are dominated by alder, oak, and birch, with coppiced hazel, as well as conifer plantations. The path around the ponds is suitable for wheelchairs.

Soudley Valley Geology Trail (5)
An excellent leaflet, published by the Gloucestershire Geology Trust, describes the geology of this part of the Soudley Valley, with details of 10 sites. Only a few of the more important features will be mentioned here, and the Trail is well worth walking on its own. The rocks on the left of the cutting belong to the Devonian Old Red Sandstone and were deposited in a large river system. They are quite steeply dipping, but the Brownstones (mudstone, sandstone, and conglomerate) are overlain by, and are therefore older than, the pebbly Quartz Conglomerate. The two rock units are separated by an unconformity, which represents a period of erosion, and therefore a time gap. Outcrops further along on the right, before the old railway tunnel, consist of Tintern Sandstone (the upper, youngest part of the Old Red Sandstone), followed by the Lower Limestone Shale and Lower Dolomite (both part of the Carboniferous Limestone Series). The composition of the latter rocks shows that the area had by then been covered by the sea. They can be seen in Blue Rock Quarry, reached up steps on the right before the railway tunnel, and near the far end of the tunnel.

The Hod Boy (6)
Cyril Hart describes the use of hod boys in the collieries in his Industrial History of Dean (1971). *"Owing to the thinness of the seams it was necessary to be sparing in the driving of roads, and where the gradient of the seam was steep, say above 6°, hod-roads were driven to the rise. The underground haulage system was of a primitive character, and in the steep measures coal was brought down to the loading stages in*

hods, shallow wooden boxes about 2½ft long x 1½ft wide x 4in deep, mounted on two slides or trotters in the style of a sleigh. The hods were generally drawn by boys (paid about 6d [=2½p] a ton in 1889) with a harness, called a girdle – a wide leather strap, split in the middle to slip over the head, so that part rested on each shoulder; the two ends were brought together at the bottom, before and behind, and a chain with a hook was attached. The hod-roads were usually cut 4½ to 5ft high by 5ft wide, but owing to the heaving-up or 'pucking up' of the floor the height did not usually exceed 2½ft. Such exacting conditions in which young boys had to work (women up to about 1810 also did the same task) are difficult to imagine. Fortunately this often cruel and always exhausting operation was abolished before the close of the nineteenth century." The sculptor of the Hod Boy was John Wakefield, who, together with Graham Tyler, also produced the Miners' Memorial at New Fancy picnic site.

King's Furnace was erected here in 1612–3, during the reign of James I. It had a stack 28 ft square at the base and utilised a 22 ft diameter water wheel. The ironworks supplied shot to Royalist forces during the siege of Gloucester in August 1647. It was probably demolished soon after the trial and execution of Charles I in 1649, when Parliament ordered the destruction of all the ironworks in the Forest. A short distance downstream, on the opposite side of Soudley Brook, is Brinchcombe Limestone Level, which seems to be the one shown as an "Ironstone Level" on the 1878 Ordnance Survey map. It has wide passages (about 7 x 8 ft) and is thought to have been used as a source of limestone for flux in nearby blast furnaces.

Shakemantle Iron Mine and Limestone Quarry (7)

Shakemantle Iron Mine, which has a complex history, was the southern point in an extensive area of iron-mine workings which extended 2½ miles to the north. In 1829 the Cinderford Iron Co. sank a shaft (Lime Kiln Iron Mine), which may have been on the Cinderford Iron Mine gale on which the Shakemantle shafts were situated. Several other gales were added to the area to form part of Buckshaft Iron Mine, about ½ ml to the north, which was leased to Richard Cooper in 1834; a shaft was sunk here in 1835. In 1841 the gales were awarded to William Crawshay of Cyfarthfa Castle and Moses Teague of Cinderford, who were also involved with Cinderford Ironworks and Lightmoor Colliery. A shaft was sunk in 1849 on the St Annal's gale, about 2 mls to the north, which was added to the area, and a second shaft (Deep Pit) at Shakemantle in the 1850s. Shakemantle Mines thus comprised four shafts: St Annal's (657 ft deep), Buckshaft (or Buckshraft, 620 ft), Shakemantle Land (at least 230 ft), and Shakemantle

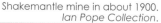

Shakemantle mine in about 1900.
Ian Pope Collection.

Deep (about 470 ft). There were four levels, driven in the Crease Limestone, connecting these workings, together with two crosscuts to ore in the Drybrook Sandstone. As the workings extended to a depth of nearly 900 ft there were problems with water, and a 36-inch pumping engine was installed on the Land Pit and a 60-inch engine on the Deep Pit. There was a siding on the GWR's Forest of Dean Branch, but most of the ore was sent to Cinderford Ironworks on Crawshay's private tramroad. Output declined during the

1890s due to closure of the ironworks in 1894, the increasing difficulty of extraction, and cheap imports of Spanish ore. An attempt at further development in 1898 was unsuccessful, and the mine was closed in September 1899, the remaining 160 men and boys being paid off. The total output of the Buckshaft–Shakemantle–St Annal's group of mines between 1841 and 1899 was 1 650 000 tons of ore.

The iron mine site was purchased by Arthur Morgan, a director of H. Crawshay & Co., in 1907. The intention was to develop an old quarry near the site to produce railway ballast and road metal. Following a dispute with the Crown over royalty fees, the quarry was assigned to the Basic Lime & Stone Co. Ltd in 1911. The stone was to be loaded onto wagons at Shakemantle Siding on the Forest of Dean Branch, but there was another dispute with the Crown, who wanted the use of these facilities for loading timber. The lease of the quarry was transferred to the Porthywaen Lime & Basic Co. Ltd in 1916, but it was some years before it was working. This company was taken over by the Steetley Lime & Building Stone Co., who operated the quarry until 1948. It was being worked by the Shakemantle Quarry Co. by 1962, although a proposal to send railway ballast from the quarry was foiled by closure of the branch. It belonged to Foster, Yeoman & Co. Ltd by 1971. Shakemantle Quarry worked almost the entire thickness (168 ft) of the Lower Dolomite and 35 ft of the overlying dolomitic Crease Limestone, both part of the Carboniferous Limestone Series. The rocks dip westwards at 50–60°. Remains of some buildings and structures (e.g., loading facilities and screens) survive.

Perseverance Iron Mine (8)

The Perseverance and Findall Iron Mine gale was owned by Edward Protheroe and William Crawshay by 1841, although Perseverance Pit and Findall Level *(see 11)* were worked separately at that time. The Perseverance shaft (sunk at some time before 1855) was 385 ft deep and there were two levels, each nearly a mile long. There were also two surface levels, including Findall Level, which were used for drainage. All the underground levels were driven in the mineralised Crease Limestone. In later years the mine was worked by Henry Crawshay & Co. Ltd and a cut-out was driven from the bottom of Perseverance Shaft to Shakemantle Mine. 1537 tons of ore were produced in 1880. There was a siding on the Forest of Dean Branch, but much of the ore may have been sent to Cinderford Ironworks on Crawshay's private tramroad. The mine closed at the same time as Shakemantle, in September 1899.

Sandstone Quarries (9)

These quarries were dug in the Drybrook Sandstone, the upper, youngest part of the Carboniferous Limestone Series. The sandstones, with minor shales and conglomerates, are thought to have been deposited by a large river, which indicates that the area had by then been uplifted above sea level.

Eastern United Colliery (10)

The Eastern United Colliery gale was one of seven areas into which the deep gales of the coalfield were amalgamated by the 1904 Dean Forest (Mines) Act. It was acquired by Henry Crawshay & Co. Ltd in 1907. Driving of two sloping adits or 'dipples', the larger 10 ft wide by 7 ft high, on the site of the old Findall Colliery began in 1909, but the Walmer's shaft was retained for ventilation. The object was to work the lower part of the Upper Coal Measures, containing mainly steam coals, including the Coleford High Delf Seam. Sidings connected to the Forest of Dean Branch were completed in 1909, and the first coal was sold in 1910. However, it was not until 1916 that serious geological problems were overcome: the seams were lost in the main headings due to folding of the strata and were only re-located by driving lengthy cross dipples. The larger dipple was used for tub haulage, using a steam-powered endless rope

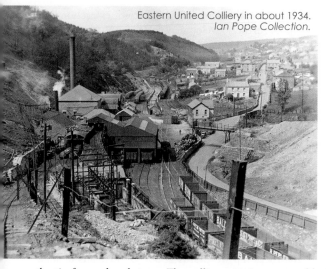

Eastern United Colliery in about 1934.
Ian Pope Collection.

system (electric locomotives were later used in some parts of the mine), and electric pumps were installed. Coal output increased from 58038 tons in 1920 to 239747 tons in 1930 and 283666 tons (the peak) in 1937, by which time new screens had been installed. Thereafter, costs rose due to declining production (112187 tons in 1955), geological difficulties, and water ingress. The colliery, by then owned by the National Coal Board, closed from 30th January 1959. 23 fatalities are known between 1911 and 1957. As can be seen, an attempt was made to rework the tip for coal and stone. The colliery site is now used by light industrial firms, although a two-storey house by the site entrance, which was originally the mine offices, and the brick pithead baths building (across the Cinderford–Blakeney road) survive.

Findall Iron Mine (11)

The Perseverance and Findall Iron Mine gale was owned by Edward Protheroe and William Crawshay by 1841, although Perseverance Pit *(see 8)* and Findall Level were then worked separately. Findall (or Scilly Point) Level had been driven before 1841. It produced ore for Protheroe's blast furnaces at Soudley, but these temporarily closed in 1842. The level was sold to a Mr James of Lydney in 1845, and may have passed to Benjamin Gibbon when he bought the Soudley furnaces in 1857. Both the level and furnaces went to Maximilian Low in 1873, but production ceased in about 1877. There was a connection, via a tramroad, to Scilly (or Silly) Point Siding on the Forest of Dean Branch. Findall Level was connected underground to another level in Perseverance Mine. The 45-ft sandstone ventilation chimney, complete with firebox, on the hillside above was connected via stone flues down a scowle hole

Findall iron mine ventilation chimney and 'scowles'.

(part of Cudleigh Holes) and underground workings to Findall Mine. The ancient near-surface workings known as 'scowles' *(see Walk 9)* closely follow the outcrop of the Crease Limestone, which hosts most of the iron ore in the Forest. In later years Perseverance Mine was worked by Henry Crawshay & Co. Ltd and Findall Level was used for drainage of Perseverance and possibly Shakemantle, both of which closed in September 1899. The chimney and firebox were restored in 1975–6.

Staple Edge Bungalows (12)

After excessive timber felling by Sir John Wintour (or Wynter) in the mid-17th century, the Dean Forest (Reafforestation) Act of 1668 allowed the enclosure of 11 000 acres, divided into six Walks, each with a lodge, which housed a keeper *(see Walk 5)*. Further problems led to a new Enclosure Act in 1808. This allowed construction of 24 new lodges, including one here at Staple Edge (dated 1809). The original lodge was demolished (only an outbuilding remains) and a bungalow built on the site in 1926.

Bradley Hill woods in spring.

Bradley House (13)

Bradley Forge dates from 1628, and was rebuilt in about 1770. In 1820 Samuel Hewlett converted the old forge into a foundry, which supplied tram plates and mileposts for Forest tramroads. There was a tramroad connection to the Forest of Dean line at Haie Hill Tunnel. The works were later acquired by the Great Western Ironworks, owners of Soudley Ironworks. Bradley House was the home of Samuel Hewlett.

Soudley Ironworks (14)

Iron has been worked in the Soudley area since 1565. A pair of blast furnaces was erected by Edward Protheroe in 1836–7, but only worked until 1842. The works were served by a branch tramroad of the Forest of Dean Railway. For the next 30 years, the ironworks had a chequered history, with long periods of closure, under several owners. The Great Western Iron Co. Ltd was formed in 1875 and a modernisation programme begun. Waste gases from the furnaces were recycled through the blast furnace stoves and the boilers of the blowing engines, thus saving fuel. Unfortunately the venture was not a success, and only one of the modified furnaces was ever used, and that only until 1877. The cost of importing Spanish ore had become prohibitive, and the company was wound up in 1879. The site was later use by the Cinderford Crushing Co., which produced ballast derived from ironworks slag, exported via newly-constructed sidings. In 1899 such ballast was used in construction of the Severn and Wye Railway's Cinderford extension and the new Ruspidge–Blakeney Road. The ironworks chimneys were demolished in the same year, but the site was not finally cleared until about 1907.

Haie Hill Tunnel (15)

The major engineering feature on the Forest of Dean Railway was the 1064 yard long Haie Hill Tunnel, originally constructed in 1809 as part of the Bullo Pill Railway's tramroad and enlarged to accommodate broad-gauge trains in 1851–4. When built, it was one of the longest railway tunnels in the world *(see also Walk 12)*. The nearby Bradley Hill (299 yds) and Blue Rock (109 yds) tunnels were only constructed at the time of the conversion to broad gauge to avoid the tight curves of the tramroad.

Good river views, historic riverside hamlets, and some interesting railway remains. A fairly hilly walk, mostly across fields (may be muddy in parts) and along lanes; 19 stiles.

START at the end of the minor road in Gatcombe, reached from the A48 Gloucester to Chepstow road in Blakeney. Please park carefully, leaving space for other cars to turn: GR SO 679054. **Refreshments:** Cock Inn, Nibley; other facilities (pub, shop) in Blakeney. **Bus:** 73 (Gloucester–Chepstow) to Nibley.

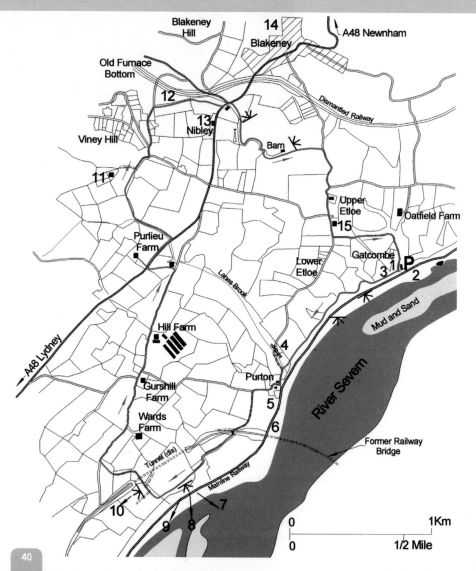

THE HAMLET OF GATCOMBE *(1)* has long been associated with the traditional fisheries of the River Severn. Start the walk by taking the footpath downstream between the railway line *(2)* on your left and a wooded slope on your right. Note the old wharf and the fast-decaying stop boats *(3)*. After crossing two stiles and a small stream the path goes up steps to another stile and then into a field. Turn left to follow the field boundary to a stile on the left, which leads to a path between wire fences. There are good views of the river and the Cotswold Hills beyond, with Stinchcombe Hill being prominent. Regain the field edge via another stile, and then take the next stile on the left after 50 yds, which leads to a path descending through woodland (bluebells in spring) and over a footbridge. The path curves left and right, climbs steps up the side of the gully, and again follows the cliff edge, with views of Purton ahead. It descends to another footbridge, crosses a stile, and regains the cliff top. After about 300 yds, cross another stile in the field corner and descend to yet another footbridge, followed by a stile, to emerge onto a road.

Turn right here for 200 yds to see Purton Viaduct *(4)*, then retrace your steps and follow the road through Purton *(5)*, passing Old Severn Bridge House on the right and Purton Manor on the left. Some 200 yds after the latter, climb a stile on the left to follow a gravel track. Bear left under a stone bridge, which passes through the embankment of the former Severn & Wye Railway's line over the now-demolished Severn Railway Bridge *(6)*. Go through the right-hand gate and follow the left-hand edge of a field, keeping left down a grassy track to a gate, which leads to another field. The trees to the right conceal the entrance to a tunnel on the Severn Bridge line. Go through a gate on the left, then turn right to follow a fence uphill. There are more good views of the river, with another Purton, Sharpness Docks, the Gloucester & Sharpness Canal *(7)*, and Berkeley and Oldbury Nuclear Power Stations *(8)*, on the other side. Ahead, beyond some cliffs, is the jetty of Lydney Docks *(9)*.

Where the fence ends, bear slightly left across the field to go through a kissing gate in the far left-hand corner, turning right to follow the fence to another kissing gate. This leads to a dirt track, which you follow straight ahead. The spire of Lydney Church can be seen to the left, with the imposing house of Lydney Park on the hillside beyond *(10)*. The track bends left through a gap in the hedge (with views of the Severn Bridge – *see Walk 2*) and follows the right-hand field edge to another gap, where you bear right across the field beyond towards a pylon. Pass through a kissing gate and turn right on a dirt lane, which soon becomes a tarmac road. Follow the road ahead for nearly a mile, past two road junctions to left and to right. Go past Hill Farm and downhill to Lensbrook Cottage, where you turn left through a field gate. Cross the field diagonally to the far corner, where a stile leads to a main road.

Cross the road with care and turn right along the roadside footpath to the bottom of the hill. Turn left over a stile at a footpath sign and follow the left-hand field edge to another stile. Continue with the hedge on your left for 60 yds, climb a stile on the left, and turn right uphill, now with a stream and hedge on your right, to a stile near a gate in the field corner. Cross this and follow the right-hand field edge, with Hayes *(11)* up to the left, to another stile by a gate. This leads to a gravel/tarmac track and then to a road. Turn left, then after 50 yds turn right onto Pollards Lane. After about 350 yds, cross a stone stile on the right, opposite a red-brick house. Go down the field to a stile in the bottom left-hand corner. The stone viaduct on the left belonged to the Forest of Dean Central Railway *(12)*. Continue to a gate and stile to the right of a house.

Beyond the stile is a main road, with the Cock Inn at Nibley *(13)* just to the right. However, the walk goes left for 100 yds, before crossing the road and taking a waymarked footpath up a drive to the left of Old Nibley Farmhouse. The right-of-way goes through two wooden gates and ahead on a grass path for 20 yds. Turn sharp right to head uphill to the left of trees to a stile in the field corner. There are good views back to Viney Hill and Blakeney Hill from here. Continue, with the hedge on your right, to the top of the hill (near a mast), following the field boundary as it bends left, then right, into the next field. Follow the field edge for another 50 yds or so and cross a stile (or go through the adjacent gap) on your right. Turn left, now with the hedge on your left. Continue past a barn, with good views of Blakeney *(14)*, the Severn, and the Cotswolds, keeping ahead down to a road. Turn right to a T-junction, where you go right (signposted Etloe). Continue for 400 yds, passing Etloe House *(15)*, then turn left to Gatcombe to return to the start.

Gatcombe (1)

Gatcombe stands on a pill (tidal inlet) at the end of a wooded valley. By 1583 it was a hamlet of six or seven houses, similar to the present day. Nevertheless, it has long been a centre for the river trade, fishing, and even ship building. Drake's House, on the eastern side of the pill, is so-called from an unconfirmed tradition that Sir Francis Drake stayed here, possibly while visiting Sir William Wynter *(see 10)*. It certainly dates back to the 16th century and was formerly an inn, originally called the Gatcombe Boat and later the Sloop, which closed in the late 1800s. The Court House, across the pill, incorporates an early 17th-century range. In the early 19th century it was the Ship Inn, later becoming the Court House where the manor court met. Just up the valley is the early 17th century Oatfield Farm, the home of the Hooper family until the 18th century, later passing to the Hagloe estate. Gatcombe was an important port by the 15th century, when it was one of Gloucester's chief trade outlets as many larger vessels would not venture further upstream. Much trade continued to pass through Gatcombe in the 18th century, with copper and maltsters' coal from South Wales becoming particularly important. Iron from Blakeney furnace and Forest coal were exported. There was trade with Ireland, mainly oak bark and cider. Gatcombe was a centre of the timber trade in the late 18th and early 19th centuries. During the Napoleonic Wars it was one of the main shipping points for oak timber from the Forest to the naval dockyards. Shipbuilding was established by 1608, and vessels of up to 600 tons are said to have been built here in the 18th century. However, construction of the South Wales Railway along the foreshore in about 1850 would have prevented the building of all but very small craft and also obstructed access to the timber yards. In any case, much trade would have already been lost to Bullo Pill and Lydney, which had better facilities, including tramroad access to the centre of the Forest, since about 1810.

GWR Castle class loco on a steam special passing Gatcombe, with 'Drake's House' on the left.

South Wales Railway (2)

The main line of the South Wales Railway (SWR) ran from Grange Court Junction, north of Westbury, to Neyland in Pembrokeshire, via Cardiff and Swansea. It opened in stages between 1850 and 1856, with the section between Grange Court and Chepstow East opening on 19 September 1851. However, the tubular suspension bridge over the River Wye at Chepstow, designed by I.K. Brunel and built by Edward Finch of Liverpool and later Chepstow, was not completed until the following July. The Gloucester and Dean Forest Railway, from Gloucester to Grange Court Junction, also opened on 19 September 1851, and a line from the latter to Hereford (the Hereford, Ross and Gloucester Railway) opened between 1853 and 1855. All these lines were later amalgamated with the Great Western Railway, the SWR itself on 1 August 1863. The SWR was built to broad gauge, but converted to standard gauge over a single weekend in 1872 (how long would the job take today?). At various times there were stations (or halts) at Grange Court, Newnham, Ruddle Road (Bullo), Awre Junction, Gatcombe (actually at Purton, and closed when Awre Junction opened), Lydney Junction, and Woolaston. Today the former SWR is the only surviving railway in the area (other than the preserved Dean Forest Railway), being part of the busy main line from Gloucester and the Midlands to South Wales. The only station still open between Gloucester and Chepstow is Lydney Junction, to which the DFR also operates.

Severn Fisheries (3)

Fishing has been carried out in the Severn for millennia, probably since at least the Mesolithic. Remains of fish weirs and wicker fish baskets, the latter dated to about 900 AD, have been found further downstream. Salmon has long been the most sought-after fish, and the first recorded attempt to prevent over-fishing dates back to 1285, when Edward I introduced closed seasons. Several distinct methods of fishing have traditionally been used. *Stopping nets* were deployed from stop boats, sturdy flat-bottomed boats about 23 x 8 ft, up to six of which would be attached to a fixed anchor cable tied to the bank. The boats were broadside on to the tide, and the net was spread between two poles in the form of a V, the point of which was propped up in the boat, the wide part being in the water. When a fish was detected, the fisherman would kick the prop away, thus allowing the counterbalanced net, hopefully with fish, to rise out of the water. A stop net fishery was operated by the Morse family at Gatcombe for nearly a century, until rising costs and dwindling salmon stocks forced them to give up in 1986. Another fixed fishery method used *putts and putchers*, conical wicker baskets tied to frameworks of wooden poles near the river bank. Putts were up to 14 ft long and made in three sections, whereas putchers were smaller (about 5–6 ft long); they generally faced upstream to fish the ebb tide. There were once thousands of putcher ranks on the river, mostly downstream of Awre. The remains of the some of the frameworks can still be seen between Gatcombe and Purton. *Long nets* were about 90 yards long and 12 ft deep; they were suspended beneath cork floats. They were paid out in a semicircle into the river using a Severn punt, one end (the debut line) being held on the bank, and the other (the muntle line) being returned to the bank. The two ends were brought together and the net then winched ashore. Long nets were mainly used upstream of Awre. *Lave nets* were hand-held bag-shaped nets about 6 ft across held on a Y-shaped frame with a handle. They were used to fish in pools and channels at low water, mostly in the estuary downstream of Lydney. Given the enormous tidal range and moving sandbanks in the Severn,

Decaying stop boats and salmon putchers at Gatcombe.

this method could be hazardous, even to someone with intimate knowledge of the river. The Severn salmon fishery is now almost, but not quite, extinct, owing largely to over-fishing in the adult feeding grounds off Newfoundland and Greenland, although it is to be hoped that conservation attempts will be successful. For now, a few fishermen, mostly using lave nets, still maintain the tradition, notably at Black Rock, near the Welsh end of the new Severn Bridge. At the time of writing putchers were still in use at Woolaston, albeit using non-traditional materials. One other fishery which should be mentioned is that of *elevering*, the use of hand-held fine-mesh nets to catch elvers, young eels which arrive from their breeding grounds in the Sargasso Sea each spring. Again, elver numbers have dwindled alarmingly in recent years.

Purton Viaduct (4)

This three-arch red sandstone viaduct over the Etloe to Purton Road was built in about 1832 for the proposed Purton Steam Carriage Road from Purton Pill to a new colliery at Foxes Bridge, between Speech House and Cinderford. Planned at about the time that the Stockton and Darlington Railway first ran, it failed to obtain an Act of Parliament and was never completed. However, it did have a considerable effect on local politics at the time, and the Forest of Dean Central Railway was eventually built near much of the proposed route *(see 12 below)*. The finance was to come from a prominent ironmaster, Charles Mathias of Lamphey Court, Pembrokeshire, and Moses Teague was a prominent supporter. The viaduct is an important survival of a scheme which would have involved the first crossing of the Severn on a moveable bridge.

Purton (5)

Like Gatcombe, the small hamlet of Purton was once a port that exported Forest timber for the Royal Navy, as well as other products. It was also the location of a ferry, which was in existence by 1282 when it was operated by "Hamelin the Ferryman". By the 18th century it was known as the Purton Passage Ferry; in 1798 James Inman charged 3d per person, 9d (about 4p) per horse, 3d or 6d per calf, and 2/9d (about 14p) for 20 sheep or pigs. The ferry remained in operation until the late 19th century, and the stone quay and slipway can still be seen. Purton's existence as a port came to an end in 1850 with the construction of the South Wales Railway. Purton Manor, on high ground at the southern end of the hamlet, is a 16th century stone house which retains many of its original features. The early 19th century Old Severn Bridge House was until recently the Severn Bridge Hotel. There was also a Purton Passage Inn here in the 18th and 19th centuries.

Severn Railway Bridge (6)

An 1872 Act of Parliament authorized the building of the Severn Bridge Railway. This was to run from Lydney Junction, on the former South Wales Railway (by then GWR), to a bridge over the Severn between Purton and Sharpness, where it would join the Midland

Railway's proposed Sharpness Branch from Berkeley Road on their Bristol–Gloucester main line. The bridge, designed by G.W. Keeling and G.W. Owen, was begun in 1875 and completed in 1879. It was formed of a series of bowstring girders on tubular piers and had a pair of wide central spans and 19 lesser spans. The total length was 4162 ft, and there was a swing bridge over the canal at Sharpness. Severn Bridge Station (a modest affair of two platforms with wooden

From an old postcard.

shelters) was built on the approach to the bridge near Purton and the station at Lydney Junction was replaced by another at the start of the new line. The railway opened on 17 October 1879 as the Severn and Wye and Severn Bridge Railway, having been amalgamated with the Severn and Wye Railway. In 1894 this became the Severn and Wye Joint Railway (Great Western and Midland Railways), which incorporated the MR's Sharpness Branch (opened in 1875) from Berkeley Road. There were about six daily services each way between Berkeley Road and Lydney in 1900, many of these going to or from Lydbrook Junction. Although the S&W's passenger services north of Lydney Town were withdrawn in 1929, the Berkeley Road to Lydney Town service lasted until 1960. Then, on the foggy evening of October 25th 1960, two fuel barges (*Arkendale* and *Wastdale*) missed the entrance to Sharpness Docks and collided with the bridge, demolishing one of the upright columns and causing two spans to fall onto them. The impact caused the barges' cargo of around 5000 gallons of petrol to ignite, setting the Severn on fire around the bridge. A 12-inch gas main which crossed the bridge was also severed, adding to the blaze. Five men lost their lives, but it could have been much worse, as maintenance workers on the bridge had taken a break in the signal box at Severn Bridge Station to listen to a radio broadcast of a boxing match involving Henry Cooper. In spite of proposals, the bridge was never repaired and was finally dismantled in the late 1960s. Thus was lost, not only the local passenger and freight services, but also a useful diversionary route in the event of the Severn Tunnel being closed. The foundations of the bridge piers can still be seen at low tide, as can the remains of the two barges a little way upstream. The stone piers of the canal swing bridge on the opposite bank also survive.

Gloucester and Sharpness Canal. (7)

The original plan for a ship canal between Gloucester and Berkeley was authorised by an Act of Parliament in 1793. The aim was to bypass the narrow winding stretch of the River Severn below Gloucester, but the Company ran out of money when only one third of the canal had been completed. Work eventually started again on a route to Sharpness, which was seen to be better placed for access from the River Severn, and the canal was completed in 1827. At first there were no facilities for cargo handling at Sharpness and ships (of up to 600 tons) travelled up the canal to discharge in the basin at Gloucester Docks, where wharves and warehouses were built to accommodate the increasing traffic. Many of the imports were carried onwards by boats on the Severn or canal network, and later by rail.

A new dock and tidal basin were built at Sharpness in the 1870s to accommodate larger vessels unable to pass up the canal, the original canal entrance eventually being closed. Warehouses were built beside the new dock, principally to accommodate imported grain, and barges and lighters towed by tugs gradually took over much of the canal traffic. Railway lines connected to both the Midland and (via the Severn Bridge) Great Western main lines could also be used for goods traffic. Commercial traffic on the canal had virtually ceased by the 1980s due to competition from pipelines and road transport. However, Sharpness still handles bulk cargoes, such as cement, fertilizer, and scrap metal, while the canal is much used by pleasure craft. A mile north of Sharpness, at Purton (not to be confused with the hamlet on the Dean side of the river), the canal runs very close to the river bank, and a large number (over 50) of boat hulks was placed between river and canal to prevent erosion. They included a variety of barges, trows, and other vessels, many of which can still be seen, albeit gradually rotting away.

Berkeley and Oldbury Nuclear Power Stations (8)

Berkeley had two Magnox reactors producing 276 MW and was the first commercial nuclear power station in the United Kingdom. After 27 years of successful operation, generating enough electricity on a typical day to serve an urban area the size of Bristol, it was also the first in the country to be decommissioned following closure in 1989. Further downstream is Oldbury Power Station, construction of which started in 1962. Since it was opened in 1968, it has produced electricity around the clock, supplying 435MW on a typical day. The station has two reactor vessels, each containing 26 400 fuel elements, and draws unlimited supplies of cooling water from the River Severn. It was to have ceased operations at the end of 2008, but is now expected to continue running for several more years. After closure, fuel will be progressively removed from the reactors and sent to Sellafield for treatment. This is expected to take about three years, after which decommissioning can begin. There were two other nuclear power stations near the mouth of the River Severn in Somerset: Hinkley Point A (closed in 2000) and B (due to close in 2011).

Ian Pope Collection.

Lydney Docks (9)

Lydney Pill has probably been used as a port since Roman times, and there is a record of a river trade by 1270, but it was the development of tramroads which really made improved dock facilities essential. Lydney Docks were built in 1810–3 by the Severn and Wye Railway and Canal Co., whose horse tramroad from Lydney to Lydbrook had opened in 1810. A one-mile length of canal connected Lydney with the harbour (tidal basin). There was an earlier narrow tub-boat canal from Middle Forge to Lydney Pill (Pidcock's Canal, built in about 1790), and the upper 1.5 miles of this remained in use for some years transporting coal and iron from nearby pits and forges down, via a tramroad connection, to the wharves. The outer harbour was not completed until 1821 and the tramroad was then extended along the north bank of the canal, with a branch over a swing bridge to coal tips on the south side of the basin. The entrance to the docks was via a tidal basin to the lower and upper basins of the canal. The tramroad was converted to a broad-gauge locomotive railway in about 1868, and new mechanical coal tips replaced the old wooden ones. However, like the South Wales Railway, the Severn and Wye's line was soon converted to standard gauge. The importance of Lydney as a market town with better communications with the heart of the Forest, and the much superior facilities at Lydney Docks meant that trade was soon diverted from smaller ports like Gatcombe and Purton. The docks were very busy throughout the 19th century and in 1867 handled about 200 000 tons of trade, mainly coal, pig iron, bark, timber, and stone. 244 200 tons of coal were shipped in 1881–2, mainly to Bridgwater and Bristol, but also to 29 other ports, including some in South Wales and Ireland. Trade began to decline after the Severn Bridge opened in 1879, allowing Forest coal and other products to be exported via the new Sharpness Docks, which could handle larger vessels. The ailing company was taken over to become the Severn and Wye Joint Railway (Great Western and Midland Railways) in 1894. Sail was giving way to steam ships by this time, but sailing vessels continued to call at Lydney well into the 20th century. The final export of coal from the harbour was in 1960, although logs for use in plywood manufacture were imported until the 1970s. However, things are looking up, as the docks have recently (2005) been refurbished with new lock gates to create a marina and harbour area for sea-going yachts and motor boats, with further improvements planned. The Lydney Yacht Club is based here and the *MV Balmoral* occasionally calls on its pleasure cruises in the Bristol Channel. The cliffs upstream of the docks (and north to Gatcombe) consist of Lower Devonian Old Red Sandstone rocks of the Raglan Marl Group (marl, sandstone, and shale). At the base is a thin layer of 'Fish Conglomerate', which includes numerous fragments of primitive fish.

Lydney (10)

Lydney (est. pop. 9160 in 2006) is one of the most important towns in Dean, being situated on an ancient route between Gloucester and South Wales. The area around the Iron Age hill fort in Lydney Park was taken over by the Romans, who mined for iron there and in the 4th century built a large temple complex dedicated to Nodens. Iron mining and smelting continued to be important and Lydney became a market town in 1268. In 1588 Admiral Sir William Wynter (Wintour), Vice-admiral of the Fleet, was granted the manor of Lydney by Elizabeth I in recognition of his

Naas House.

services against the Spanish Armada. His grandson John became an important figure in Forest history *(see Walk 5)*. The Wintour estate passed to the Bathurst family, who still own it, in 1723.

The present Lydney Park house was designed by C.H. Howell. It was built in 1877 of coursed limestone, with a tile roof and multiple chimney stacks. Most of the present town dates from the 19th and 20th centuries, as new industries and facilities were introduced and houses were built. However, the fine church dates mainly from the 13th century, albeit heavily restored in Victorian times. Near the docks is Naas House, an early 17th century house, fortified by Parliamentarian forces laying siege to Whitecross Manor, home of Sir John Wintour, during the Civil War. Herbert Howells (1892–1983), the composer, was born in Lydney.

Hayes (11)

The Hayes was the manor house of Blakeney, and dates from around the late 16th century. Originally timber-framed, it was much modified in the 17th and 19th centuries. The house stands at the eastern end of a terraced area which was formerly partly walled and suggests a formal garden of the late 17th or early 18th century. More unusual is the grade II listed privy, which can be seen at the bottom of the garden. This is constructed of finely-coursed stone rubble, has a tile roof with gabled ends, and probably dates from the 17th century. It is a very rare survival of an early privy. The house belonged to the Barrow family by the late 16th century, but had passed through the female line to George Savage by the late 18th century. Sir Thomas Crawley-Boevey of Flaxley owned it in 1794, and the Hayes was bought by William Ambrose, owner of the Hagloe estate, in 1820. It apparently belonged to J. Mathias in 1879, but by the early 20th century the Hayes was the farmhouse of a small farm owned by the Hayman family.

Forest of Dean Central Railway (12)

The Forest of Dean Central Railway gained its Act of Parliament in July 1856 for a line from Awre Junction, on the South Wales Railway (SWR), to Howbeech (or Howbeach), with branches to Foxes Bridge and New Fancy Collieries, and to a dock on the Severn at Brimspill. Financial problems delayed construction and the line, as far as Howbeech, was not opened until 29 May 1868. The branches to Foxes Bridge and Brimspill were never completed. Worked by the Great Western Railway from the start, and absorbed into that company in 1923, the line was laid to broad gauge, but converted to standard gauge at the same time as the SWR in 1872. Traffic was disappointing, and even that from New Fancy was soon lost to the Severn and Wye Railway when its mineral loop was opened in 1872. Howbeech Colliery closed in 1895, although there seems to have some production in the 1920s. With little or no goods traffic by then (there was never a passenger service), the section of line beyond Blakeney was officially closed in 1932, leaving only a service to the goods station (opened in about 1870) there. The last train to Blakeney ran on 29 July 1949, after which the line closed for good. West of the viaduct, the line climbed up Old Furnace Bottom, between Viney and Blakeney Hills. Interesting buildings here include the former Malt Shovel Inn, Old Tump House (another former inn), a mill (now cottages), and the 17th century farmhouse.

Cock Inn, Nibley (13)

The Cock Inn dates from the 18th century, and in 1822 it was a staging post for a South Wales coach. But why does the inn sign show a horse rather than a bird? A cock horse was a spare horse which was kept ready to assist another horse with a heavy load up a hill. "Ride a cock horse to Banbury Cross" refers to the fact that children would do just that when the horse returned to its station at the bottom of the hill. The term was apparently also applied to the extra steam locomotives used on steep sections of a railway, although 'banker' came to be more generally used. Old Nibley Farmhouse, on the opposite side of the road, was recorded from 1678, but was rebuilt in about 1800. Two other old farmhouses nearby, at Upper Viney and Lower Viney, date from the 17th century and 1741, respectively.

Blakeney (14)

Blakeney grew up on the Gloucester–Chepstow road near the junction of the Soudley and Blackpool Brooks, which powered a number of mills. The village had become a trading and industrial centre by the late 13th century. Corn-milling, tanning, grindstone manufacture, nail-making, and weaving were all of some importance, and many of these industries continued into the 19th century. The tanners used oak bark from the Forest, which also provided timber for various uses. The oldest part of the village is probably around Church Square, which today is surrounded by attractive, mostly 18th and 19th century buildings, nearly all of them listed. The oldest is the 16th century timber-framed Swan House, formerly the Swan Inn. The Yew Tree (currently closed) dates from the early 19th century, and the nearby King's Head is late 18th century. The early 18th century All Saints Church was rebuilt in about 1820 by Samuel Hewlett, and the sanctuary was added in 1907. The late 18th and 19th

Furnace Valley, with the Forest of Dean Central Railway's viaduct prominent. *From an old postcard.*

centuries were the time of Blakeney's greatest prosperity, with tradesmen and shopkeepers serving the growing settlements on the hillsides above, as well as traffic on the turnpike road. Over 40 different trades were represented in 1851. A brewery was opened before 1870 and operated until about 1915. There were still 20 shopkeepers and 15 other tradesmen and small businessmen in 1931, but trade declined as Lydney grew into an important business and shopping centre.

Etloe House (15)

An estate based on Etloe House was built up by the A Deane family, which was recorded at Etloe from the early 16th century and owned it until the late 19th century. The present Etloe House is a three-storey sandstone building with dormer windows and a Welsh slate roof. It is dated 1730, and has a listed 18th century five-bay stone barn adjacent. However, the original Etloe House Farmhouse is much older: 16th century or earlier, built mainly of coursed rubble-stone, but with a rendered and timber framed east gable. It is further along the road to Purton, about 200 yds past where the walk route turns left to return to Gatcombe.

Historic collieries, an attractive lake, the Speech House, and a sculpture trail. A relatively flat walk along forest tracks and paths and gravel cycle tracks, with just a couple of short ascents and descents; 3 stiles.

START at the Forestry Commission's Beechenhurst Lodge Car Park off the B4226 Coleford to Cinderford road (charge): GR SO 614121. **Refreshments:** Café at Beechenhurst, Speech House Hotel (upmarket). **Bus:** 30 (Gloucester–Coleford) to Speech House.

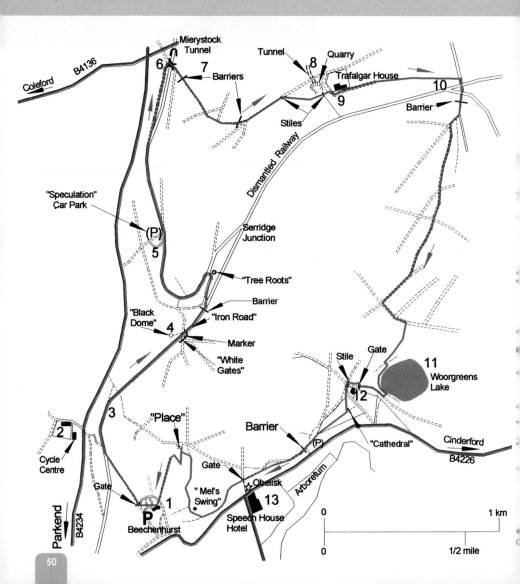

BEECHENHURST LODGE, where there are toilets, shop, café, and picnic area, was the site of Speech House Hill Colliery (1). The walk starts in the direction indicated by the "Cycle Track" sign on the large post just behind the lodge. Our route follows red marker posts diagonally across the car park and through an area of large trees. Go past several fenced-off depressions (possibly old shafts), across a tarmac road, and through a wooden gate onto a gravel cycle track. Bear right at a junction, signposted to Drybrook Road Station, and ignore the left turn to the Cycle Centre. Across the main road a short distance to the left is the site of Cannop Colliery (2), now housing a council depot as well as the Cycle Centre. You are now following the trackbed of the former Severn & Wye Railway from Lydney to Lydbrook (3). After about ½ mile a sign ("White Gates") is reached, with a metal "Beechenhurst Inclosure" marker of 1896 by a gate on the right. In the trees back to the left here is 'Black Dome', which is one of the many features of the Beechenhurst Sculpture Trail (4). We will see a few more of the sculptures on this walk, but the whole trail makes a worthwhile walk in its own right. Keep directly ahead past a barrier, ignoring the left fork to Drybrook Road, and continue past another sculpture: 'Iron Road'. At the next junction, just beyond another barrier, take the left-hand uphill gravel track ahead, signposted to Lydbrook. (Serridge Junction, where the railway line to Lydbrook diverged from that to Drybrook Road and Cinderford, was a short distance along the track which forks right here.) The gravel track bends sharp left, then curves right, with an open area and adjacent car park soon appearing down on your left. This was the site of Speculation Colliery (5).

Just after passing above the car park, bear left onto a grassy track (cycle track to Lydbrook), which continues along the old S&WR trackbed (the Lydbrook Branch). Follow this track, which later diverges left of the railway trackbed to follow the original tramroad route, for about ½ mile

to Mierystock Bridge (6). Turn right to cross the bridge over the former railway, noting the tunnel to the left. Follow a path uphill past a barrier, with the forested tip of Arthur & Edward (or Waterloo) Colliery (7) on the left. Keep straight ahead over a gravel track, continuing uphill under powerlines and past a track junction on the left, before passing a barrier onto a gravel road. Bear left on this (joining the Wysis Way, see Walk 13) for about 300 yds and cross over a stile on the right onto a narrow footpath, which heads downhill (note colliery tips on the right) to another stile. Just to the left of this second stile, in an overgrown quarry, is the tramroad tunnel between Strip-and-at-it (8) and Trafalgar (9) Collieries. Climb the stile and turn right on the gravel road. On the right are the sites of the two main shafts of Trafalgar, now marked by large stones. The road bends left past Trafalgar House, where teas can sometimes be obtained. Continue along the now grassy track (the line of the original Trafalgar Tramroad, later replaced by a standard-gauge connection) to a tarmac road.

Turn right on the road, which in a short distance crosses a grass track and then a gravel cycle track. This is the site of the S&WR's Drybrook Road Station (10), the platform having been on the grass crossing track, just to the right of the tarmac road. Keep ahead past a metal barrier, and, about 100 yds after this, bear right onto a gravel track, following a Gloucestershire Way (GW, see Walk 14) arrow. After another 100 yds, turn left onto a grass path, still following the GW. Continue ahead on a generally wider track over two crossing tracks and bearing right at a junction to emerge onto a broad gravel track at a bend. Turn left here (leaving the GW) and 50 yds after a left-hand track junction, take a narrow, rather muddy path on the right. This goes through pine forest to a path junction, where you keep ahead up a short bank to the edge of Woorgreens Lake (11). Turn right along the lake shore for about 150 yds to where there is a good open view of the lake, and turn right here on a path for 20 yds. Turn right again onto a dirt track. This leads to a gate by some buildings, but keep right of the gate, following a path to a stile.

Turn left on the dirt road beyond, then bear half right opposite the house (Kensley Lodge, *12)* onto a path into trees following blue waymark arrows. This leads to a surprise: a stained glass window ('Cathedral'), another part of the Sculpture Trail. Turn right near the window, still following blue arrows, along a path through the woods towards a parking area. Keep ahead onto a dirt track which passes just to the right of the car park. Bear slightly right

past a wooden barrier, then bear left at each of two forks (both with waymark arrows) to reach a wooden gate. To the left is Speech House *(13)*, the most important of the original Forest Lodges. Beyond the gate we will again follow the blue arrow trail. This goes ahead at first, then swings right past two path junctions on the left (and 'Melissa's Swing' on the right), and eventually turns left and then right at junctions to reach a giant chair ('Place'). From here there are good views of the Cannop Valley and Nagshead Plantation beyond. Retrace your steps for 10 yds and turn right on a gravel path which zig-zags downhill to Beechenhurst Lodge.

Speech House Hill Colliery (1)

The first recorded working of the Royal Forester gale was in the 1830s and 40s by Richard James, but it was bought by the Brain brothers, who had the adjoining Rose-in-hand gale, in 1847. The Speech House Hill Colliery Co. had taken over by 1869, followed by the Great Western (Forest of Dean) Coal Consumers Co. Ltd (a Crawshay company) in 1873. A branch to the S&WR was constructed in 1874. 56976 tons of coal were produced in 1880. The winding shaft (eventually 420 ft deep) reached the Churchway High Delf Seam (3 ft 3 in. thick) at 393 ft. The colliery had a rather chequered history, passing through a succession of owners, until it was bought by Henry Crawshay & Co. Ltd, owners of the adjacent Lightmoor Colliery, in 1903. The barrier to the latter colliery was opened up and

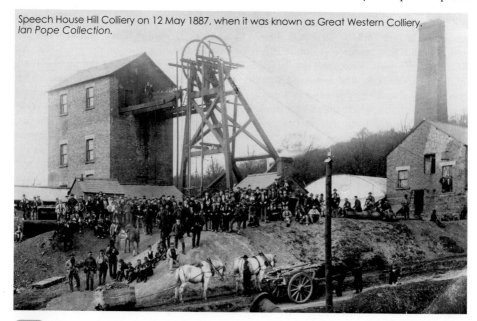

Speech House Hill Colliery on 12 May 1887, when it was known as Great Western Colliery. *Ian Pope Collection.*

most of the surface works at Speech House Hill, no longer being required, were closed by 1906. However, the main shaft was maintained as an emergency exit for Lightmoor until the gale was surrendered in 1937. The area has now been landscaped and forms the Forestry Commission's Beechenhurst Lodge Picnic Site. A few fenced off depressions north of the lodge may be old shafts or collapses.

Cannop Colliery (2)

The Cannop Coal Co. Ltd was formed in June 1906, taking over the Union & Cannop and Prince Albert deep gales from Henry Crawshay & Co. Ltd. The aim was to work the Coleford High Delf Seam beneath the workings of the Speech House Hill Colliery. A drift mine (Cannop Drift) was driven a short distance up Wimberry Slade to work the Yorkley and High Delf Seams while two shafts were being sunk. The 4 ft 9 in thick High Delf was reached at a depth of 612 ft in no.1 pit by November 1909. Sidings and a connection with the Wimberry Branch of the Severn and Wye Railway were installed. Winding of coal from the deep pit began in 1912, output reaching 1000 tons/day by March 1915. Production peaked in 1937 (402784 tons), making it the largest colliery in Dean, and the workforce was about 1040 around this time. The colliery was an extremely wet one and was flooded on several occasions. Electric pumps were used and 1140 million gallons were pumped in 1928. The high cost of pumping was a major factor leading to closure in September 1960. There were 23 fatalities between 1908 and 1960. The license to work the Yorkley Seam was taken by Harvey Gwilliam, who opened a new drift (New Cannop Drift Mine) in Wimberry Slade, although the original Cannop Drift was retained as a second exit. This small mine is one of three still operating in the Forest, currently being licensed to Richard and Steven Harding. The Cannop Colliery buildings are now part of a Council depot, and a cycle hire centre occupies the mine offices. The overgrown tip and the brick-lined entrance (now gated) to the Cannop Drift mine survive. The nearby ponds were used for cooling water.

Severn and Wye Railway (3)

The Severn and Wye Railway and Canal Co. opened a 3 ft 6 in. gauge horse tramroad from Lydney to Lydbrook, via Serridge Junction, in 1810. The main line was eventually converted to a standard gauge railway. A mineral loop line from Tufts Junction, near Whitecroft, to Drybrook Road *(see 10)* was opened in 1872. The Lydbrook Branch ran from Serridge Junction, between Parkend and Cinderford, to Lydbrook Junction on the Ross and Monmouth Railway. The first passenger train ran from Lydney to Lydbrook on 23 September 1875, and an extension to Cinderford opened in 1900. Regular passenger services from Lydney to Lydbrook and Cinderford ended on 6 July 1929, and closure to goods trains came on 30 January 1956. *(See Walk 7 for more details of the S&WR.)*

'Cathedral'

Beechenhurst Sculpture Trail (4)

The Sculpture Trail, which opened in 1986, is a co-operative project between the Forest of Dean Sculpture Trust and the Forestry Commission. It now comprises nearly 20 sculptures inspired by various aspects of the Forest, from trees and wildlife to industrial history. The complete trail is 4.5 miles long, but there are shorter alternatives of 2.2 and 3 miles. An informative leaflet, produced by the Forestry Commission can be purchased at Beechenhurst, and the trail is well recommended.

Speculation Colliery (5)
Sinking of a shaft, by Corneleus Brain, was well underway by 1853 and the Churchway High Delf Seam was eventually reached at a depth of 308 ft. 18694 tons of coal were produced in 1880, and there was a siding connecting with the Severn and Wye Railway. The colliery was leased by the Wye Colliery Co. from about 1873 to the late 1880s, when it passed back to the Brain family and was then worked by the Trafalgar Colliery Co. Ltd. By this time the pumping engine may only have been used to help keep Trafalgar dry. When the latter colliery unexpectedly flooded in 1919 and was bought by the managements of Lightmoor and Foxes Bridge Collieries to protect their own workings, the Speculation gale was also transferred. It was surrendered after closure of Trafalgar in 1925. Only the levelled tip and a filled-in shaft remain to be seen.

Mierystock (6)
Mierystock (the spelling varies) was the junction of the 1½ mile long Churchway Branch tramroad of the Severn and Wye Railway. However, this was abandoned by 1877, by which time traffic had been diverted onto the Great Western Railway's Forest of Dean Branch

between Cinderford and Bullo Pill Junction on the South Wales main line *(see Walk 3)*. In 1908 sidings were laid for use by the Lydney and Crump Meadow Colliery Co. Ltd, owners of the nearby Arthur & Edward Colliery. They were removed after the colliery closed in 1959. The most obvious features of the former S&WR are the beautifully-built stone bridge and the southern portal of the 242 yd-long Mierystock tunnel. There are plans to divert the cycle track to go through the tunnel, thus avoiding a major road crossing *(see also Walk 8)*.

Mierystock tunnel.

Arthur & Edward (Waterloo) Colliery (7)
Arthur & Edward Colliery dates from the mid-1830s, but only in 1908, when the new North-Western United deep gale was acquired by the Lydney and Crump Meadow Collieries Co. Ltd, did it become one of Dean's major producers *(see Walk 8)*. Tub loads of coal were transported by means of an endless rope-hauled tramway or 'creeper' to screens at Mierystock across the Monmouth–Mitcheldean Road. The screens, which were near the pond to the right of the tip, were connected to a siding on the former S&WR. The colliery closed on 23 December 1959.

Strip-and-at-it Colliery (8)

The Strip-and-at-it gale was worked by John Harris from 1832. Two pumping engines were in use by 1841, and production was 11502 tons in 1856. The pit worked the Rocky and Churchway Seams through a 381 ft (in 1841) shaft, and was notorious for the thinness (20 ins) of its seams. Coal raising ceased in 1861 and the gale was surrendered to the Crown in 1864. It was then acquired by Corneleus and Francis Brain, owners of the nearby Trafalgar Colliery, who used the shaft for pumping (a 44-inch Cornish engine was working in 1880) and as an emergency exit. There was a spur to the S&WR's Churchward Branch by 1842, and this was connected by a short tunnel to Trafalgar Colliery in 1860, although the latter colliery soon had direct rail access to both the GWR's Forest of Dean Branch and the S&WR's main line. Strip-and-at-it closed, along with Trafalgar Colliery, in 1925.

Trafalgar Colliery (9)

The Trafalgar gale was granted to Corneleus Brain in 1842, but work on a pit does not appear to have begun until about 1860. There were two shafts, worked by the same winding engine, down to the Churchway High Delf Seam at a depth of 586 ft. A narrow-gauge tramway (Brain's Tramway) was soon built to the GWR's Forest of Dean Branch at Bilson, but after 1872 there was also a connection with the

Tramroad tunnel near Trafalgar Colliery.

S&WR. The colliery was unique in Dean in being lit by gas, and electric pumps were installed underground in 1882, the first recorded use of electric power in a mine. Trafalgar was one of the larger pits, employing 800 men and boys in 1870, and producing 88794 tons of coal in 1880 and about 500 tons/day in 1906. However, the main dip roadway was unexpectedly flooded in 1919, and the colliery was bought by the managements of Lightmoor and Foxes Bridge Collieries to protect their own workings. It closed in 1925. 29 fatalities are recorded between 1863 and 1922, an indication of the dangers inherent in coal mining. Trafalgar House (still a dwelling) was the home of Sir Francis Brain.

Drybrook Road Station (10)

Drybrook Road Station was where trains on the Severn and Wye Railway's main line between Lydney and Lydbrook (*see 3 above*) reversed. It was also the junction of the mineral loop line from Tufts Junction, near Whitecroft, which opened in 1872. The first passenger train from Lydney to Lydbrook ran on 23 September 1875, and an extension to Cinderford opened in July 1900. Although regular passenger services from Lydney to Cinderford and Lydbrook ceased on 6 July 1929, there were occasional excursion trains after that date. There was a single platform and a signal box on the down side. The original wooden station building was replaced by that from Cinderford old station in 1901. The grass crossing track is the former main line from Lydney via Serridge Junction to Cinderford, whereas the gravel cycle track follows the route of the mineral loop.

Woorgreens Lake (11)

The lake was created after open-cast coal mining activity (by Northern Strip Mining) ceased in 1981. Prior to that open-cast mining had been carried out near Steam Mills, north of Cinderford, where a small lake is now used by fishermen. Royalties received from licensing mining operations at Woorgreens were used by the Forestry Commission to construct the lakes at Mallard's Pike, now a popular picnic area. Woorgreens Lake and Marsh is now a nature reserve belonging to the Gloucestershire Wildlife Trust, and is one of Dean's best dragonfly sites, 17 species having been recorded. The reserve attracts heathland birds (including whinchat, stonechat, skylark, tree pipit, cuckoo, nightjar, kestrel, and sparrowhawk), waders (spotted redshank, greenshank, green sandpiper, and curlew) and other water birds (little grebe, moorhen, mallard, teal, and tufted duck). It is also an important habitat for butterflies and marsh plants.

Kensley Lodge (12)

After excessive timber felling by Sir John Wintour (or Wynter) in the mid-17th century, the Dean Forest (Reafforestation) Act of 1668 allowed the enclosure of 11 000 acres, divided into six Walks, each with a lodge, which housed a keeper (*see below*). However, further problems, including neglect, theft of timber, and illegal grazing of animals, continued throughout the 18th century. Admiral Nelson's visit to the Forest in 1802 and his report of 1803 thus led to a new Enclosure Act in 1808. This allowed construction of 24 new lodges, including Kensley Lodge (dated 1811).

Speech House (13)

In 1640 timber and mineral rights over 18000 acres of the Forest were granted to Sir John Wintour (Wynter) of Lydney by Charles I, with an obligation to supply timber to the Crown for ships and charcoal for the King's ironworks. However, his overzealous cutting of timber,

Speech House

as well as his enclosures of areas used by local people for grazing, etc., made him very unpopular, and he was deprived of his grant by Parliament in 1642. During the Civil War, as a Royalist in a largely Parliamentarian area, Wintour was forced to flee to France, after burning his residence at Whitecross Manor, near Lydney. It was at about this time that he made his famous escape from Parliamentarian troops by riding his horse over the cliffs ('Wintour's Leap') above the Wye at Woodcroft, near Chepstow. Wintour was imprisoned in the Tower in 1649, but after the restoration of Charles II in 1660, he re-established control of much of the Forest. By 1667 he was again under investigation by Parliament for excessive tree clearance, and was forced to relinquish his rights in 1668. The resultant Dean Forest (Reafforestation) Act of 1668 allowed the enclosure (not without local opposition) of 11 000 acres, divided into six Walks, each to have a lodge, which housed a keeper. The first of these was King's Lodge or Speech House, built by 1676. The others were York, Danby, Worcester, Latimer, and Herbert.

Speech House was badly damaged by rioters in 1688 and had to be rebuilt. It has since had several extensions and is a handsome sandstone building, with deeply overhanging eaves. A Verderers' Courtroom, where the verderers meet to deal with offences (illegal cutting of trees, encroachment, poaching, etc.) and disputes involving the vert (trees) and venison of the Forest on behalf of the Crown, was opened in 1680. The Verderers' Court had been held at Kensley House, which stood in the centre of the Forest, from as early as 1338, and the court was sometimes held on Speeches Day. The house continued to be used for the Court, increasingly called the Speech Court, into the early 17th century, and the site is where Speech House now stands. Similarly, the mining industry is controlled by gavellers, who grant 'gales' (mining licence areas) to 'Free Miners' to work for iron, coal, or stone *(Walk 7)*. Speech House was leased as an inn in 1841, and is now a hotel. The Bledisloe Monument opposite is said to mark the centre of the Forest. The nearby Arboretum, which covers 15 acres, includes broadleaf trees and conifers planted from 1915 from the collection of Frank Wilson. It is named after Cyril Hart, the Senior Verderer of the Forest of Dean, who has served as a Verderer since 1952, when he was the youngest person in recent history to have been elected to that office. His knowledge of the Forest and its history is immense, and he is the author of the classic *The Industrial History of Dean*, among many others.

A Norman castle and church, natural dams, ancient woodland, and Wye Valley views. A hilly walk, mostly on field and woodland paths, with some steep ascents and descents; 9 stiles.

Park on side of road on Wye Valley side of St Briavels Castle: GR SO 558045. **Refreshments:** pubs in St Briavels. **Bus:** 69 (Chepstow–Monmouth) to Bigsweir Bridge.

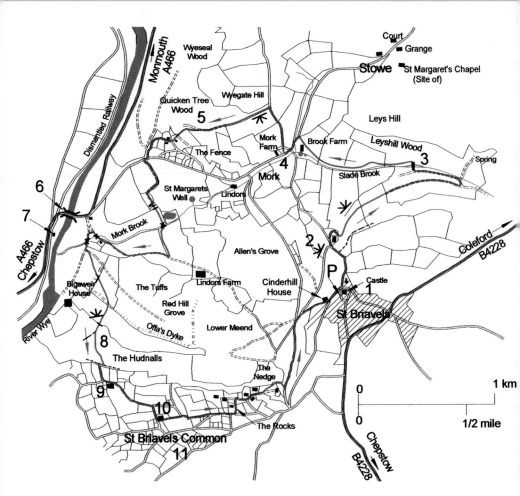

ST BRIAVELS AND ITS CASTLE *(1)* have a long history, which is intimately associated with that of the Forest of Dean. Starting with your back to the castle gatehouse, go down

Mork Road, just to the left of the church, passing Church Farm on your left. Where the road bends sharp left near a mast, bear right onto Mork Lane. There is a lovely view of the Wye Valley (2) from here. After 60 yds, turn right at a footpath sign along a driveway, and onto a grass track. Keep right of wooden posts to a stile at the top of a field. Descend diagonally left across the field, keeping to the right of an overgrown hedge and then contouring around to the right to reach a stile in the wire fence ahead. (Take care not to descend too far to the left here.) There is a nice view of the Slade Brook Valley, Mork, and Wyegate Hill beyond. Keep ahead across the next field to a stile about half way down the edge of woodland. Enter the woods and follow a grassy track for about 600 yds to a junction, where you go sharp left, then left again after about 60 yds onto a track which goes down the valley a little to the left of a stream. About 400 yds from the junction, look out for a narrow footpath leading down to a footbridge on the right. Cross Slade Brook over two footbridges, from which can be seen some of the travertine dams over which the stream flows (3). The path then goes left, keeping near the stream, to a stile at the edge of the woods.

Continue just above the stream over three more stiles to emerge onto a road at Mork (4). Turn left, past 'Sladbrook', to a byway sign on the right. This leads steeply up past Mork Farm, through a gate to a tarmac lane. Continue uphill on the lane (Coxbury and Wyegate Lane, an 18th century turnpike road), which soon becomes a grassy and then a stony, sunken track. Turn sharp left over a stile by metal railings and take the footpath beyond this, which follows a wire fence. There are nice views of St Briavels and Hudnalls Wood from here. Continue on a wider path through woods (5), then fork left onto a narrow waymarked downhill path beside a fence. Cross a gravel track beside houses and take a path ahead by a low wall, between more houses, onto a tarmac lane at The Fence. Turn right, following the lane to a road.

Take the footpath gate opposite and follow the gravel track to the left around the edge of a field. Turn left in front of a converted barn, and go down to a metal gate. Continue through a second gate, and along the left-hand side of a field to another gate. Turn right and follow the field boundary up to a dirt track, where you go right. About 100 yds past a bungalow, just beyond a small bridge, turn left and left again onto another dirt track. Bigsweir Bridge (6) can be seen on the right, with St Briavels Station building (7) in the trees directly across the river to its left. Recross the stream and, just past an Offa's Dyke Path sign, bear left onto a grass track. After 20 yds a narrow footpath forks right across a field to a gate on the far side. Continue in the same direction, aiming for a gap near the top of the right-hand field boundary, by a waymarked stile. Note the low earthwork of Offa's Dyke (see Walk 14) on your right. Go through the gap and a line of ancient sweet chestnut trees, and continue straight ahead across the next field (avoid going too far to the left) to a gate, which soon comes into view on the edge of woodland. The view back to the River Wye, Bigsweir Bridge, The Fence, Wyegate Hill, Staunton and the Kymin hill (Walk 13) is superb. Enter Hudnalls Wood (8), taking the left fork to follow the Offa's Dyke Path as it winds steeply uphill. This section of path may not be too obvious, so keep a good lookout for yellow arrows painted on trees and rocks. It may also be muddy and slippery after rain, so take care. Turn right near the top at a T-junction of paths in front of a ruined stone wall, and then left after 20 yds, between walls to a tarmac road.

Turn left past Birchfield House (9), with more good views of the Wye Valley, and follow the road for about 500 yds to a restricted byway sign. Go right here, turn left onto another byway just past the Gideon Chapel (10), and then turn right onto the tarmac road. This area is part of St Briavels Common (11). Continue along the road, turning left at a T-junction, and taking the next road on the left (The Rocks). Take the first right and turn left down a tarmac driveway (The Nedge) opposite a stone barn. Turn right along a grass track in front of 'Overdale', then, after 200 yds, bear left on a grass path (waymark on tree), just past two wooden sheds. Follow the path over a stone stile, and then keep right down to a stream, which is followed up to a footbridge. Cross, go up steps onto a dirt track, and turn left to reach a tarmac road. Bear left, with views to the left of the Black Mountains on a clear day, to a junction. Take the right-hand of the three roads ahead, going uphill. There is a final good view of Llandogo and the Wye Valley on the left before you pass Cinderhill House (which dates, in part, back to the 14th century) and the well. The castle and starting point are just beyond.

St Briavels (1)

The village of St Briavels (pronounced Brevels) is sometimes said to have been named after the 5th century Celtic (Welsh) Saint Brieuc (or Brioc), although recent studies suggest that St Briavel was an 8th century Welsh prince, born at Cleddon, who spread Christianity in the area and founded several churches. However, until the 12th century the village was known as 'Ledeneia Parva' (Little Lydney). It is situated in a commanding position above the River Wye, and is close to Offa's Dyke *(see Walk 14)*. The centre of the village is dominated by the Norman Castle, said to have been built (of local red sandstone) by Milo Fitz Walter, Earl of Gloucester in about 1130, to guard the Welsh border during the reign of Henry I. Milo became the first Constable of St Briavels and Warden of the Forest, guarding the King's rights and collecting taxes. He was killed in 1143 by an arrow whilst hunting in the Vale of Castiard (Flaxley Valley). The castle and the Forest of Dean were taken over by Henry II in 1160, and the castle was used as a royal hunting lodge by succeeding monarchs, notably King John (1199–1216), whose visits are remembered in the rhyme:

> *St Briavels water and Whyral's wheat*
> *Are the best bread and water King John ever eat.*

The much modified hall range (royal apartments) date from this time, and the imposing gatehouse and a chapel were added about the end of the 13th century. St Briavels Hundred was created, probably in the early 12th century, to provide an administrative structure for the Forest of Dean. A 'hundred' is said to have been the area that could supply a hundred fighting men when called upon by the King. The history of the hundred and of the Forest remained closely entwined. St Briavels Castle was the administrative and judicial centre of the Forest of Dean, being the official residence of the Constable and Warden of the Forest (hence the Constable's horn on top of the chimney).

For centuries it was used for sittings of the Verderers', Miners', and Manor Courts *(see Walk 5)*, and the gatehouse was also used as a prison. Graffiti on one of the walls of the latter include the inscription: *"Robin Belcher The day will come that thou shalt answer for it for thou hast sworn against me 1671"*. During much of the 13th century, the castle was a major production centre for quarrels — the iron bolts fired from crossbows. As many as a million may have been manufactured here. There is a 'Quarrel Field' south of the village, on the edge of the common, and part of the Hudnalls Wood *(see 8)* was probably cut down to make charcoal for the forges. The castle had largely fallen into a state of disrepair by the 18th century, when the keep collapsed, but parts were later used a school and a private house. After restoration it is now used as a Youth Hostel, and the grounds may be visited in the afternoon.

Opposite the castle is the Parish Church of St Mary the Virgin. The original Norman sandstone church (late 11th/early 12th century) was much enlarged in the late 12th and 13th centuries by the addition of the north aisle, north and south transepts, tower, and chancel. The tower was replaced by a south porch tower in about 1830 as the original had become unsafe. The Norman font has an unusual 16-lobed shelf, and there are some interesting tombs, including one to Robert, Abbot of Lire, who died here in 1272, and that of William Warren, his wife Mariana, and their four children (late 16th century). The ancient custom of distributing small pieces of bread and cheese among the congregation after the evening service (which includes the sermon for the Whittington Purse) on Whit Sunday is thought to date back to the 12th century, when villagers successfully defended their rights to pasture animals and cut timber in nearby Hudnalls Wood *(8)*. Each person who claimed the 'dole' had to pay a penny to the Earl of Hereford (this was Milo Fitz Walter from 1141–3). There are a number of attractive late 18th and early 19th century houses facing the castle walls and moat (now filled in). St Mary's Chantry is now a dwelling, but incorporates parts of a 16th century chantry chapel. Church Farmhouse dates from the 16th century, but has since been much modified. Below the castle, by Cinderhill (a reference to the former industrial activity here) is St Bride's Well; the present well head is probably 19th century, but the well is ancient. There are two pubs: the 16th century George and the Crown. Unfortunately, the village shop, post offce, and tea rooms have all recently closed, although there is still a primary school, Congregational Chapel, craft shop, Assembly Rooms, and sports pavillion. The areas of Upper Meend and Lower Meend (meend refers to common land) are situated on the slopes leading down towards the Wye Valley. The population of the village has increased only gradually over the last 150 years or so, in spite of a significant amount of new housing being constructed in the 20th century; 1331 people lived here in 1991. Interestingly, a recent aerial survey has shown evidence for extensive, probably medieval, earthworks beyond the current built-up area, suggesting that significant contraction has occurred at some stage of its history. Did this result from one of the Great Plagues (1348 or 1665) or from depopulation caused by conversion of common lands to sheep pastures?

Wye Valley Gorge (2)

In this part of the Lower Wye Gorge, the river has cut its way down through the Devonian Upper Old Red Sandstone rocks (Tintern Sandstone and Quartz Conglomerate) into the Lower Old Red Sandstone Brownstones *(see Walk 1)*. The valley profile here is somewhat less steep than the sheer cliffs which characterise the gorge in areas of Carboniferous Limestone, such as around Symonds Yat. The low-lying cultivated ground below the viewpoint was once within a meander of the Wye (the Bigsweir Meander), abandoned when the river cut down through the neck of the meander. The fields are underlain by river terrace gravels, and to the right of these is the unusually named hamlet of The Fence. There is another, even more spectacular, abandoned meander a couple of miles upstream, between Redbrook and Newland. The Wye was once the main means of transport in the area, being navigable at least as far up as Hereford. Llandogo, the village seen on the Welsh side, was once, like Brockweir *(Walk 14)*, a boat-building centre and an important port for small sailing vessels, which worked to South Wales, Bristol, and elsewhere. The importance of the river trade is indicated by the 36-vessel fleet of ships and trows owned by James Hodges of Llandogo in the early 1800s. These conveyed timber and bark, much of it to Ireland, with the return cargo being iron ore from Furness, Lancashire. The Sloop Inn, which was built as a cider house and mill in 1707, is a reminder of these times. In the latter part of the

19th century, it was owned by Alfred Williams, a master mariner and barge owner. The Bristol connection is shown by a pub in that city called the Llandoger Trow, originally a mid-17th century timber-framed merchant's house. A trow (rhymes with 'crow') was a flat-bottomed sailing barge used on the Severn and the Wye. A typical example is the 'Hannah Louisa', built at Llandogo in 1868, which was 71 ft 2 in. long, with a beam of 12 ft 7 in., a draught of 6 ft 2 in., and a weight of 56 tons. The last surviving trow is the *Spry*, now on display at the Blist's Hill Museum at Ironbridge in Shropshire. The bell of *The William and Sarah*, one of the last Chepstow barges to trade on the river, can be found in the bell tower of Llandogo's St Oudoceus church, which was built in 1860. Until the turnpike road between Monmouth and Chepstow (now the A466), which crossed the river at Bigsweir Bridge, was opened in 1828, the main overland route was over the hills through Trellech, a short distance away on the Welsh side. It is hard to believe that this quiet village was once one of the most important towns in Medieval Wales: in the late 13th century it was larger than Cardiff or Chepstow. The opening of the Wye Valley Railway in 1876 *(see Walk 13)* continued the use of the Wye Valley as a major transport route, but was one of the final nails in the coffin of the up-river trade *(see also Walk 14)*. Just above Llandogo are the waterfalls called Cleddon Shoots (near which St Briavel may have been born), best seen after heavy rain.

Slade Brook Travertine Dams (3)

This remarkable series of dams (at least 60) occurs over nearly half a mile of Slade Brook. They completely dam the stream, which is from 3 to 30 ft wide, and range from about 1 to 18 inches in height, with an average of about a foot. Such dams are formed when spring water, near-saturated in lime, runs over obstructions in the stream bed, when loss of dissolved carbon dioxide results in deposition of travertine (a porous, friable type of limestone). Development of dams may well have been initiated by water running over accumulations of twigs and branches across the stream. The dams are colonised by various species of moss and algae, which become encrusted by travertine as the dams build up, and they have considerable conservation value. Most of the water in the stream is discharged from a large spring, which emerges from the Carboniferous Limestone bedrock near the head of the valley. The Slade Brook dams are possibly the best example of such structures in the country. On no account should they be touched, as they are easily damaged.

Mork (4)

The hamlet of Mork has some interesting listed buildings. White-painted 'Sladbrook' dates from the late 18th or early 19th century, and once included a watermill. It was also used as a smithy, but is now a private dwelling. At the back of the cottage the roof is swept down and the building is partly over Mork Stream. Mork Farmhouse was built in the 16th or 17th century of local sandstone, with a Welsh slate roof. The hamlet of Stowe, about half a mile up the road towards Clearwell, includes the 16th century (with 19th century additions) Stowe Grange farmhouse, reputed to date from 1563. Nearby are the sparse remains of the medieval Chapel of St Margaret, now part of a group of farm buildings which includes a large 18th century sandstone rubble field barn.

Stowe Court is a large detached house dating from the 17th, 18th and 19th centuries, with an adjoining walled garden enclosure. There is evidence for much older human activity near here: a concentration of flint artefacts on the hill just north of Slade Brook suggests a Mesolithic camp site. Neolithic stone axes have also been found, and there is a particular concentration of Neolithic flints on the Bearse, between St Briavels and Bream, indicating that the area was being settled by that time. Bronze Age flints have also been found in the latter area, and there was once a large standing stone, the Broadstone of probable similar age, nearby.

Bigsweir Wood (5)

The Lower Wye Valley's native woodlands form some of the best examples of ravine woodlands remaining in Europe. They occur on nutrient-rich soils on the valley sides and bottoms, along about 18 miles of the Lower Wye Valley AONB. The woodland is dominated by ash, beech, and yew, with an intimate mix of other native woodland trees, including small-leaved lime and oak, although there are also commercial conifer plantations. There are nationally important populations of plant and animal species, such as Tintern spurge, narrow-leaved bittercress, greater and lesser horseshoe bats, dormouse, and white admiral butterfly. As such the Wye Valley is one of the most important areas for woodland conservation in Britain. However, the survival of these woods is threatened by the decline of traditional woodland management techniques, like coppicing, and by overgrazing by wild fallow deer, which prevents regeneration. Fortunately, these issues are now being addressed. Much of the woodland on the eastern side of the Wye Valley between here and Redbrook is owned by the Woodland Trust. Bigsweir Wood is dominated by oak, small-leaved lime, and beech, but elsewhere there are large areas of conifers. The latter will gradually be restored to native woodland, as some of the original woodland trees (oaks, yews, and limes) and herbs persist in parts of the wood, while the seeds of other plants are lying dormant in the soil. The conifers will initially be thinned to give space to the surviving broad-leaved trees and to allow light to penetrate to the forest floor and stimulate the re-growth of woodland flora. The remaining conifers will eventually be harvested and replaced with the original forest species.

Evidence of former industrial activity can still be seen in the woods. Because timber holds too much water to produce the very high temperatures needed for smelting operations, it was necessary to first convert it to charcoal. This was produced by piling dried wood on a platform (a flat area of ground), covering it with a layer of turf, and then igniting it, so that only partial combustion occurred. Thin sections of wood, commonly oak, were obtained by coppicing to ensure a constant supply. The sites of these charcoal platforms can still be seen, the product being used in forges at places like Redbrook and Tintern. Towards the top of the valley side are a number of small quarries, where Quartz Conglomerate was obtained for making millstones, which were then lowered down to the Wye for transport. Unfinished or damaged millstones can still be found amongst the boulders which litter the hillside on both sides of the valley between Brockweir and Redbrook, and others can be seen in the river when the water is low, presumably having been lost when being transported downhill or during loading onto boats. Although not easy to pick out on the ground, the late 8th century earthwork of Offa's Dyke *(see Walk 14)* passes through Bigsweir Wood. Its course has recently been confirmed by a lidar survey *(see Walk 10)*.

Bigsweir Bridge (6)

Bigsweir Bridge formed part of a toll road along the Wye Valley between Monmouth and Chepstow, which was authorised in 1824. The road replaced earlier routes over the hills on each side of the Wye, via Redbrook, St Briavels and Tidenham Chase, and via Trellech and Tintern Cross. It was opened in 1828 and incorporates a stone toll house at the western (Welsh) end. The bridge was designed by

Charles Hollis and the ironwork was cast at Merthyr Tydfil. It consists of a single cast iron arch of 164 ft span with four ribs of dumbbell section; the spandrels have N-pattern bracing. The arch is supported on circular stone piers and is surmounted by a cast iron balustrade. In the mid 19th century, two masonry flood arches were added at each end, bringing the overall length to 321 ft. In 1876 the Wye Valley Railway opened, and St Briavels station was built near the western end of the bridge. The bridge now carries considerable traffic on the A466 between Chepstow and Monmouth, but its restricted width (12 ft) necessitates one-way traffic controlled by lights. It was named after Bigs Weir, about 600 yds downstream, near which there was once a wharf. Just above the weir (on the English side) is Bigsweir House, a large mid-18th century country house, once the seat of the Rooke family. The house is built of cut sandstone blocks, with a Welsh slate roof, and the front entrance has a Roman Doric portico with pediment, approached by steps.

St Briavels Station (7)

The Wye Valley Railway from Wye Valley Junction, near Chepstow, to Wyesham Junction, near Monmouth, was opened on 1 November 1876 *(see Walk 13)*. Passenger services ceased in January 1959, and the line finally closed to goods in January 1964. St Briavels station was actually situated in Wales, and was nearly 2 miles by road from the village it served (a long way uphill to carry your shopping). Originally named Bigsweir, it was renamed St Briavels and Llandogo in May 1909, before becoming simply St Briavels on 1 February 1927, prior to the opening of Llandogo Halt.

The small stone station building and single platform were on the western (up) side of the line, and there was a signal box adjacent to the level crossing on the A466 road. There was a loop and sidings in a small goods yard, which had a goods shed and storage shed, as well as 30 cwt and 5 ton cranes. The station closed to both passenger and goods traffic on 5 January 1959. The station building is one of only two on the line to survive (the other is Tintern), and is now used by a fishing club. The goods shed also survives, but in a derelict condition.

The Hudnalls (8)

The earliest reference was in 1282, when the Forest Eyre recorded that "The Hudnalls wood is a desmesne wood of the Lord King and is cut down by the men of St Briavels, who claim the liberty of taking from there at will and have always taken from there in this way". It was part of the Royal Manor of St Briavels, and hence extraparochial, until 1842, when most was incorporated into St Briavels Parish, the rest going to Hewelsfield. Most of the flatter land on the plateau was settled and enclosed in the late 18th/early 19th centuries *(see 11 below)*, but the steeply sloping hillsides above the River Wye and Lindors Brook survived as an important example of ancient semi-natural woodland. The section above the Wye has recently been bought by English Nature as a National Nature Reserve. The woods consist mainly of beech, pendunculate and sessile oaks, ash, and small-leaved lime, with hazel, holly, and yew in the underwood; there are also a few wych elm and field maple. Birch, cherry, and rare aspen are found in disturbed areas, and alder on wet ground. The beech- and oak-dominated areas have been much coppiced in the past. Fallow deer are often seen in the woods and nearby fields. A number of small streams flow down boulder-filled gullies, and evidence for human activity includes a few ruined buildings, broken-down stone walls, and abandoned millstones. The Hudnalls is the subject of some of the oldest commoners' rights in England, where men of St Briavels have long been permitted to take wood (estovers), graze animals (herbage), and run pigs for acorns and beech mast (pannage). These rights are thought to date back at least to the time of Milo Fitz Walter, builder of St Briavels Castle, who seems to have granted them on the urging of his daughter, Margaret. However, it is quite likely that Milo was merely confirming rights which were already old, and that he was acting on behalf of King Henry I. Interestingly, there are several references to a Margaret in the area, notably St Margaret's Chapel at Stowe *(see 4)*, and St Margaret's Well, near The Fence. The rights in the Hudnalls are intimately associated with the Bread and Cheese Dole, described above *(1)*. Whatever their origin, these unique rights still exist, being registered in 1977 under the 1965 Commons Act, although they are now rarely exercised.

Birchfield House (9)

This unusual house, whch has two narrow, but lofty front gables, was built in 1908. It appears to have been an extension to a late 18th century building, the rather plain block set against the gable wall. The latter was used until recently as a Child Development Centre. There is a lovely view up the Wye Valley towards Monmouth from in front of the house, which can be seen from afar.

Gideon Chapel (10)

This originated as a school in 1852. It seems to have been used as a chapel by 1908, when the Congregational Church at St. Briavels had an outlying mission there. In recent years the Gideon Chapel has been used mainly as a youth centre by young members of the St. Briavels congregation and by visiting groups from other churches.

St Briavels Common (11)

Together with the adjoining Hewelsfield Common, St Briavels Common was originally part of the woodland of the Hudnalls, a tract of extraparochial common land. In medieval times, most of the flatter uplands seem to have been relatively open woodland, with grassy clearings used as pasture. Much of this was settled and enclosed by squatters between about 1750 and 1810, leaving only the steeper slopes above the Wye as woodland *(see 8)*. The result was an unusual landscape of small fields, isolated cottages, and small patches of woodland, separated by narrow winding lanes and footpaths *(see Walk 14)*.

Old tramroads and collieries, stone quarries, a famous iron works, a nature reserve, and a typical Forest village. The walk is mainly on forest tracks and old railway trackbeds, with one steady climb up Bixslade and a short steep descent towards Darkhill. The 7 miles/11 km route includes the Nagshead detour.

START at the lay-by opposite the Forest of Dean Stoneworks (or the one beside the works) at the southern end of Cannop Ponds on the Parkend–Lydbrook Road (B4234): GR SO 607099. **Refreshments:** Pubs and shop in Parkend. **Bus:** 727 (Lydney–Parkend) to Parkend.

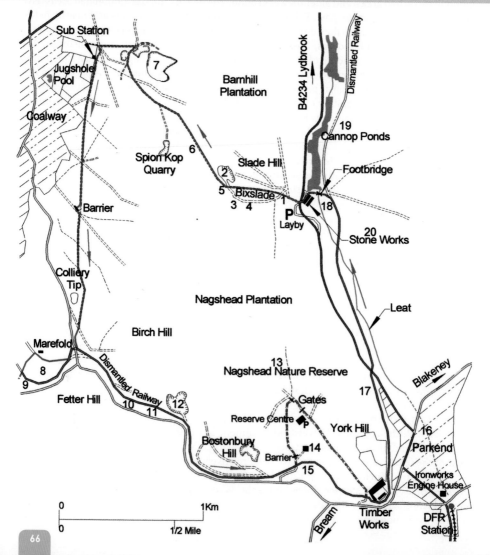

66

THE WALK STARTS along the gravel road just across the main road from the Forest of Dean Stone Firms' stoneworks, briefly following the Gloucestershire Way *(see Walk 14)*. After 100 yds, where the gravel road bends right, bear slightly left onto a footpath. Note the stone blocks of the Severn & Wye Railway's Bicslade (sic) Tramroad *(1)*, which was the last horse-drawn tramroad operating in Dean. Cross a gravel road and continue up the valley (Bixslade), with more stone blocks visible, to a small clearing with a quarry entrance on the right. This is Mine Train Quarry *(2)*. About 50 yds back along a gravel track on the left is a memorial to the disaster at Union Colliery *(3)* in 1902, which killed four men, and just beyond that is Monument Mine *(4)*, one of the few remaining coal mines in the Forest.

Return to the clearing, and in a dip opposite the quarry entrance is Bixslade Low Level, part of Bixslade Colliery *(5)*. Go past two large rocks and follow a footpath up the valley. Bixslade High Level *(6)* is down on the left after about 350 yds, but in summer may be hidden behind undergrowth. Continue past other old mine and quarry workings to a junction, where a side path goes left under powerlines. Keep straight ahead here for 150 yds to a clearing, where the track bears slightly right between fenced-off quarries. Continue for about 100 yds, noting some old iron tramroad plates in the fence on the right, and then turn left on a track which initially follows powerlines. Alternatively, you can turn right here for a short distance to see (from outside the fence) some of the extensive workings of Bixhead Quarries *(7)* before returning to the track junction. Follow the track to the next junction, where you turn left and then almost immediately bear right onto a footpath. This passes to the left of an electricity substation and then follows powerlines as a mostly wider track, with pine forest on the left. After about ¾ mile, the track bends right to a barrier, beyond

which you turn left on a forest road. Take the next track on the right, again following the powerlines and ignoring side paths, for a further ½ mile until you come out onto a gravel road. Cross this and take the narrow footpath almost opposite, which goes steeply downhill to emerge onto a tarmac road at a cycle track crossing.

The walk can be shortened by about ½ mile here by turning sharp left through the gate onto the cycle track. Otherwise, cross over the main road, follow the cycle track for 50 yds, and then fork right onto a footpath by a large boulder. The remains of Darkhill Ironworks *(8)* are soon seen on the left, and note the stone tramroad blocks along the path. Turn left between stone posts onto a descending footpath just opposite the entrance to Marefold (note the large lumps of slag here). On reaching a gravel cycle track, go left. This is the trackbed of the former Severn & Wye Railway's Coleford Branch *(9)*. There are more views of the ironworks, a memorial to the Mushet family, and an information board before the track returns you to the main road.

Cross the road and follow the cycle track, soon passing the sites of Darkhill *(10)* and Hopewell Engine *(11)* Collieries on the right. The circular shaft of the latter is just beside the track. The disused Point Quarry *(12)* is on the left, about 200 yds further on: note the line of the original tramroad from the quarry, which passed under the railway through a short tunnel here and continued towards Parkend below and to the right of the railway. Where the cycle track crosses a tarmac lane just before some cottages, a worthwhile half-mile detour can be made to Nagshead Nature Reserve *(13)*. To visit this, turn left here, following a waymarked footpath, the Gloucestershire Way, past the driveway to Western Lodge *(14)* on the right, and passing a barrier onto a gravel track. Follow this through a gate, turn right to go past the visitors' centre and car park, and continue ahead along the gravel access road. This eventually takes you back to the cycle track, where you turn left, near sawmill buildings. Otherwise, keep ahead past the site of Venus and Jupiter Colliery *(15)* to a Parkend sign, where the detour rejoins from the left, continuing with the sawmill on your left and a road on your right.

Follow the cycle track signs left at Hughes Terrace, then right behind houses. This is Parkend *(16)*, which has several points of interest worth a detour around the village green. The cycle track passes the site of Coleford Junction, before continuing along the trackbed of the former Severn & Wye Railway's main line *(17)*. Cross a main road and continue along the cycle track. Visible at several points (including one behind some stone walling on the right and another where the track crosses it) is the leat which fed water from Cannop Ponds to Parkend Ironworks. A few yards before reaching a Cannop Wharf (sic) nameboard (and signpost to Dilke Bridge) are the remains of Bicslade Wharf *(18)*, with several large stone blocks, on the left. Turn left just before the nameboard to cross a footbridge at the end of Cannop Ponds *(19)*, keeping right of the stoneworks *(20)*. As you climb up to the main road and parking area, look down to spot the last piece of tramroad track still in situ.

Ian Pope Collection.

The tramroad today.

Bicslade Tramroad (1)

The Bicslade Tramroad was a branch of the Severn and Wye Railway's tramroad from Lydney to Lydbrook *(see 17)*, which opened in 1810. The ¾-mile branch was built to serve collieries and stone quarries along Bixslade and had opened by June 1812. Horse-drawn 4-wheeled wagons were used for transporting coal and twin-bogie wagons for stone. The original track consisted of L-section cast iron plates, 3 ft long and weighing 42 lbs, spiked to 14 inch-square stone blocks (or setts) with single iron nails. Later track utilised longer plates, set on chairs which were attached to the blocks with two tapered bosses. The gauge was nominally 3 ft 6 in., but this tended to widen with time. After 1874, when the main tramroad was abandoned in favour of a standard-gauge line, traffic was transhipped to the latter at Bicslade Wharf *(18)*. Traffic declined in the 20th century, the last load of stone being taken out on 25 July 1944 and coal traffic had ceased by

November 1946. However, the short section between the stoneworks and Bicslade Wharf remained in use into the 1950s. This was the last working tramroad in the Forest. Note that the S&WR used the spelling 'Bicslade', whereas most maps show 'Bixslade'.

Mine Train Quarry (2)

There was a quarry here by 1835, at least, working the Pennant Sandstone of the Upper Coal Measures. Together with many other Forest quarries, it was taken over by Messrs. Trotter, Thomas & Co. in 1836. The firm was amalgamated into David & Sant Limited in 1892, and this was acquired by the Forest of Dean Stone Firms in 1900. In 1910 the United Stone Firms was formed to operate all the major quarries in the Forest, and the quarry is still active today, owned by Robert and John Tainton and providing stone for customers as far away as Scotland. In 1899 stone from Mine Train Quarry was supplied to the Marquis of Bute for use in Cardiff Castle. The quarry workings have intersected part of Birch Hill Iron Mine, which was galed to Mr Stopford of Macclesfield in 1858, and produced 3600 tons of hematite between 1906 and 1932. This mine was unusual in being located in Pennant Group rocks, whereas most of the Dean iron mines are in or near the underlying Crease Limestone. Thin veins of hematite can be seen in some of the large sandstone blocks outside the quarry entrance.

Union Colliery (3)

The Union gale was leased by James and Robert Morrell, Oxford bankers, in 1824 to allow further extension of their interests along Bixslade. They had leased Miles Level, near the southern end of Cannop Ponds, since 1815, and Hopewell Engine gale since 1822; all of these were eventually connected underground. By 1841, Union Pit (or Bixhead Slade Pit) on Miles Level was 75 ft deep and producing about 8400 tons of coal per year from the Coleford High Delf and Yorkley Seams. Work had ceased by 1877 when the gale was surrendered. In 1892 the gales were bought by the Parkend Deep Navigation Collieries Co. Ltd, who re-opened Slade Pit (as the Royal Union Steam Navigation Colliery), the shaft ultimately being 252 ft deep. About 100 men were employed and about 100 tons of coal per day were produced. The latter was taken down the Bicslade Tramroad for transhipment onto the S&WR at Bicslade Wharf. However, the coal was of inferior quality and there were serious problems with water. On 4th September 1902 the colliery was flooded by an influx of water from abandoned workings, trapping seven men, of whom three were found alive after five days. The colliery was then closed, the gale being sold to the Princess Royal Collieries Co. Ltd, who worked the remaining coal from the Fetter Hill direction. The site is now largely overgrown and there is little to be seen, apart from a stone structure on the site of the shaft, and a nearby adit, now marked by a steel pipe used by bats. The disaster is commemorated by a

statue of two trapped miners (the James brothers) embracing, commissioned by the Forest Freeminers, and a plaque. The statue is the work of sculptor Matt Baker, and is carved from Pennant Sandstone from nearby Mine Train Quarry.

Monument Mine (4)

Formerly known as Hayners Bailey or Bixslade Free Mine, Monument Mine (named after the nearby Union Pit Disaster Memorial) is one of only a handful of small mines (3 at the time of writing) still producing coal in the Forest. It works the Yorkley Seam of the Pennant Group via a 200 yd inclined drift. A typical working Forest mine, it includes the drift entrance, tramway with tubs, and a coal-loading wharf with screens. The mine is currently operated by Ray Ashley, Neil Jones, and Richard Daniels. The origin of the ancient rights of Free Miners to mine a gale (a mining licence area) are thought to have been awarded to Forest miners as a reward for undermining the walls of Berwick Castle during one of the sieges by either Edward I or III in the late 13th or early 14th century. To qualify, a miner must be male, have been born in, and abide in, the Hundred of St Briavels, be over the age of 21 years, and have worked in a mine for a year and a day. The gales are granted on behalf of the Crown, subject to compliance with the 1841 regulations, by the Gaveller or his deputy.

Bixslade Low Level (5)

There was a colliery in Bixslade at least by the 1790s, when James Teague was a partner in Bixslade Water Engine Pit. Bixslade Low (or Deep) Level was begun in 1809 by Thomas Halford and David Mushet to exploit the Coleford High Delf Seam. By 1841 Bixslade Colliery (which included the High Level) was producing about 30000 tons of coal per year, which was transported on the Bicslade Tramroad, but production seems to have ceased by about 1871. Martin James was killed by a fall in 1853, his age being recorded as 8 years! In 1908 the Bixslade Colliery Co. employed 20 people, and the tramroad was conveying coal until 1946. Since then, free miners have worked parts of the Bixslade gale via several new levels. The stone-lined entrances to Bixslade Low and High Levels survive, as do several infilled shafts.

Bixslade High Level (6)

Bixslade High (or Land) Level was driven in 1826 by David Mushet and, like the Low Level, worked the Coleford High Delf Seam, as well as draining a large area west of the Cannop Valley. There are two shafts nearby.

Bixhead Quarries (7)

There were around 20 quarries in the area in 1675, working the Pennant Sandstone for building stone and other purposes. The Bicslade Tramroad had opened by 1812, and stone, as well as coal, could then be transported to the Severn & Wye Railway's main line at Cannop.

Various quarries at Bixhead were owned by Messrs. Trotter, Thomas & Co., T. Porter, and E.R. Payne in 1877. The first two became part of David & Sant Ltd in 1892, which had 41 quarries by 1899, but further amalgamations resulted in formation of the Forest of Dean Stone Firms Ltd in 1900. The United Stone Firms was formed in 1910 to operate all the major quarries in the Forest, but went into liquidation in 1913. It was re-organised in 1926, but went

into receivership again in 1931. Work continued under the receiver until 1939, when the firm was acquired by the present Forest of Dean Stone Firms Ltd who still operate the largest quarry. Until recently, a large crane was used to lift stone blocks from the quarry floor. There are extensive underground workings, and a large area southeast of the present Bixhead Quarry has been quarried over the centuries. The abandoned quarries make good habitats for ferns, and one of them, Spion Kop Quarry a little way down the valley, is a nature reserve.

Darkhill Ironworks (8)

These were built in 1818 by David Mushet, a Scottish metallurgist who had originally come to Coleford in 1810 to run Whitecliff Furnace *(see Walk 9)*. At Darkhill, he developed a method for producing high-quality iron by direct smelting. In 1845 the works were transferred to his three sons, who, unfortunately, were not on good terms, which led to many problems. Robert became manager, and developed the steel used in the first successful steel railway rail. This was rolled by the Ebbw Vale Iron Co. and laid

in Derby Station in 1857. Its manufacture involved adding spiegeleisen (a type of pig iron rich in manganese and carbon) to the molten iron. Unfortunately, due to lack of funding and poor health, Robert Mushet lost his patent, and the technique was adopted by Henry Bessemer in his Bessemer Converter method. Bessemer later admitted that his success was due to Robert's experimental work, and, at the urging of Robert's daughter, Mary, paid off his debts of £344 14s 10d. Robert went on to develop self-hardening steel, which contained titanium and could be used for making drill bits. To manufacture this he built the Titanic Steelworks, immediately to the west. However, economic success was still not achieved, and the Titanic Co. was wound up in 1874. Today the Darkhill site is difficult to interpret, due in part to the secrecy with which much of the work was done. The blast furnace and blowing-engine house near the bottom of the site date from the later period of operation. There are also remains of experimental furnaces, as well as brick-making kilns and drying rooms. Little survives at the Titanic Steelworks site.

Coleford Branch (9)

This originated as the Milkwall (or Darkhill) branch of the Severn & Wye Railway's tramroad, one of about 10 branches. The first section from Parkend to Dark Hill opened not long after the main tramroad, in about 1812. It served stone quarries and collieries around Fetter Hill and Dark Hill, and iron mines at Milkwall. The tramroad remained in use until the Coleford Branch railway was opened to goods traffic on 9 December 1875, and to passenger trains the following month. However, a short section of tramroad to Point Quarry was retained for some time after this. In 1900 there were 5 or 6 daily passenger trains each way on the Coleford Branch, most of which connected with Lydney/Berkeley Road or Lydbrook services at Parkend. Regular passenger services ceased on 6 July 1929, but goods services lasted longer: stone from Whitecliff Quarry (actually situated on the remaining stub of the Coleford Railway, *see Walk 9*) was carried until 1967.

Darkhill Colliery (10)

There was a colliery at Dark Hill by 1813 when it was sold to John Hawkins. The gale was confirmed as being awarded to David Mushet in 1841, and by 1847 he had also obtained the neighbouring Shutcastle gale. Dark Hill (or Darkhill) level was close to the S&WR's Milkwall (later Coleford) Branch, and after about 1875 was served by Fetterhill Sidings. It worked the Coleford High Delf Seam (6 ft thick here). On Mushet's death in 1847, the colliery, together with his Darkhill Ironworks and Shutcastle Colliery, were put up for auction, but did not sell and passed to his three sons, soon being held by David Mushet (Jr) alone. Darkhill was worked intermittently thereafter, only 4206 tons of coal being produced in 1880. It was bought by Thomas Bennett Brain in 1899. Little work seems to have been done after his death in 1914, although the gale continued to be worked from several adjoining gales. Nearby was Darkhill

Hopewell Engine Colliery shaft beside the former Severn & Wye Valley Railway's Coleford Branch.

Brickworks, which were also owned by Mushet in 1841. A brickworks at or near the same site was owned by Messrs Wanklyn and Grindle from the mid-1850s until about 1900. There were also stoneworks here, using stone from local quarries. E. Turner and Sons operated one in the early 20th century, and Thomas Pullen owned one from 1920 until at least the 1950s, after which it was taken over by Simpsons.

Hopewell Engine Colliery (11)

There was a colliery here in 1836, when Thomas and James Bennett (presumably the lessees) applied to erect a steam engine at 'Hope-Well

Pit', although the gale had been held by James and Robert Morrell since 1822. The pit was open in 1863, and a connection was made with the S&WR's Milkwall (later Coleford) Branch. Sidings at Fetterhill, laid in 1875, served several collieries, including Hopewell Engine and Darkhill. Like the latter, Hopewell presumably worked the Coleford High Delf Seam, and 4331 tons of coal were produced in 1880. A dispute arose with the S&WR in 1889–90 over workings causing damage to the line. In 1909 the colliery was up for sale, and by 1913 it was owned by the Parkend Deep Navigation Collieries Co. Ltd, who used it simply to protect their other interests from flooding. It was transferred to the Mapleford Colliery Ltd in 1928, but it is uncertain if any more work was done.

Point Quarry (12)

Sandstone of the Pennant Group has been worked for building stone and other uses for centuries. Point Quarry is one of several in the valley (Quest Slade) between Fetterhill and Parkend, others being on Birch and Bostonbury Hills. It was owned by Edwin Payne in the 1870s and Richard and Juliana Payne in the 1890s, the family firm dating back to 1760. A new company, E.R. Payne & Son, was set up in 1905, and a well-equipped stone works was opened in the quarry soon after. The Paynes also had quarries at Dark Hill, Wimberry, Bixhead, and Barnhill. Sidings were provided when the S&WR's Coleford Branch was opened in 1875, although there had been a tramroad connection to Parkend since about 1812. Like many others, Point Quarry was taken over by the United Stone Firms Co. Ltd in 1910, but seems to have closed by 1939, although some stone may have been quarried after WW2. A few stone blocks and remains of the loading wharf survive, but the quarry is much overgrown. The stone-lined tramroad tunnel under the Coleford Branch trackbed is in good condition.

Pied flycatcher.

Nagshead Nature Reserve (13)

This reserve, run by the RSPB, covers 435 acres, more than half of which is covered by oak trees planted in the early 19th century for use in naval ships. A wide variety of breeding and visiting birds can be seen at different times of the year, notably blackcaps, bullfinches, crossbills, dippers, goldcrests, grey wagtails, nuthatches, pied and spotted flycatchers, redstarts, redwings, siskins, tits, treecreepers, wood warblers, and woodpeckers. Buzzards and goshawks may be seen circling overhead. The reserve is also home to many species of reptiles (lizards, adders, slow worms, grass snakes), amphibians (frogs, toads, and newts), butterflies, and dragonflies.

Western Lodge (14)

After excessive timber felling by Sir John Wynter in the mid-17th century, the Dean Forest (Reafforestation) Act of 1668 allowed the enclosure of 11 000 acres, divided into six Walks, each with a lodge, which housed a keeper *(see Walk 5)*. Further problems continued throughout the 18th century, resulting in a new Enclosure Act in 1808. This allowed construction of 24 new lodges, and several more were built later in the 19th century. Western Lodge is a typical example.

Venus and Jupiter Colliery (15)

Venus & Jupiter gale was granted to George and James Baldwin in 1841, who sold it to Thomas Protheroe and Thomas Phillips. A pit (known at that time as Great Western Colliery) was sunk to the Yorkley Seam (Pennant Group), but little useable coal was found and there were major problems with water; the gale was surrendered in 1887. The Venus Colliery Co. Ltd was formed in 1895, but also met with little success and the company went into liquidation in 1900, the only coal produced having come from old workings. A siding from the Severn and Wye Joint Railway's Coleford branch was laid in 1895, but was removed around 1903. The gale passed to Princess Royal Colliery Co. Ltd in 1900.

Parkend (16)

Probably the most typical of the Forest villages, Parkend was once a thriving industrial centre, but is now a peaceful backwater surrounded by woodlands. The parish of Parkend was not founded until 1822, prior to which the area was part of the Royal Hunting Forest. There was an iron furnace, using charcoal, and a forge here in 1612, but Parkend only became an important iron-making centre with the coming of blast furnaces which could use coke made from local coal. A new ironworks was set up in 1799, and much of the present day village was built as a result. The works fell idle in about 1807, but were bought in 1824 by Edward Protheroe, who then leased them to the Forest of Dean Iron Co., set up by Moses Teague, Benjamin Whitehouse, and William Montague. A new blast furnace was built, together with a 51ft diameter water wheel to operate the furnaces and forge hammers, using water from Cannop Ponds to the north. Unfortunately, the wheel was not a great success and a new steam engine also proved to be necessary. Booming business led to a third furnace being built in 1871. The ironworks and nearby tinplate works were bought by Edwin Crawshay in 1875, but by this time the industry was in decline and the works closed in

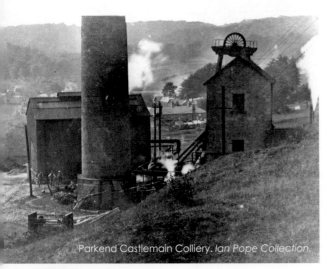

Parkend Castlemain Colliery. Ian Pope Collection.

1877. Iron ore came from mines in the Oakwood Valley, and coal from pits at Fetterhill and Parkend. Edward Protheroe was one of the biggest coal owners in the Parkend area, having interests in the Parkend gale from around 1820 until his death in 1856. By 1827 his pits included Park End Main, Park End Royal, and Castlemain, as well as New Fancy, a mile to the northeast. Production from the Parkend pits was 31364 tons of coal in 1841, 57266 tons in 1845, and 86973 tons in 1856, the latter being the highest in Dean that year. The pits closed in 1880, following a slump in the coal trade, but under the management of Thomas Deakin they were soon prosperous again. Working was integrated with that of New Fancy Colliery, the combined output averaging 80000 tons/year in the 1880s. A rail connection was made in 1887 by extending the Furnace branch of the Parkend ironworks (the Parkend Royal branch), which joined the S&WR near Coleford Junction. Parkend had one pumping shaft (Castlemain, 476 ft deep) and two other shafts (Parkend Royal, the deeper being 590 ft).

Castlemain shaft today.

Pumping was carried out by a 72-inch Cornish engine, installed in 1877. The workings were in the Supra-Pennant Group, which includes the 3 ft-thick Parkend High Delf Seam. Although Parkend itself ceased to produce coal in 1929, it remained connected underground to New Fancy to provide an emergency exit, with Castlemain shaft used for pumping and ventilation, until final closure in 1944.

Parkend has a number of interesting buildings. The ironworks engine house (1849) became the first Forestry Training School in 1908, and is now the Dean Field Studies Centre. Castlemain Mill was formerly the colliery offices. St Paul's Church, designed by Richard James and built in 1822, has an unusual octagonal shape. Parkend County Primary School, built in 1822, has a fine Gothic-style window. There are two pubs, the Fountain (late 18th century) and the Woodman. Parkend Station was on the S&WR between Lydney and Lydbrook, which opened to passengers on 23 September 1875. It was the junction for the Coleford Branch, which opened to passengers in January 1876. There were two platforms, with the wooden station building on the down side, and a small shelter on the up. Regular passenger services ended on 6 July 1929, but goods services to Lydney ran until 1976. Happily, it is still possible to travel from Lydney to Parkend by steam train: the volunteer-run Dean Forest Railway operates regular services at popular times *(see Walk 2)*. A useful leaflet (Parkend Village Walk, by Keith Webb) is available from the DFR at Norchard.

Severn and Wye Railway (17)

Originally authorised by Act of Parliament as the 'Lydney and Lydbrook Railway' in 1809, the name was changed to the Severn and Wye Railway and Canal Co. the following year. Two of the original subscribers were Edward Protheroe, who went on to become chairman, and David Mushet, both prominent industrialists. The company opened a 3 ft 6 in. gauge horse tramroad from Lydney to Lydbrook via Serridge Junction in 1810. The main line, together with a number of branches, was built to serve collieries and stone quarries in the area. The southern part of the main tramroad was converted to broad gauge in 1868, and steam locomotives were introduced. A mineral loop line from Tufts Junction, near Whitecroft, to Drybrook Road *(see Walk 5)* was opened in 1872. This served several important collieries, including New Fancy, Lightmoor, Foxes Bridge, and Crump Meadow, as well as other industries. The broad-gauge lines were soon converted to standard gauge, and the first passenger train ran from Lydney to Lydbrook on 23 September 1875. With

Bicslade Wharf in 1948. *Ian Pope Collection.*

the opening of the Severn railway bridge in 1879, the company became the Severn and Wye and Severn Bridge Railway. This, in turn, became the Severn and Wye Joint Railway (Great Western and Midland Railways) in 1894. An extension to Cinderford opened in 1900. In that year there were five daily passenger services each way between Lydbrook Junction and Lydney Town, most of which worked to or from Berkeley Road over the Severn Bridge; additional trains served the Coleford Branch. Regular passenger services from Lydney to Cinderford and Lydbrook ceased on 6 July 1929, although the service from Berkeley Road (on the former Midland Railway's Gloucester–Bristol line) to Lydney Town was only terminated by the collapse of the Severn Bridge in 1960 *(see Walk 4)*. Freight traffic generally lasted longer: the Lydbrook branch was closed to goods on 30 January 1956, although there had been little or no traffic for over three years; stone from Whitecliff Quarry was transported over the Coleford Branch until 1967; and the Parkend to Lydney section survived until 1976.

Bicslade Wharf (18)

After 1874, when the main Severn & Wye tramroad was abandoned in favour of a standard-gauge railway, traffic from the Bicslade Tramroad was transhipped at Bicslade Wharf, near Cannop Ponds. The main traffic was coal and stone, but this declined in the first half of the 20th century. Stone was moved by cranes erected by the quarry owners, such as E.R. Payne, Turner & Son, and David & Sant, and there were still two in situ in the 1940s. The short section of tramroad between Bixslade Stone Works and Bicslade Wharf did not close until the 1950s, and a short section of L-section tramroad rail can still be seen nearby. The wharf is badly overgrown, but large stone blocks, which once held down a Scotch derrick, a type of tripod crane, can still be seen.

Cannop Ponds (19)

Cannop Ponds were constructed in the early 19th century to supply water, via a stone-lined leat, to Parkend Ironworks. The water powered a 51ft diameter water wheel, which operated the blast furnaces and forge hammers. The ponds area is now an attractive place for walking, picnics, and bird watching, mandarin ducks and other water birds being common here. The mixed plantations in the Cannop Valley include oak, beech, sweet chestnut, Norway spruce, and Douglas fir.

Forest of Dean Stone Firms Stoneworks (20)

The original Forest of Dean Stone Firms Ltd was formed in 1900 to operate many of the Forest quarries. Further amalgamations resulted in the formation of The United Stone Firms Co. Ltd in 1910. This was eventually acquired by the present Forest of Dean Stone Firms Ltd. The stoneworks were built in 1901 by Messrs E. Turner & Sons of Cardiff, who operated a quarry in Bixslade. Only in recent years has it been modernised with the introduction of computer-controlled stone-cutting saws. Bixhead Quarry is still used as a source of stone by the company. Miles Level, which exits below the stoneworks, is about 4 miles long and drains a large area below Bixslade and Birch Hill.

Railway and colliery remains, a Tudor house, and lovely views of Wales and Herefordshire. The walk is mainly on woodland tracks and an old railway trackbed (now a cycle track), with some field paths and lanes; one steady climb; 8 stiles.

START at 'Piano Corner' on minor road (Pludds Road) between Brierley and The Pludds (about 500 yds from junction with A4136 Monmouth–Mitcheldean road): GR SO 621154. Park on gravel area by metal barrier on left-hand side of road when travelling away from Brierley and the A4136. The name is said to have originated when a piano fell off a truck here! **Refreshments:** pubs in Lower Lydbrook. **Bus:** 24 (Gloucester–Joy's Green) to Joy's Green; 31 (Gloucester–Coleford/Berry Hill) to The Swan at Brierley.

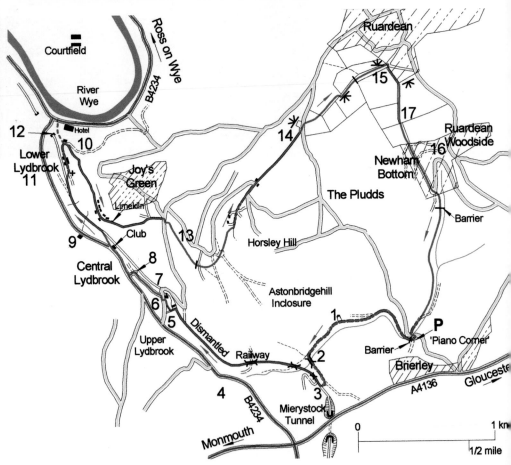

GO PAST THE BARRIER and follow the dirt track down the valley to the right of the stream (i.e., do not cross road). Keep left at a fork, still following the stream (Greathough Brook). An outcrop of Pennant Sandstone (part of the Coal Measures) is seen on the right, after about 250 yds. Just after this, opposite a small open area, is a small cutting with a pipe protruding from the blocked-up adit of Favourite Free Mine *(1)*. Note the small rock carving, now badly weathered, on the left of the cutting. At the next junction, after another 300 yds, turn left to cross the brook over what was originally a tramroad bridge *(2)*. Turn right onto a gravel cycle-track at a T-junction, and then right again after a few yards. This is the track bed of the former Severn & Wye Railway *(3)*, with the recently unearthed portal of Mierystock Tunnel *(Walk 5)* just behind you. Cross three bridges, of which only the stone abutments are original, after which views of the Lydbrook Valley can be seen on the left. The site of Waterloo Colliery *(4)* is on the opposite side of the valley. Pass a massive retaining wall, near which 'Quarry Siding', used by Lydbrook Colliery *(5)*, was situated. Keep straight ahead at a junction where the cycleway goes right uphill, with views of Upper Lydbrook (nameboard) on the left. After 150 yds, turn left in front of a house to go through a gate onto a footpath. Turn right over a stile and cross the churchyard to a gate just below the church *(6)*. Turn right up the road.

After 50 yds, just opposite the church, take the sign-posted public footpath to the left, beside a fence. This soon emerges, via steps, onto a gravel track at a bend. Keep left along this track, going downhill; the site of Upper Lydbrook Station *(7)* is up to the right. Bear left at the bottom, noting the Iron Mine Level *(8)* in the bank on the right. Turn right along the main road past terrace houses. After about 200 yds, just past the Social Club, bear right across a car park to a public footpath sign. Follow the path uphill to emerge onto the old railway track bed again, where you turn left. The ancient half-timbered Sarah Siddon's House *(9)* can

soon be seen in the valley below. Continue on the level track, ignoring a fork downhill to the left, but soon bear right uphill by a fence (with a former chapel up to the right) onto a grass track between houses (part of the former Severn and Wye's tramroad which preceded the railway). This comes out at the end of a tarmac lane. To the right, a dirt track follows the route of the Bishopswood Tramroad *(10)*, and there was an incline down to the Wye here. Ahead, to the left of 'Wye Crest' are steps which lead steeply down to the River Wye at Lower Lydbrook *(11)*, where refreshments may be obtained at the Forge Hammer or Courtfield Arms. To the left of the steps can be seen one of the abutments of Lydbrook railway viaduct *(12)*. Return up the steps if you make this detour.

Follow the tarmac lane uphill for nearly half a mile to 'Limekilns', just past which, on the left, are the sparse remains of an old lime kiln (note the fused rocks). Continue uphill, bearing right at a junction just before a playground to reach a T-junction in Joy's Green. Cross the road here with care, and after a few yards go up a bank onto a footpath into the woods. After 200 yds, some stonework and steel girders on the left are all that remain of Lydbrook Deep Level Free Mine *(13)*. After a further 200 yds, pass a metal barrier, cross a tarmac lane, and continue on the path ahead. Follow this straight ahead, passing a rather overgrown path on the right and continuing over a crossing track to reach a gravel clearing (parking area). We now join a path which heads uphill from the far left-hand corner of the clearing. Follow the path uphill under power lines, bearing slightly right out of the trees and then bearing left alongside a hedge onto a gravel road.

Continue past houses on your left, keeping ahead on a grass track where the gravel one goes right. Lovely views of the Wye Valley begin to open up to the left. The track comes out onto a tarmac road, where you bear left. Follow this for about 150 yds to a sharp bend, but take the public bridleway straight ahead between buildings. Follow this green lane to come out at another road, where there is a viewpoint and seat on the left. The view of the Wye Valley from here *(14)*, weather permitting, is superb. Cross the road behind the viewpoint and take the signed footpath over a stile, bearing half left across the field (where orchids flower in May–June) to another stile. Keep the hedge on your right until you reach a stile in the far right-hand corner. Cross this and turn left, now keeping the hedge on your left to arrive at a stile (there are good views of Ruardean Woodside and Dean from here). Follow a track between hedges, which leads to another lovely viewpoint over Ruardean *(15)*. Turn right onto a narrow footpath to the right of houses, between a wall and hedge. Cross a stone stile into a field, where there are good views of Ruardean Woodside, with several old colliery waste tips visible *(16)*, and Newham Bottom.

Follow a wire fence, and then a hedge, to a stile in the bottom right-hand corner of the field (behind an old tip of True Blue Colliery, *17)*. Now bear slightly left to another stile in the far left-hand corner of the next field, which takes you down onto a road. Follow the road downhill for about ¼ mile to where the road turns sharply left, but keep ahead here onto a downhill path. This goes past a barrier and continues down the valley to the right of the stream, through attractive woodland between conifer plantations (Astonbridgehill Inclosure), with good displays of bluebells in spring. The path joins a gravel road, which will soon return you to the parking area across the road. Brierley is only ¼ mile to the left. The village was the birthplace in 1914 of Winifred Foley, author of *A Child in the Forest*, and other books on the area.

Photo by Dave Morris.

Favourite Free Mine (1)

In 1842 the Favourite gale was granted to William Court in order to sink a pit about 200 yds south of Brierley to get coal between the Coleford High Delf and Churchway High Delf Seams. By 1873 the pit was owned by Messrs Holden and Illingworth, major shareholders in the New Bowson Coal Co. It was idle by 1900. In more recent years, Favourite Free Mine was worked by Eric Morris to exploit coal seams in the Pennant Group via a drift above Greathough Brook. It is distinguished by a small carving of St Piran, patron saint of Cornish miners, which was produced in 1976 by Vanilla Beer. The carving is on the rock face to the left of the former drift entrance, but is now badly weathered.

Severn & Wye Tramroad (2)

The Severn and Wye Railway and Canal Co. opened a 3 ft 6 in. gauge horse tramroad from Lydney to Lydbrook in 1810. Together with a number of branches, it was built to serve collieries and stone quarries in the area. The tramroad was connected to a wharf on the River Wye at Lower Lydbrook by an incline, but this was out of use by the mid-1850s as goods traffic on the tramroad was by then going via Lydney.

Severn & Wye Railway (3)

The Severn and Wye's tramroad was eventually converted to a standard-gauge railway. This section was part of the Lydbrook Branch, which ran from Serridge Junction, between Parkend and Cinderford, to Lydbrook Junction, where there was a station, on the Ross and Monmouth

Railway. The first passenger train ran from Lydney to Lydbrook on 23 September 1875. In 1900 there were five daily passenger services each way between Lydbrook Junction and Lydney Town, most of which worked to or from Berkeley Road over the Severn Bridge. Regular passenger services from Lydney to Cinderford and Lydbrook ceased on 6 July 1929, and final closure to goods trains came on 30 January 1956, although there had been little or no traffic for over three years. At the time of writing, the northern portal of Mierystock Tunnel had been cleared of spoil which had been dumped in the cutting, with a view to re-routing the cycle track through the tunnel. *(See Walk 7 for more details of the S&WR.)*

Arthur & Edward (Waterloo) Colliery (4)

The Arthur & Edward gale was worked by Benjamin Gwilliam and Thomas Butler from the mid-1830s, two shafts being sunk to work the Coleford High Delf Seam. 12857 tons of coal were produced in 1856, when the pit was being worked by the Arthur & Edward and Miery Stock Colliery Co., but the company was wound up in 1859. There appears to have been little subsequent production until the new North-Western United deep gale was acquired by the Lydney and Crump Meadow Collieries Co. Ltd in 1908. The Coleford High Delf was reached at a depth of 273 ft in No. 1 Shaft, and was followed by dipples down to about 1050 ft. There were two winding engines (18 in. and 16 in.) and a pumping engine. Tub loads of coal were transported by means of an endless rope-hauled tramway or 'creeper' to screens at Mierystock across the Monmouth–Mitcheldean Road *(see Walk 5)*, the screens being connected to a siding adjacent to the former Severn and Wye Railway. In 1928 the colliery was completely electrified and mechanical coal cutters and conveyer belts were installed. At its peak the colliery was producing over 4000 tons of steam coal per week (192172 tons in 1938, but down to 147254 tons in 1946). On 30 June 1949 the pit was flooded when a breach was made into the water-filled workings of East Slade Colliery. 177 men escaped by means of the cage up the shaft, and 5 missing men were eventually contacted and rescued via the old Pluds' Colliery shaft, which had recently been re-opened for ventilation purposes. Unfortunately, others were not so lucky, as there were 18 fatalities between 1919 and 1953, the last when a misfire exploded as two men tried to make the explosives safe, killing Harold Ward. Closure of the pit came on 23 December 1959.

Lydbrook Colliery (5)

Lydbrook Colliery comprised three gales (Lydbrook Deep Level, Birchen Grove, and Pluds'), the history of which are complex. Theophilus Creswick began work on Scotts and Lydbrook Deep Levels in 1862, and the Lydbrook Deep Level Collieries Co. Ltd, incorporating all three gales, was formed in 1866. The colliery exploited the Yorkley and Coleford High Delf Seams. A siding on the Severn and Wye Railway's Lydbrook branch had been laid by 1877, and a bridge to carry coal tubs from the Deep Level over the railway to a loading point on the siding was constructed in 1885. A new shaft, Pluds', was sunk in 1892–3 and reached the Coleford High Delf Seam (4 ft thick) at a depth of 394 ft, but it still proved difficult to make the colliery pay. It had a number of owners and lessees between 1866 and 1912, finally being closed by the British Red Ash Collieries Co. Ltd in 1917. Little evidence remains on the site today, and part has been built over. In 1934 a recreation ground was constructed on the site of the large spoil heap (the 'Blue Mound').

Lydbrook Church (6)

Holy Jesus Church was designed in 14th century decorative style by Henry Woodyer, and was completed in 1851. The tower has a saddle-back roof. Bath stone was used for the interior and local sandstone for the exterior. The church was restored in 1903.

Upper Lydbrook Station (7)

The station opened on the first day of passenger services, 23 September 1875. It had a crossing loop and two platforms, with the wooden station building on the up side and a small wooden shelter on the down. There were signal cabins at each end of the loop, and Lydbrook Colliery Sidings were nearby. Regular passenger services ended on 6 July 1929, but there were occasional summer seaside excursions after that date, even though the station building had by then become a private dwelling.

Iron Mine Level (8)

Variously reported as Bay Head and Lydbrook Iron Mine Level, this was an exploratory level for iron ore. Although the Carboniferous Crease Limestone, the main host of iron-ore deposits in the Forest, in this area shows traces of mineralisation, it seems that no economic deposits were found. The presence of a small pool in a cavern cut by the level gave rise to rumours of an "underground lake". The level was apparently used as an air-raid shelter during the war.

Sarah Siddon's House (9)

This timber-framed house on a stone base dates from the early 16th century, but was extended in 1718. Originally a yeoman's house, it was owned for many years by the theatrical Kemble family, whose daughter Sarah (1755–1831) became Britain's leading dramatic actress. On Hangerberry Hill, across the valley, is an ancient beech wood, now a nature reserve. The route of the first tramroad in the Forest ran along the hillside here. This was built by James Teague (a free miner) to carry coal from his pits in the Mile End area to the Wye at Lower Lydbrook. It was finally completed in about 1803, amidst considerable opposition from the authorities, and closed in 1815 when the pits were abandoned. Opposite Sarah Siddon's House is the Anchor Inn, which may date from the 17th century. It was bought in 1856 by William Russell, a Bishopswood ironmaster, whose family owned mills and forges in Lydbrook, including the adjacent wire works. Just to the north were tinplate works, the horses from which were stabled at the Anchor. Closure of many of the works by 1930 eventually resulted in most of Lydbrook's pubs also closing. The Anchor went in 1954, but re-opened in 1980.

Bishopswood Tramroad (10)

The Severn & Wye Railway's mile-long branch tramroad to serve Bishopswood Ironworks and wharves upstream on the Wye was authorised in 1810, but not completed for several years. Unfortunately, the ironworks, which were operating by 1602, closed soon after (in about 1817). Nevertheless, some coal was still being carried to Bishopswood in 1858, after the incline at Lower Lydbrook had closed. Traffic had ceased by 1869. Another short-lived tramroad, Scott's Tramroad (1820-3), which linked Millway Moorwood Level to the Wye, crossed the Bishopswood Branch just east of Lydbrook.

Lydbrook Viaduct crossed the valley above the far end of the village.

Lydbrook (11)

Lydbrook nestles in the long valley of the Lyd Brook, which has provided power for water mills since at least the 13th century. Seven iron-making sites, including forges (charcoal blast furnaces), wireworks, and ironworks have been recorded, the first of which opened in 1590. In 1770 there was a large wharf on the River Wye "where coals were shipped for Hereford and other places". Lower (c.1610, situated near the present Forge Hammer Inn) and Middle (c.1590) Forges were eventually incorporated into the Lydbrook Tinplate Works, which were started in 1806 by Thomas Allaway. In 1817 he leased Lower and Middle Forges from John Partridge and his son, also John. The works then consisted of three forges, rolling and bar mills, and a tin house. Richard Thomas leased the works in 1871 and later acquired them. They finally closed in 1925 after a somewhat chequered history. The expansion of industry in the first half of the 19th century was accompanied by building of many workers' houses, as well as more palatial accommodation for the bosses, such as Lydbrook House (c.1827) in Lower Lydbrook, which was bought by ironmaster William Allaway in about 1840. At one time, there were more than 30 shops, and Lower Lydbrook alone had seven pubs, of which only the Courtfield Arms (formerly the Waterside Inn) and Forge Hammer survive (together with the Anchor a little way up the valley). A small Baptist Chapel was built in 1823, but was replaced in 1864, the original becoming a public reading room. A Primitive Methodist Chapel of 1828 was rebuilt in 1852, and replaced by a larger one in 1913. Another major employer in

the area was the Lydbrook Cable Works, about ½ mile below Lower Lydbrook, near Lydbrook Junction Station. The works opened in 1912, and employed over 1200 people at its peak. It closed in 1965, by then being owned by the AEI Group. Reed Corrugated Cases (later part of the SCA Group) took over the premises in 1966, but the factory finally closed in 2002.

From an old postcard.

The Viaduct Lydbrook

Lydbrook Viaduct (12)

Lydbrook viaduct, on the Lydbrook branch of the Severn and Wye Railway (see 3), was designed by George W. Keeling. It was begun on 9 November 1872, and completed and ready for goods traffic on 26 August 1874. The masonry work (three arches at the southeastern end, two arches at the northwestern end, and two intermediate 90-foot piers) was carried out by contractor J.E. Billups. Three girder spans (120, 150, and 120 feet in length) were manufactured by the Crumlin Viaduct Works Co. Lower Lydbrook Station was near the southeastern end of the viaduct. It had a single platform, a loop, and two sidings which served the nearby wire works and tinplate works. Poor passenger traffic resulted in closure of the station in April 1903. The branch was finally closed to goods traffic on 30 January 1956, but the viaduct was not demolished until 1965. Viaduct Cottage and Viaduct House were originally almost beneath the viaduct.

Lydbrook Deep Level Free Mine (13)
The original Lydbrook Deep Level was part of Lydbrook Colliery, but a free mine of this name was worked by Mervyn Bradley, who moved to Monument Mine in Bixslade in 2000 *(see Walk 7)*. An inclined drift probably worked the Coleford High Delf Seam.

View of Wye Valley (14)
There is an excellent view of the meandering River Wye cutting through the hills *(see Walks 1 and 6)*. To the left is Joy's Green, above Lydbrook, with Coldwell Rocks (haunt of peregrine falcons) and Symonds Yat Rock beyond. Ahead is Coppet Hill, with Goodrich Castle to the right and Welsh Bicknor church and Courtfield House, a former religious foundation, across the river in the foreground. The latter may be near the site of a church founded by St Dubricius in the 5th or 6th century. Ross-on-Wye is just behind the hills to the right. In the distance can be seen the rounded summits of Graig Syfyrddin and Garway Hill, with the Black Mountains beyond. Almost the whole of this area is underlain by rocks of the Devonian Old Red Sandstone, which gives the fields of large areas of Herefordshire their distinctive reddish colour, similar to that in large parts of Devon, from which, of course, the name Devonian was derived.

Ruardean, with the Malvern Hills in the distance.

Ruardean and view (15)
Most of Dean's ancient churches are situated on the fringes of the Forest, and the Church of St John the Baptist at Ruardean is a good example. It dates from about 1110 and is particularly noteworthy for a sculptured tympanum of St George and the Dragon over the south door, the work of the Herefordshire school of Norman sculpture. Displayed on the south wall is a small carving of two fish, which was discovered in a nearby cottage about 50 years ago and probably came from the same source. The south aisle dates from the 13th century, the tower is late 14th, the chancel was rebuilt in the 15th, and much of the exterior was renewed in 1890. The village developed along an ancient road from Mitcheldean to Monmouth, but the population increased significantly in the 19th

century, with the expansion of mining and other industries. Two pubs survive, the Angel and the Malt Shovel. Both are at least as early as the 18th century, but it is claimed that the latter is much older, possibly even 12th century and "the oldest pub in England"! James Teague (1750–1818), who, together with his brothers and sons (notably Moses, 1792–1840, born at Whitecliff near Coleford), became one of the most important industrialists in Dean, was born in Ruardean. James and William Horlick, who developed the famous malted milk drink, lived here, although whether this work was carried out in the local malt house, as some claim, is uncertain. Below the church are the scanty remains of an ancient manor house, said to have been destroyed during the Civil War. The view beyond takes in the Wye Valley, the hills above

Ross-on-Wye (Chase Hill and Penyard Park), and, in the right distance, the Woolhope Dome (with the TV mast above Much Marcle) and Malvern Hills. The hills of the Woolhope Dome consist of Silurian rocks, which underlie the Old Red Sandstone, and the Malvern Hills are much older still, being Precambrian in age *(see Walk 11).*

Ruardean Woodside, with old colliery tips visible.

Woodside Colliery (16)

Although the gales were not granted at that time, work on Woodside Colliery, by Giles Griffiths and others, was begun in 1832. The Woodside gale was worked in conjunction with East Slade gale, and there were two shafts of about 180 ft which exploited the Coleford High Delf Seam. However, the colliery was not working in 1841 and the gale may have been sold off soon afterwards. By 1852 it was being worked by the Woodside Colliery Co., but seems to have closed in the mid-1860s. There was a tramroad from the colliery to Churchway by 1850, and sidings were provided on the South Wales Railway's (later Great Western Railway's) Churchway Branch in 1854. The Woodside gale was later worked as part of East Slade Colliery, about ½ mile to the southeast.

True Blue Colliery (17)

This is only one of at least a dozen pits in the area to the southwest, south, and southeast of Ruardean Church named 'True Blue' on Thomas Sopwith's 1835 map. A True Blue Pit had been in production since at least 1788. True Blue and Newham Bottom were leased to a group of shareholders (from a Free Miner) in 1841 to work the 'Hill Delf' (presumably Coleford High Delf) Seam in land drained by True Blue and Newham Bottom Levels. In 1859 the Gloucestershire Coal Mining Co. Ltd was formed to acquire True Blue, Newham Bottom, Woodside, and Birchen Grove Collieries, but this was soon wound up. In 1884 True Blue and Newham Bottom were galed to Moses Hale, and the pits were being worked by T.B. Brain by 1899, but were abandoned in about 1910. They were acquired by the Forest Syndicate Co. Ltd, which, in 1919, formed the Premier Briquette Co. to produce compressed coal briquettes. This company was liquidated in 1923, by which time True Blue Colliery included five gales. The colliery was conveyed to the Wigpool Coal and Iron Co. Ltd, owners of Harrow Hill, in 1925. It was producing 100–150 tons of coal per week in 1927 and finally closed in the 1950s.

Two attractive villages, the 'Cathedral of the Forest', a historic furnace, and ancient iron mines. A hilly walk on field paths and green lanes; 23 stiles.

START at the Clearwell Caves car park off the minor road between Clearwell and Milkwall, about ¼ mile northeast of Clearwell village: GR SO 578083. Note that the car park barrier is closed when the caves close for the day (see signs or check at the caves for times). If parking outside the barrier, please take care not to obstruct access. If starting in Coleford, follow Newland Street from the Market Place to point 5. **Refreshments:** Café at Clearwell Caves; pubs in Clearwell and Newland; range of facilities in Coleford. **Bus:** 30, 31, 35, 721, etc. to Coleford.

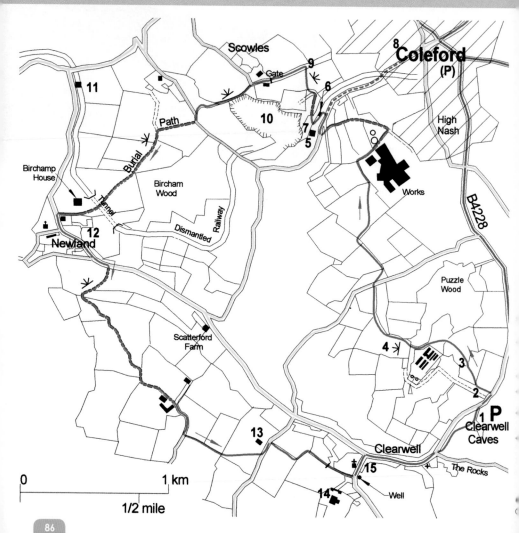

CLEARWELL CAVES *(1)* are ancient iron mines, open to the public for underground tours and well worth a visit. Leave the car park by walking down the tarmac entrance road to the main road. Turn right for about 100 yds, then go left over a stile at a footpath sign. Follow the path downhill and after 100 yds one of the entrances (gated) to Old Ham Iron Mine *(2)* can be seen under a tree on the left. Climb a stile and follow the path as it bears right into woodland, continuing over another stile into an area of ancient iron workings or 'scowles'*(3)*. The path here may be rather indistinct, but is marked by yellow arrows. Note the yew tree on an isolated pillar of rock just before a short steep climb. Soon after this you bear left to emerge at a stile on a field boundary. Bear half left across the field to a stile by a gate at the left-hand edge of woodland. Continue past a chicken farm and over two more stiles into a field with lovely views of Newland and the Welsh mountains *(4)* on a clear day. Bear right to join the right-hand edge of the field going downhill. Keep bearing right, along the right-hand field margin, to climb a stile, before continuing down to a kissing gate.

Cross the road beyond, climb a stile opposite, and bear right diagonally uphill to a stile in the field corner. Follow the right-hand field edge for about 250 yds, past a gateway on the right and into the next field. After a few yards, turn right through a gap and follow the right-hand field edge for 150 yds to a marker post by some large rocks. The right of way goes diagonally left across the field here, towards a stile in the far corner just to the left of factory buildings. Cross this and continue by the fence to climb a metal gate/stile. Turn right and follow the field edge to a dirt track between a large storage tank and factory buildings. After 100 yds turn left at a T-junction onto a path between hedges, and later stone walls, which leads down to a gravel road. Taking the narrow path opposite will bring you onto a road, just opposite Whitecliff Furnace *(5)*.

Turn right for 150 yds, then cross a stile by a footpath sign on the left. Go straight ahead and follow the path uphill, turning left at the top of the field, past overgrown limekilns *(6)* for about 80 yds to a marker post. Turn sharp right onto the old trackbed of the Coleford Railway *(7)*, but after 30 yds bear left uphill on a rocky track. Immediately after the track bends sharp left, turn right onto an uphill path, aiming a few yards to the right of a power-line post to a stile in the field corner. Cross this and keep ahead across the next field (with good views of Coleford *(8)* on the right) to a stile and gate, which lead to a tarmac footpath about 40 yds ahead. Turn left here. This is the old Burial Path *(9)*, which we will eventually follow all the way to Newland. The Path goes between houses onto a tarmac road. After about 60 yds, where the road bends right into the hamlet of Scowles (unsurprisingly there are more scowles here), turn left at a footpath sign. The Path passes Whitecliff Quarry *(10)* to the left, with more views of the Welsh peaks to the right. Cross a stile and follow the left-hand field boundary (the pathway has stone edging here), bearing left to yet another stile, which leads via steps to a tarmac road. Turn left and after 80 yds take the track on the right. Follow this uphill to a T-junction, where you go left, ignoring (probably with relief) the stile ahead. There are further views into Wales from here, but also look back to the right after about 100 yds to where the former Newland Station *(11)* can be seen in trees in the valley bottom, just left of a white house and metal-roofed barn. The large Stowfield limestone quarry can also be seen. The track becomes increasingly sunken, and muddy, eventually becoming tarmac at the entrance to Birchamp House. It soon emerges onto a road in the village of Newland *(12)*.

Turn left to pass the Ostrich pub, with the church and almshouses on the right, and continue to the bottom of the hill at the end of the village. Just past the traffic bollards, turn right onto a sunken lane, which climbs steadily uphill. Just before a left-hand bend there is a nice view of Newland to the right.

After ¾ mile the lane comes out onto a road, where you keep ahead past barns on the right. After 200 yds turn left through a gateway at a footpath sign and follow the left-hand hedge to the field corner, with a stile (and gateway). Cross this and the field ahead, aiming just to the right of some buildings (and a mast on the hill beyond) to reach a stile, which leads onto a road. The building on the left was once a tithe barn *(13)*. Turn left on the road for 80 yds, then climb a particularly high stile on the right. Follow the wire fence on the left, with nice views of the Clearwell valley, to a stile in the far left-hand corner of the field. Cross this and follow a stone wall to climb another stile on the right, continuing with the wall, and then a fence, on your right. There is a good view of Clearwell Castle *(14)* from here. Climb one last stile and follow a track, and then a lane, down to a main road in Clearwell *(15)*. Turn left past the church, then right at the Cross into High Street, passing Tudor Farmhouse and the Butcher's Arms. The road bends left past a chapel, then, immediately after 'The Rocks' lane on the right, take a footpath bearing right uphill. Keep ahead above the road and bear slightly left onto a gravel track, which goes past the Clearwell Caves café and up to the car park.

Clearwell Caves (1)

In the 1960s some of the shallower working of Old Ham Iron Mine (**see below**) were made accessible for public tours by Ray Wright. Much of the iron-ore was deposited in ancient cave systems in the Crease Limestone, part of the Carboniferous Limestone Series *(see 3)*. Several of these old caverns, known as 'churns' and now largely mined out, can be seen on the tour. A visit to this genuine Forest iron mine is highly recommended.

Old Ham Iron Mine (2)

In 1841 Old Ham, together with Old Bow, was galed to Benjamin Hutchings. It had passed to William Talbot by 1856, but the pit was idle by 1859. It was worked by the Talbots from 1870–4, but was then leased to William Fryer, who constructed a tramroad connection to sidings on the Severn & Wye Railway's Sling Branch in 1876. The Forest Hematite Co. Ltd was formed in 1891 by Messrs Bonsor and Scrutton, who had acquired the Old Ham and Lambsquay pits from Fryer. The gales were surrendered in 1903. Old Ham was re-granted to Amos Morgan and 16 other Free Miners in 1909, and they sold it to the Coleford Iron Co. in 1917. Between 1846 and 1900 it produced some 62000 tons of ore, with 3000 tons coming from outcrop workings between 1909 and 1916. Only 18 tons were produced in 1925. Old Ham Pit was acquired by the British Colour & Mining Co. Ltd in 1927, who worked ochre from Old Ham and Lambsquay. It was one of the 'Land' or shallow pits, and had connections underground with New Dunn, Old Sling and Old Bow pits. In the 1960s some of the Old Ham workings became the tourist mine called Clearwell Caves.

Scowles (3)

Here in Lambsquay Wood are good examples of the earliest, near-surface, iron-ore workings in Dean, known locally as 'scowles'. These consist of hollows, channels, quarry-like rock faces, and rock pillars, as well as underground workings. They generally follow the outcrop of the Crease Limestone (part of the Carboniferous Limestone Series), which is the main host to the iron-ore deposits. It is thought that the iron was derived from eroding Coal Measures rocks, rich in iron carbonate and pyrite, during Permo–Triassic times. Descending iron-bearing solutions then deposited most of this iron in the open-textured, relatively cavernous Crease Limestone, with smaller amounts in the Lower Dolomite and in dolomite units within the Drybrook Sandstone.

The presence of iron ore at the surface would have attracted the first miners to the area. Recent detailed studies have shown that scowles are, to a large extent, natural features, representing ancient cave systems in the Crease Limestone. Nevertheless, significant modification of such ancient 'karst' topography *(see Walk 14)* during mining activity over many hundreds of years is evidenced by the presence of pick marks, drill holes, and spoil heaps, as well as the volume of material which must have been extracted. Although direct evidence is scanty, it is likely that some of the workings may date back to Iron Age or Roman times. Royalties from mining were being paid to the Crown in the 13th century, and there were six small pits in the mid-1700s. Once the near-surface ore was worked out, mining was extended underground. Lambsquay underground mine was a relatively small 'land' or shallow pit, and produced only small amounts of iron ore (around 3000 tons) in the 1800s. However, some ochre was obtained from old outcrop workings after 1927. In the late 19th century, some of the scowles in Great Lambsquay Wood were converted into an area of scenic walks named 'Puzzle Wood', still open to visitors. Probably the most spectacular and best-preserved examples of scowles are in Noxon Park, near Bream. They are now home to ancient beech and yew trees, as well as a variety of ferns.

Viewpoint (4)

The view from here includes several Welsh peaks, including the Sugar Loaf, Skirrid, Black Mountains, and, on a particularly clear day, the Brecon Beacons. Newland Church can be seen ahead, and somewhat closer is the white-painted late 17th century Scatterford Farm.

Whitecliff Furnace (5)

This coke-fuelled blast furnace for smelting iron ore was built in 1798–1810. (A datestone appears to read 1806.) Coke was made on site and, together with the ore, was fed in at the top. The surviving furnace, with its charging bridge, is thought to be the second, built when an earlier uncompleted furnace was swept away by floods. The ironworks attracted metallurgist David Mushet to Coleford in 1810, although he soon opened his own works at Dark Hill *(see Walk 7)*. A little way up the road towards Coleford is Whitecliff House, which is partly late 16th century,

but enlarged in 1790. It was bought in 1816 by industrialist James Teague, but he died before he could take up residence. Not far beyond this the the stone bridge of the former Coleford Railway *(see 7 below)*, and just beyond the bridge is the mid-19th century folly called Rock Castle (now a dental practice). Coleford town centre is only a short distance further along this road.

Limekilns (6)

This is typical of the many limekilns which survive in the Dean area near limestone quarries, most of which worked various units of the Carboniferous Limestone Series. Many are built entirely of stone, but this one has brick-lined arches. The charge (limestone, which is essentilly

$CaCO_3$, and a fuel such as coal) was loaded into the top of the kiln, which was commonly built against a hillside or embankment to facilitate this. The product was quicklime (CaO), which was raked out of draw-holes, usually protected by arches or recesses. The quicklime would be slaked by mixing with water to form slaked lime ($Ca(OH)_2$) before it was spread over the fields. At one time quicklime was sometimes dispersed in small heaps over a field and allowed to slake there before being ploughed in. Transport of quicklime in wooden carts was somewhat dangerous, as the heat generated when quicklime is wetted generates considerable heat, with the risk of setting the cart on fire! Lime was also in demand for mortar, and limestone was also quarried for building purposes. The few surviving limestone quarries in Dean produce crushed aggregate for use in road construction and concrete manufacture.

Coleford Railway (7)

This replaced the Monmouth Railway, a horse-drawn tramroad, which ran from Broadwell, via Coleford, Newland, and Redbrook, to May Hill, near Monmouth, and which was opened in 1812 *(see also Walk 13)*. The Coleford Railway Act, authorising construction of a standard-gauge line from Wyesham Junction (where the Coleford, Monmouth, Usk and Pontypool and the Wye Valley Railways met), near Monmouth, to Coleford, was passed on 18 July 1872. However, construction did not begin until 1880, with Reed Bros & Co. of London as contractors. The 5-mile line was finally opened on 1 September 1883. It was worked by the Great Western Railway from the start, amalgamation with that company occurring on 1 July 1884. The line followed much of the old tramroad track, but deviated to avoid the sharper curves of the latter. It climbed some 500 ft between Monmouth and Coleford on gradients mostly between 1 in 40 and 1 in 67, and it had several sharp curves, so it was a difficult one to work. Stations were provided at Newland and Coleford, the latter adjacent to, but initially quite separate from, the Severn and Wye Railway's establishment. There were 3 or 4 passenger trains each way per day in 1900, but traffic, even goods, was never very plentiful, and the line closed as from 1 January 1917, most of the track soon being lifted for the war effort. However, the section from Whitecliff Quarry to Coleford and the former S&WR line continued in use for carriage of limestone until 1967.

Coleford (8)

Coleford (pop. 8351 in 2001) is a thriving community and is now the administrative centre of the Forest of Dean. It was first recorded as Colevorde in 1275, when it was part of the Royal hunting forest. Coleford was the scene of a battle during the Civil War. On 20 February 1643, the townspeople fought 1500 cavalry and foot soldiers allied to Royalist Prince Rupert, and the market hall was burnt down. There were 160 houses in 1710, but it was only in the later 18th and 19th centuries that increasing industrialisation (particularly production of stone, coal, and iron) transformed Coleford in an important market town. It was served by two railways: the Severn & Wye Railway (opened 1875), and the Coleford Railway (opened by the GWR in 1883), which initially had separate stations. The former GWR goods shed is now an interesting railway museum. The market place is dominated by the tower of the original octagonal parish church, built in 1821 and mostly demolished in 1882. Around the square are some attractive 18th and early 19th century buildings. Of the many pubs, the King's Head, Angel, and Old White Hart (17th century) are still in business. Also noteworthy are the classical late 18th century Bank House off Bank Street, now the Forestry Commission offices, and the early 17th century Poolway House in Gloucester Road. Tump House, now the Forest House Hotel, was leased by David Mushet in 1810. The present Parish Church of St John was built in 1880 to a design by F.S. Waller. The Baptist Church dates from 1858. The large factory passed on the walk is owned by GlaxoSmithKline and makes the well-known drinks *Lucozade* and *Ribena*. A number of famous people have lived in Coleford: Robert Mushet, industrialist *(see Walk 7)*; James Teague, industrialist (*see 5 above and Walk 8*); Mary Howitt, Quaker and Victorian writer; Angus Buchanan VC, World War 1 hero; and Dennis Potter (1935–83), author and playwright.

Burial Path (9)
Before Coleford had its own parish church, burials took place at Newland, nearly two miles from the centre of Coleford. This necessitated the carrying of coffins along the 'burial path'. There are several such burial paths (known elsewhere as 'corpse roads') around the Forest, linking outlying communities with their parish church.

Whitecliff Quarry (10)
Limestone was quarried near Whitecliff before the 17th century, and limekilns are recorded here in the 18th. The opening of a tramroad from Coleford to Monmouth in 1812 stimulated quarrying, and there were three new kilns in 1836. The tramroad was converted to a standard-gauge railway by the Great Western Railway in 1883, and there was an agreement between the GWR and the Whitecliff Lime Co. for a private siding in 1885. Monmouth Steam Sawmills Co. Ltd took over the quarry in 1904, Thomas Swan & Co. Ltd in 1930, and Fred Watkins (Whitecliff Quarries) Ltd soon after World War II. Ownership passed to Man-Abell (Whitecliff Quarry) Ltd in the mid-1960s, stone for tarmac, aggregate, blast-furnace flux, and railway ballast being produced from the massive Lower Dolomite, part of the Carboniferous Limestone Series. After the line to Monmouth was closed in 1917, stone was transported onto the Severn & Wye Railway's branch at Coleford until that closed in 1967. The quarry was disused by the 1990s, by which time it was quite extensive (500 yds across). Part of the site now houses some light industrial units, but most is a 4-wheel drive training centre.

Newland Station (11)
The only intermediate station on the Coleford Railway *(see 7)* was at Newland, although this was situated ½ mile north of the village near Cherry Orchard Farm. The main station building included the booking office and was on the western (down) side of the line. It was constructed of stone with a small canopy, and was similar to that at Coleford. The up platform was on a loop and had a small stone, canopied shelter. Behind this was a further loop, and two short sidings serving a platform supporting the stone goods shed and a crane. A wooden signal box was situated to the east of the running line by the level crossing over the Berry Hill road, and the station master's house was almost opposite. The station closed with the line from 1 January 1917, but the site was used by the Royal Air Force (59 Maintenance Unit) during World War II, the tunnels at Redbrook and Newland being used for storage of ammunition. Most of the station buildings have been preserved. The two passenger station buildings have been much modified and incorporated into a private residence, but the goods shed (and platform) is, externally at least, in near-original condition. Two of the level crossing gates survive, but the signal box has gone. The former station master's house is still lived in.

Newland (12)
Newland is an attractive village, dominated by its magnificent All Saints' Church, known as the 'Cathedral of the Forest'. The church was founded by Rector Robert de Wakering (1215–37), but the present church dates mostly from c.1280–1300, when Edward I's historian, John of London, was rector. In 1305 Edward I added the small chapel adjoining the porch to contain the chantry of King Edward's Service. The church comprises a west tower,

nave with five arches, very large north and south aisles, south porch, chancel, and chapels. There are many interesting monuments within the church. An effigy of Jenkin Wyrall, Forester of Fee (d. 1457), shows details of hunting costume of the time. An early 17th century forester with bow and horn is shown on an incised slab. On a tomb in the south chapel is the famous 'Miners' Brass', showing the figure of a medieval miner, with his hod and pick in his

hands and candlestick in his mouth. This has become the symbol of the Forest Free Miners. The steps of the cross in the churchyard are 14th century, but the rest is Victorian. Near the churchyard is a row of almshouses with a panel inscribed: *These Almhouses for eight men and eight women Parishioners of Newland and the habitation adjoining for a lecturer, were founded A.D.1615 by Mr. William Jones, Citizen and Haberdasher of London; and he appointed the Worshipful Company of Haberdashers Governors.* The Ostrich Inn dates back to at least 1694. Other listed buildings nearby include Bell's Old Grammar School (c.1638), Dower and Spout Farm Cottages (early–mid-17th century), Dower House, the

Lecturage, and Tanhouse Farm (late 17th–early 18th century), and Birchamp House (early 19th century). In the fields north of the church is the Great Oak of Newland, which is claimed to be one of the biggest in England

Tithe Barn (13)

This is an L-shaped 17th century stone tithe barn with two extensions. There were two opposed cart entries, originally with large double boarded doors. Like many other barns in the area, this one has been converted into a private residence.

Clearwell Castle (14)

Clearwell Castle was built in Gothic style on the site of a Tudor manor by Roger Morris for Thomas Wyndham in 1727. Built of Forest stone, it was England's first neo-Gothic mansion, but was burnt down in 1929 and left in ruins until 1953. It was known as Clearwell Court until 1908. The entrance front has a 2-storey central portion flanked by symmetrical 3-storey towers, all with

embattlements alternately carved with the Wyndham lion. The house was restored after the fire, and many of the ceilings are facsimiles rather than original. It has had several owners who have used it for various commercial ventures, including a recording studio, and is presently available for hire, being especially popular as a wedding venue. The adjacent Castle Farm includes a particularly handsome early 17th century stone barn, which may have been a tithe barn. One of the cart entries is a gabled projecting structure with pointed archway.

Clearwell (15)

Nestled in a pleasant valley, it is hard to imagine that this quiet village originated in Saxon (or maybe even earlier) times as an iron-mining settlement. The presence of abundant clear water from springs encouraged the development of tanning and nail-making industries and gave the village its name. That considerable wealth was generated is shown by the many fine buildings in the village, many built of local reddish sandstone. Some date back to the 16th century (Baynams, Platwell

House, Tudor Farmhouse, and the Wyndham Arms), whereas others are 17th (Stank Farmhouse) or 18th (Cross House) century. The base of the cross in the centre of the village is medieval, but the rest is mid-19th century. There are three pubs: the Butcher's Arms, the Lamb, and the Wyndham Arms. St Peter's Church, designed by John Middleton of Cheltenham (who also restored the medieval cross), was built in 1866. A 19th century stone wellhouse is tucked away behind the Wyndham Arms, and there is another wellhead opposite the entrance to the castle.

Village cross and sandstone houses in Clearwell.

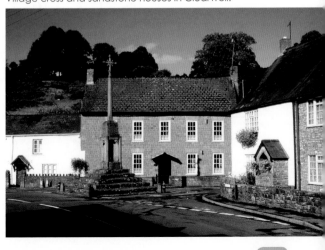

Old mills and iron mines, St Anthony's Well, an Iron Age hill fort, Flaxley Abbey, and a miners' church. A fairly hilly walk, mainly on field paths and forest paths and tracks; 7 (or 9) stiles.

START at the parking area near the top of Plump Hill on south side of A4136 Monmouth–Gloucester Road: GR SO 660169. Turn off the A4136 onto a gravel road opposite a minor road signposted to Wilderness; there are several places where cars can be parked a short distance along this road. **Refreshments:** none on walk route; pubs and shops in Mitcheldean.

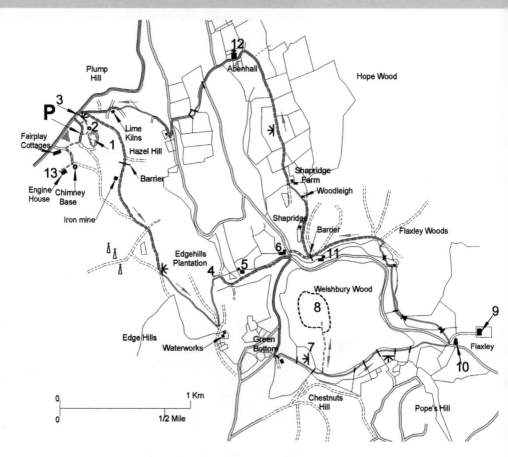

BEFORE STARTING THE WALK, there are several points of interest to look at. Go up the grassy bank, which is behind you as you face the main road. Just before the woods at the top of the hill is a quarry *(1)*. Now turn left

and descend towards the main road, keeping to the right-hand side of the grass area. Just below the quarry in a hollow near the edge of the hill is the concreted shaft of Westbury Brook Iron Mine *(2)*. A little way below this there is an excellent view over Abenhall and May Hill *(3)*. Now go down to the main road, turn right for a few yards, and right again at a lane. Keep right onto a gravel track and follow this uphill past houses, then, where the main track curves sharp left downhill, go straight ahead past a barrier. Up to the right, after about 200 yds, is a fenced entrance to Westbury Brook Mine, now used by cavers. Keep ahead where a wider track comes in from the right, and soon views towards the Cotswolds and River Severn open up. Where power lines come in from the right and the track starts to descend more steeply, look for a footpath (generally muddy) forking left downhill. This continues to descend past a stile before eventually emerging onto a gravel track near some stone waterworks buildings.

Just across this track is another (muddy) footpath, which goes sharp left following powerlines. Follow this downhill through trees, keeping straight ahead as it levels out through a more open area and then descends into a hollow which contains the stone-lined St Anthony's Well *(4)*. Turn right here and follow the stream which issues from the well down onto a dirt track. (It is usually easiest to keep right of the stream, but after heavy rain it may be necessary to go past the well and keep to the left bank.) Turn right and follow the track as it bends left, passing Upper Mill *(5)*, on the left, and, just before a road junction, Gunns Mill *(6)*, also on the left. *For a shortcut, turn left on the tarmac road beyond the latter mill, then sharp right after 40 yds onto a gravel forest road. This bends left to a barrier, just before which you turn left onto a track up a small valley.* The main route goes sharp right on the tarmac road towards Littledean and Cinderford, past the turnoff to Green Bottom, about 200 yds after which is a footpath sign pointing left. Follow a track towards a house for a few yards and then go through the field gate on your left. Climb the hill, keeping left of the fence, and go through a gate in the field corner. There are good views behind you of Green Bottom, Edge Hills, and Plump Hill *(7)*. Cross the next field and go through another gate. About 100 yds ahead, on the left-hand edge of the field, is a stile beside a gate, but only cross this if you want to see Welshbury Hill Fort *(8)*. *Just beyond the stile is a grass track. Cross this, bearing slightly left, and take the footpath ahead. Follow the path uphill for about 300 yds through Welshbury Wood to the ramparts of the hill fort. The good state of preservation of the earthworks is partly due to their location, woodland cover and low visitor numbers. Walkers wishing to visit the site are therefore asked to use existing footpaths and to help avoid causing further erosion by not climbing on exposed banks, especially after wet weather. This will help to ensure the preservation of this impressive monument for future generations. Retrace your steps to the stile, cross, and turn left.*

To continue the walk, follow the left-hand edges of several fields downhill, going over a stile and through three gates, to a kissing gate at the end of the wood. There are views of the Severn and Cotswolds ahead and Pope's Hill to the right. Bear slightly left across the field, following a track to the left of a large yew tree, with Flaxley Abbey *(9)* and Church *(10)* appearing ahead. Continue down to the bottom corner of the field, where two stiles will take you onto a tarmac road near the church. Across the road, just left of the driveway to Flaxley Abbey, is another stile. Follow the path across the field through a gate and over Westbury Brook, bearing left to go through a gate near the edge of the woods. Keep left of the stream to a gateway, and cross the middle of the next field to a stile to the left of a house. Turn left on the driveway and then right just before a cattle grid. Follow the field path back over the stream, before bearing slightly left to a stile into woodland. (There is another stile further to the left, but the intervening field is very boggy.) Cross this and climb a few yards onto a gravel forest road, where you turn left. You eventually pass, down on the left, a group of buildings which includes the former Flaxley Mill *(11)*. Just past these, bear slightly left at a track junction, go past a barrier, and immediately turn sharp right onto a narrower track which ascends a small valley. *The short cut comes in from the left here.*

Walk up the track past a house, but fork left onto a stony path just before the next house (Woodleigh), passing above it. Bear left across the green in front of Shapridge Farm, and then bear right to take the dirt track just to the left of the farm buildings. Follow this track, which soon becomes a tarmac lane, for over half a mile; there are more good views of the valley and Edge Hills on your left. The Gloucestershire Way (*see Walk 14*) comes in from the right, and we will follow this back to Plump Hill. Shortly after this, the lane bends left and passes Abenhall Church *(12)*. Continue to the junction and turn left, taking particular care, as this is quite a busy road. After 150 yds, turn right through a gate at a byway sign and follow the grassy track as it descends first left and then right to a gate in the far corner of the field. Go through this and then the second of two gates just beyond on the right before climbing up by a small stream to a gate onto a road. Turn left and after 40 yds fork right onto an uphill gravel track. Turn sharp right in front of the house, continuing up the track and keeping ahead onto a footpath where the track bends sharp left. Follow this path, ignoring side paths, as it climbs steadily to come out onto a tarmac driveway.

Bear right, then turn left onto a lane at a T-junction near old lime kilns. Follow the lane as it bends right and climbs up Hazel Hill past houses, ignoring side turnings. Towards the top of the hill you pass the site of the 1913 collapse, down on the right, before the lane emerges onto a main road. Turn left and left again to return to the parking area.

Before taking your boots off, those interested can look at the imposing remains of Fairplay Iron Mine engine house. About 200 yds from the main road junction, where the gravel road starts to bend left, there is a small clearing/parking area on the left. A short distance <u>before</u> this, but on the right, a rather indistinct footpath leads into the trees near a large oak. Follow this onto a dirt track and turn left, with Fairplay Cottages visible to the right. After about 120 yds (just before a left-hand bend), there is another indistinct (muddy!) path on the right, about 100 yds along which is the engine house (13). Return to the dirt track, turn right for about 60 yds, and just behind an old spoil heap on the right is the stone base of a ventilation chimney. You can then either return to your car by the outward route or continue along the dirt track to the next junction, where you turn sharp left back to the parking area.

Edge Hills Quarry (1)

There are a number of old quarries on Edge and Plump Hills, and quarrying has probably taken place here for centuries. They worked various units of the Carboniferous Limestone Series, mainly the Lower Limestone Shale, Lower Dolomite, and Crease, Whitehead, and Drybrook Limestones, but also Drybrook Sandstone. Much of the limestone was used for lime burning, and the 1891 OS map shows seven old lime kilns on Plump Hill alone. The large quarry seen here shows the steeply dipping Drybrook Sandstone well: the strata dip at about 65° to the west. The quarry was known as "illegal", supposedly because it began as a sandstone quarry, but was then extended into limestone without permission, being closed down in the late 1960s or early 70s. There is another, very overgrown limestone quarry (Hazel Hill Quarry) a couple of hundred yards to the east. A large limestone quarry across the main road on Plump Hill was where 36000 tons of stone were blasted in a single explosion in about 1899. At that time the quarry was owned by Aaron Simmonds. All these quarries have been abandoned for many years.

Westbury Brook Iron Mine (2)

The area has almost certainly been mined since Iron Age and Roman times, although there is little direct evidence for this. The gale of Westbury Brook was applied for by Thomas and Moses Teague and James Mountjoy, on behalf of Sir Josiah John Guest (owner of the Dowlais Iron Co.), in the mid-1830s, but was not awarded until 1841. Old Pit shaft had reached a depth of 360 ft by 1837, and the first iron ore was won in 1843. A tramroad connection to the Forest of Dean Railway's tramroad to Bullo Pill on the River Severn had been constructed by this time, but after the latter was converted to a broad-gauge line in 1854, the branch tramroad terminated at a transhipment wharf at Whimsey. Westbury Brook (also known as Edge Hills) Mine worked an area two miles long from north to south, which included the Deans Meend gale. Old Pit shaft reached two levels (Nos 1 and 2 at 280 and 360 ft below surface, respectively), and New Pit shaft had two crosscuts (No. 3 at 570 and No. 4 at 650 ft) which were driven eastwards into the Crease Limestone, and from each of which headings were driven both north and south. No. 4 level was not completed until 1884. There was also a pre-1837 shaft at Beech Pit on the southern gale boundary, which was reached by No. 3 level. Water was a major problem, and a 45-inch Cornish rotary beam engine was installed for pumping. Production of iron ore in 1880 was 12413 tons. About 958 000 tons were produced between 1843 and 1893, when the mine closed, much of it being transported to Dowlais. If the ore which must have been mined from the old workings is included, the total production could well be 2–3 million tons. The gale was surrendered in 1902, and subsequent proposals to re-open the mine in conjunction with other iron gales along the eastern outcrop did not come to fruition. Like most large mines, Westbury Brook was not free of accidents. A particularly tragic one occurred in 1860 when two children visiting the pumping engine house were scalded to death when a steam pipe fractured. Two miners, George Malsom and Thomas Moore, were killed and others injured in May 1878 when the ore cart in which they were being hauled up the shaft fell back down. On 12 October 1913, there was a major surface collapse near Old Pit, fortunately injuring no-one, but causing several cottages to be evacuated. Today the mine, which contains some enormous caverns (or 'churns'), is an important sanctuary for greater and lesser horseshoe bats. The mine reservoir, between the parking area and the main road, is now a nature reserve, noted particularly for its aquatic invertebrates (dragonflies, diving beetles, water boatmen, and water scorpions), newts, and frogs.

View (3)

The view from here takes in the Westbury Brook Valley below, Abenhall Church (which you will pass later in the walk), and the rounded May Hill, with its distinctive clump of trees on the summit *(see Walk 12)*. You are standing on Carboniferous Limestone rocks here, but the lower ground below and the ridge beyond Abenhall Church, together with the wooded Welshbury and Chestnut Hills to the right, are underlain by Lower Old Red Sandstone Brownstones. Further away, towards May Hill, are older Old Red Sandstone units (St Maughan's and Raglan Mudstone Groups), underlain by Silurian rocks, which are found in the

Blaisdon–Longhope–May Hill area. Further away again towards the Severn, beyond the Blaisdon Fault, which runs north-northeast near Newnham, Blaisdon and Huntley, are much younger Triassic (Mercia Mudstone Group or 'Keuper Marl') and Lower Jurassic (Lias) rocks. The latter subsided relative to the Devonian and Silurian rocks to the west when the Blaisdon Fault was formed *(see also Walks 11 and 12)*. At the bottom of Plump Hill, and just out of sight to the left, is the large village of Mitcheldean. By the 13th century it had already become an industrial centre, due to its proximity to iron ore deposits, and was a producer of cloth and leather. The Parish Church of St Michael is 13th to 15th century, and has an impressive spire. There are some attractive 15th to 17th century timber-framed houses in Millend and Merrin Streets, as well as some nice late 18th and 19th century houses. The arcaded sandstone Old Town Hall is early 18th century. There were once a considerable number of inns catering for the passing traffic, market traders, and townsfolk, and three survive: the White Horse and the George, both apparently dating back to the 17th century, and the Lamb. Mitcheldean brewery was the largest in Dean in the 19th century, when it was owned by the Wintle family. The original brewery building is now known as The Mews and is occupied by local businesses. On the edge of the village is a large business park which includes Xerox, one of the largest employers in the Forest of Dean. Unfortunately, in recent years this industry has been hit by recession and is now only a shadow of its former self.

St Anthony's Well (4)

Wells or springs have long been considered to be special places, the abodes of powerful spirits, and were often thought to have magical healing properties. This continued after the arrival of Christianity, when they were commonly dedicated to a saint. St Anthony's Well, in its woodland setting, is one of the largest and most picturesque of such holy wells in Gloucestershire. However, its name probably derives from the fact that bathing in the icy cold water was thought to cure skin complaints like 'St Anthony's Fire', an itching disease. The present stone-lined bathing pool probably dates from the late 18th century.

Upper Mill (5)

This appears to have been used as a fulling mill before its conversion to paper making in 1742, about the same time as Gunns Mill *(6)*. The upper storey is slatted, probably for ventilation purposes. About 100 yds downstream are the scanty remains of Middle Mill. In 1701 this was a corn mill, but later seems to have been used as a washing shed for the paper mills.

Gunns Mill (6)

Gunns (or Guns) Mill was originally a corn mill, but a charcoal iron blast furnace was built on the site in about 1628. It was owned by Sir John Wintour (or Wynter) in 1635, but was seized by the Parliamentarians during the Civil War and was later destroyed. The remains were rebuilt in 1682–3, as indicated by the dates on cast-iron lintels in the furnace house. The building was converted to a paper mill in about 1743 by Joseph Lloyd, and a wide range of paper was produced. Steam power supplemented water from about 1860, but the works closed in 1879. Gunns Mill is considered to be the finest surviving example of a charcoal blast furnace in the country and is Grade II* listed. The furnace and blowing chamber are built of coursed,

squared rubble stone and the upper storey, which dates from the rebuilding, is partly timber-framed, with a slate roof. Behind is a 25 ft long pit for an overshot waterwheel. The whole structure was encased in scaffolding and plastic sheeting by English Heritage in 2000, and it is to be hoped that it will eventually be restored to its former glory. The adjacent brick-built Gunn Mill House dates from the early 19th century, although part may be earlier; it originally had three storeys. It is now the ASHA Centre, an international retreat and conference venue, and offers B&B accomodation.

Green Bottom (7)

The view from here is in the opposite direction to that from Hazel Hill. The hillside across the valley consists of the various Carboniferous Limestone units, and just beyond the radio masts on top of Edge Hills are the overlying Coal Measures rocks, mainly sandstones. The limestones on this side of the Forest of Dean Basin dip steeply westwards (away from you) at 60–70°. Below the Carboniferous Limestone are Old Red Sandstone rocks, with much of the lower ground and hillside on which you are standing consisting of Brownstones. Green Bottom is a typical Forest hamlet of scattered cottages, although some have now been converted into up-market homes. There is a Beulah Chapel and some Grade II listed limekilns. However, probably Green Bottom's main claim to fame is that poet Leonard Clark (1905–81), who spent his childhood in nearby Cinderford, wrote about the area in his books *Green Wood* and *A Fool in the Forest*. Chestnuts Wood, on your right as you climb the hill here, figures prominently in these.

Welshbury Hill Fort (8)

The Iron Age Welshbury Hill Fort is not large (3.3 acres), but quite impressive, even though covered in trees. The layout is unusual, with triple ramparts and ditches to the south and west, and a single rampart and ditch to the north and east. The rather complex entrance is in the southeastern corner. An iron spearhead, possibly of Roman origin, was found here in 1987, and a rare late Iron Age electrum coin, of Celtic origin, was found just below the fort. Welshbury may be the site where a raiding party of Vikings was besieged by a victorious Saxon army in the early 10th century. The hill fort was one of the targets for

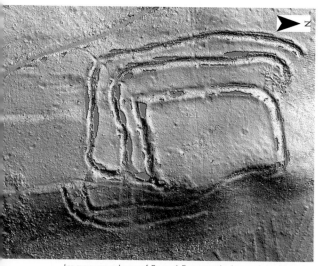

a recent airborne LIDAR (light detection and ranging) survey, in which laser light from an aircraft is reflected off the ground. The great advantage of this technique, compared with conventional aerial photography, is that it can, to a large extent, 'see' archaeological and other man-made features through tree cover. It is thus especially useful in areas like the Forest of Dean, which was one of the first places used to validate the method. Note that the image also reveals other features, such as probable field boundaries, nearby. Further details can be found at www.forestresearch.gov.uk/lidar.

Image courtesy of Forest Research, based on Forestry Commission and Unit for Landscape Modelling data.

Flaxley Abbey (9)

This Cistercian abbey was founded between 1148 and 1154 by Roger, Earl of Hereford, near the spot in the Vale of Castiard where his father, Milo (Miles) of Gloucester, was killed whilst out hunting in 1143 *(see Walk 6)*. The name suggests that flax was grown here before the site was given to the Cistercians. The abbey was initially favoured by the Crown and it was granted land by both Henry II and Henry III. However, after the Dissolution in 1536, its lands and manor were granted to Sir William Kingston, the Constable of the Tower of London. Much of the abbey appears to have been in disrepair by 1515, and was presumably demolished soon after 1536, apart from the western cloistral range which became the

manor house, still known as Flaxley Abbey. In 1648 it was sold to merchants William and James Boeve (later Boevey) of London's Dutch community. William Boevey carried out extensive alterations in the late 17th century, including a brick extension on the east side of the main range, and an orangery. The house was inherited by Thomas Crawley, who assumed the name Crawley-Boevey, in 1726. The northern part of Flaxley Abbey was destroyed by fire in 1777, following which the house was largely rebuilt to designs by Anthony Keck. The destroyed section was replaced by a cross wing matching that on the south end, and a new block on the southeast side provided an entrance hall flanked by principal rooms, all being decorated in Adam style. There were further refinements in the 19th century, and extensive repairs and alterations were carried out after 1960, when the house was bought by F. B. Watkins, a local industrialist, from the Crawley–Boevey family. It remains a private house. Formal gardens were laid out around the house by William Boevey and completed, after his death in 1692, by his wife Catharina, but they had largely been removed by the late 18th century. However, they were restored after 1960 to a modified plan. Today only a few remnants of the original abbey survive, mainly in the west wing, notably the late 12th-century rib-vaulted undercroft and two tunnel-vaulted chambers of the reredorter (latrines), with the 14th century hall or great chamber, possibly the Abbot's Lodgings or Guest Hall, above. A lower range to the east of the wing, occupied after the 1960s by the Bow Room, incorporates part of the walls of the southern cloistral range, and part of south wall of the nave survives in the orangery. Catharina Boevey (1669–1726) was the original of the 'Perverse Widow' in Joseph Addison's and Richard Steele's *Days with Sir Roger de Coverley* (1711). She was also a noted benefactor of the poor and supported a charity school.

Flaxley Church (10)
This may have originated as the gateway chapel of Flaxley Abbey. After the Dissolution it became the parish church, but was rebuilt in 1856 by Sir George Gilbert Scott, in red grit and grey Forest stone. The interior is richly decorated; there is a monument to Abraham Clark (died 1683) and tablets to the Crawley–Boevey family, who purchased the abbey in 1648. Today it is hard to believe that during the 17th century a charcoal furnace and two forges belonging to the Flaxley Estate operated on the Westbury Brook below the abbey. In the early 18th century, Flaxley Abbey ironworks included three forges, and several forges operated upstream of the abbey until at least the early 1780s. By the end of the century the ironworks, described as very large and extensive, were run by John Soule and the furnace was fed mainly with Lancashire ore shipped to Newnham. The forges hammered the iron into bars, ploughshares, and other items. The furnace was apparently abandoned in the early 1800s, but the forges probably remained in use for several more years.

Flaxley Mill (11)
Flaxley Mill House dates from before 1633 (the date on an iron fireback). The adjacent former corn mill is probably about 1750, and has a wheel pit.

Abenhall Church (12)
Abenhall is a tiny, ancient hamlet on the Flaxley to Mitcheldean road. It is notable for its Church of St Michael, built of local red sandstone. The original chapel-of-ease is late 13th century, the south aisle was added in the early 14th, and the tower in the 15th century. The beautiful mid-15th century octagonal font has the carved emblems of the free miners and smiths, as well as the arms of several noble families. The outside west wall of the tower has a modern carving of a shield with the arms of the free miners. The Pyrke family are commemorated by a brass to Richard (died 1609) and an early 18th century tablet. Just opposite the church is Church Farm House, built in 1858 for Edmund Probyn (datestone). The adjacent farm buildings are mostly of similar date, but parts are earlier. They include a cart shed, barn, stable, cow house, open-fronted shed, and a 2-storey building, the upper floor used as granary. Together they form a good example of a little-altered set of mid-19th century farm buildings.

Fairplay Iron Mine (13)

The most extensive remains of Fairplay Iron Mine are of a Cornish underbeam engine house over a masonry shaft about 350 feet deep. The date of construction of the stone and brick engine house is uncertain, but sinking of the deep pit appears to have begun by 1856. There was also a long drainage level to Nailbridge, and even a connection to the Westbury Brook tramroad. The object of the venture appears to have been to exploit iron ore in the Drybrook Sandstone, but there is no evidence for any significant production. In fact, it is said that the owners "put more iron into the mine than they ever got out". The Westbury Brook workings proved that the ore diminished and ran out at the deep boundary with Fairplay Pit, so sinking the latter was a waste of time; maybe it was a financial scam! The Westbury Brook Mine machinery and a large quantity of tramroad rails were sold in 1907 by the Chastan Syndicate, then owners of both Fairplay and the Lea Bailey Gold Mine (another abortive venture: *see Walk 11)*. About 100 yards to the east of the engine house are the filled-in remains of an air shaft with a draught opening or flue connecting the shaft to the base of an associated stone ventilation chimney, complete with hearth. These were conserved in 1980. To the south of the shafts are three small reservoir ponds for boiler water, now nature reserves. The whole area has been well mined and quarried, as, within a few hundred yards of Fairplay Mine to the west, at least three collieries once worked the Coleford High Delf Seam: Addis Hill, Inkerman and Gorbrook. After 1873 Addis Hill became part of Haywood Colliery, coal being raised through the Haywood Pit (a mile or so to the south). There was only intermittent activity at these pits during the early 20th century, and all were abandoned by about 1935. The stone-lined Gorbrook Level can still be seen in the woods.

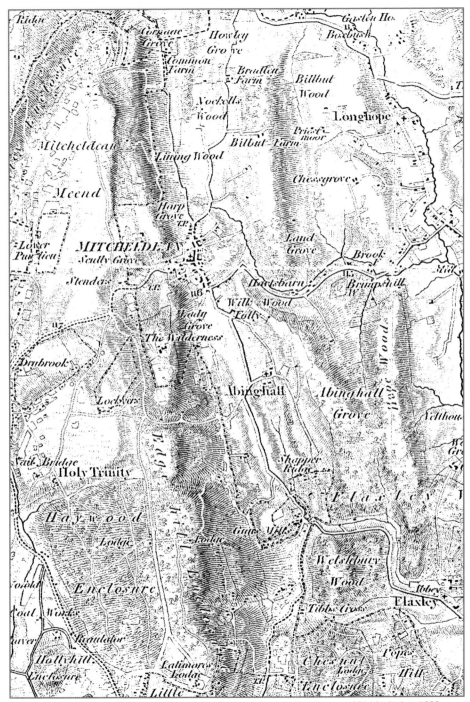

Enlarged extract from Ordnance Survey First Edition 1 inch to 1 mile map (Old Series) c. 1820

A lovely secluded valley, a gold mine, Wigpool iron mine (including a WW2 'cinema'), and extensive views. A hilly walk on field paths, woodland tracks, and lanes; can be muddy; the section around Wigpool Common requires careful navigation; 9 stiles.

START at one of the parking areas on either side of the unclassified road between Drybrook and Mitcheldean, on the sharp bend a little under a mile from Drybrook and just over half a mile from Mitcheldean (the top of Stenders Hill): GR SO 656180. **Refreshments:** none on walk; pubs and shops in Mitcheldean and Drybrook. **Bus:** 24 (Gloucester–Joy's Green) to The Stenders.

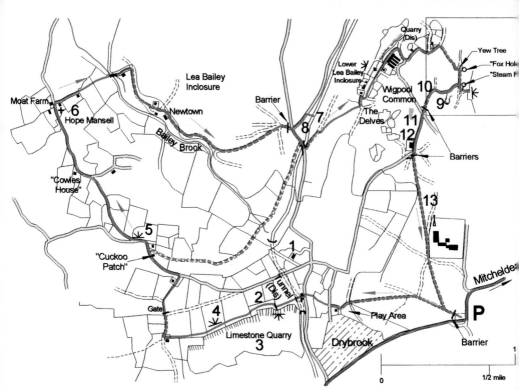

TAKE THE WIDE DIRT TRACK beyond the barrier on your left as you face towards Mitcheldean (i.e., on the inside of the bend in the main road). Keep ahead past a track junction on the right and a mast on the left. About 40 yds after the mast you turn left onto a footpath, then fork right after 20 yds and continue until you emerge from the woods. The path bears left and passes to the right of a childrens' play area. Turn right, passing a bungalow on your left, cross a tarmac lane, and climb the stile ahead.

The white house with its distinctive tower is Euroclydon *(1)*. Continue to the far end of the field, where there is a gap and a stile. Follow the narrow path beyond down to a tarmac road. Turn left and then right in front of the first house ('Greystones'). The path heads uphill, initially between stone walls, to a gate. Keeping the hedge on your left, continue uphill through another gate. Beyond this there is a good view to the left of Drybrook and Ruardean Hill, with Cinderford beyond *(2)*. Just below the path, also on the left, is Drybrook Quarry *(3)*. Still keeping the hedge (and quarry) on your left, continue over two stiles and through two hedge gaps. There are excellent views of the Herefordshire Hills and Black Mountains *(4)* to the right (north and west) along this stretch.

Climb the next stile, near a house, then turn right down an enclosed grassy track. Where this bends right, keep ahead through a gate into a field. Follow the left-hand field edge (ignoring a stile over the fence) downhill to climb a stile near a converted barn. Keep ahead down to a tarmac road and turn left. After 300 yds a byway sign near 'Cuckoo Patch' points sharp right along a grassy track, a possible short cut. *This initially follows the edge of woodland, continues past a farm, enters some woods, and finally emerges onto a road by an old railway bridge. Turn right over this to continue the walk.* Otherwise stay on the road, with good views of the lovely secluded Hope Mansell valley on the right *(5)*. Keep ahead at a junction (signed Hope Mansell) and head steadily downhill, past another junction on the right and the stone and timber-framed Cowles House (c. 1600) on the left, to Hope Mansell Church *(6)*. Just past the church, opposite Moat Farm and Mill House, turn right up a lane (signed to village hall). At the top of this lane climb the steps and stile directly ahead and continue ahead across the field to a stile. Keeping in the same direction, go downhill to pass through a hedge gap, follow a stream on your left for a short

distance, and cross a footbridge and stile. Pass to the left of a house (Bailey Brook Cottage) onto a lane and follow this uphill to a junction. Turn right here to follow a gravel track just on the edge of a conifer plantation (Lea Bailey Inclosure), keeping left past a driveway. Bear right at a junction to go behind two houses (Newtown!), and keep left at another to go up a small valley to a junction of several tracks. Take the one that goes half right past a barrier to a tarmac road (about 100 yds away).

Cross this and take the road opposite towards Lea and Mitcheldean. After about 100 yds there is a metal barrier on the right. Go past this towards a metal hut visible a short distance beyond. This is the site of Lea Bailey Gold Mine *(7)*! The mine entrance is to the left, behind the shed. After looking around here, retrace your steps to the road, turn left, left again at the junction, and cross the bridge over the trackbed of the former Mitcheldean Road & Forest of Dean Junction Railway *(8)*. *The track on the right just before the bridge is where the short cut comes in.* Just over the bridge turn left past a barrier onto a dirt track. Fork right after 100 yds onto a path, which climbs more steeply through woodland to the top of the hill, where you turn left onto a grass track. Follow this track as it bends right and then left past some cottages, but where it next turns right, keep ahead along a grass path between fences. There are chicken houses on the right and more views of the Herefordshire hills and Welsh mountains to the left. The path bends right after the chicken farm onto a dirt road, where you go right. Turn left at the next T-junction and follow this dirt road as it swings right and then left. At this point, take the grassy (and commonly muddy) track which forks right of the driveway to a house. *The next section can be a bit tricky, so please follow the directions carefully; see detailed map.*

Continue for about 100 yds, passing a driveway on the left, and then bear right at a fork. Approximately 250 yds further on, at the top of a rise, you come to a triangular junction, marked by a prominent yew tree in its centre. A few yards beyond the yew, on the far side of the crossing track in a depression, is a gated entrance (Fox Hole) to Wigpool Iron Mine. Turn right at this junction. After about 120 yds, and about 10 yds before a fork where the more obvious path bends left, is a footpath (easily missed) on the right where the route continues. *However, there are two more points of interest which you can look at first. To see these continue to the fork, bear left and, after a few yards, turn sharp left along an indistinct path for a short distance to another grid-covered mine entrance, now used by cavers. This is Steam Hole, so named because moisture in warmer air rising from the mine on a cold day will sometimes condense. Return to the track and turn left down to a gate, where there is a good view of May Hill (see Walks 10 and 12) and the River Severn. Retrace your steps past the fork to the narrow footpath mentioned earlier.* About 80 yds along this is a wire-fenced area about 20 yards to the left. This large rock-sided hole is the 'Yankee Cinema' *(9)*. About 100 yds further on you come to a junction where you turn left along a somewhat wider path. The waste heaps on the right here are from Wigpool No. 2 Pit *(10)*. The path widens into a track and soon leads out past a barrier

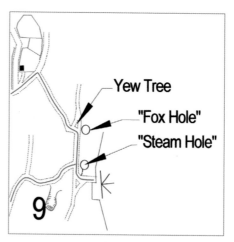

onto a tarmac road. Cross this and follow the road directly ahead, first past Wig Pool *(11)* and then the former Wigpool No. 1 Pit engine house (now a residence, *12*), both on the right. Just beyond this, where the road bends right, fork slightly left onto the first of two tracks with barriers. This grass track (often muddy) generally follows the line of the Wigpool Tramroad *(13)*. Where the track reaches the far end of the fenced water works enclosure on the left, bear left off the more obvious track, and then right to regain the line of the old tramroad. Follow this through the woods (there is at least one stone tramroad block visible), until it joins a wide dirt track, where you bear left to return to the parking area.

Euroclydon House (1)

This large black and white building has a square five-storey tower on the south side, adorned with a wrought iron balcony. It was built in the 1860s by a mine-owner, T. B. Brain, who is said to have used the tower to keep a watchful eye on his workers. The Brain family were the long-term owners of Trafalgar Colliery *(see Walk 5)*, about 3 miles to the southwest, although this cannot be seen from Euroclydon as Ruardean Hill is in the way. However, the family owned Pluckpenny Colliery, near Drybrook, in the late 1800s. The house later became a hotel and has been a nursing home since about 1980. Incidentally, Euroclydon is the name of a cold stormy east or northeast wind in the Levant that is said to have caused Saint Paul's shipwreck on Malta.

Drybrook and Cinderford (2)

The view from here takes in Drybrook in the valley, Ruardean Hill to its right, Harrow Hill to the left, and Cinderford beyond. Drybrook is a typical Forest village, workaday rather than picturesque, and based to a large extent on coal mining and stone quarrying. It only really began to expand in the late 18th century with the expansion of the extractive industries in the area. As the community developed, a range of religious, musical (including a brass band), sporting, and other activities became established. The largest collieries were situated south of the village and all worked the Coleford High Delf Seam: Pluckpenny, Newbridge Engine, Speedwell Newbridge, and Harrow Hill. However, by the end of the 19th century most of these had either closed or were in decline and only Harrow Hill, which had taken over several other collieries, survived until about 1927. Many workers therefore had to travel further afield to find employment. The coming of the railway in 1907 helped to alleviate this problem, but the depression of the 1930s hit hard. Light industries provided work after World War 2, and improving transport enabled people to commute to places such as Gloucester. Today the village has a range of facilities, including the Hearts of Oak pub. South of Drybrook is the area known as Harrow Hill (or Harry Hill), where the first Anglican church (Holy Trinity) within the boundary of the Forest of Dean was built in 1817. A Congregational Chapel, later the United Reformed Church, was built in 1858 and enlarged in 1872. The village of Ruardean Hill overlooks Drybrook from the southwest. The summit of the hill is the highest point in Dean (951 ft, 290 m). There are two pubs, the Nelson Arms and the Rose in Hand, as well as a village shop.

Cinderford is a small town with a population of 8,116 people (2001 census). Like Coleford, it lies within the original area of the Royal hunting forest, but is of somewhat more recent origin. The first settlement was a small collection of houses which grew up in the early 19th century along the eastern edge of the forest boundary. The name is derived from the slag of early ironworks in the valley bottom near the place where the Littledean–Coleford road crossed the Cinderford (or Soudley) brook; a bridge had been built there by 1674 and the Bridge Inn (now closed) is close by. Industrial development in the early 19th century, particularly the revival of the Cinderford ironworks by Moses Teague and others in the late 1820s and the development of collieries, resulted in a substantial growth in population. A church (St John's) and school were built in the 1840s. In some respects, such as the rows of terrace houses, the town resembles the coal-mining towns and villages of the Welsh Valleys. Later in the century, Cinderford grew into a small town with many of its shops, inns, and other facilities being situated to the north near the Littledean–Nailbridge road, the present town centre (The Triangle). Cinderford Station opened in 1900 and the town continued to expand in the 20th century. Closure of the last deep coal mines in the 1950s and 1960s resulted in a depression, with much unemployment. Since then, however, significant industrial development has taken place, notably in the Forest Vale Industrial Estate. Cinderford was the home of the 'Forest poetess', Catherine Drew (1784–1867).

Drybrook Quarry (3)

There was a quarry here by 1914, when Drybrook Quarry was advertised for sale. It was being worked by Thomas Roberts for road metal from the Lower Limestone Shale and Lower Dolomite, part of the Carboniferous Limestone Series. The quarry was taken over by Drybrook Quarries Ltd in 1926, and a private siding was laid by the Great Western Railway from Drybrook Halt in

1928. Nevertheless, most of the stone went out by road, and the line was closed in 1952–3. It was still owned by Drybrook Quarries Ltd in about 1970, but was later considerably enlarged by the Amey Roadstone Corporation (ARC Ltd), 25 men being employed in 1989. ARC Ltd is now called Hanson Aggregates, who are the current owners. However, owing to the recent (2008) downturn in the building industry, the quarry is currently closed. It is over 500 yds across, and there have been plans to convert part of the site into a tourist attraction. As you walk up the path above the quarry you pass an outcrop of limestone, with the beds dipping at about 20° to the south, i.e., into the quarry. There was a landslip near here in the 1970s, when part of the face fell away taking trees and hedge with it. It is easy to imagine that a massive limestone layer, possibly resting on a shale bed in the Lower Limestone Shale, would have slid down the bedding plane and into the open quarry. Such movement may well have been caused by heavy rain lubricating the shale bed.

View of Black Mountains and Herefordshire Hills (4)

The extensive views from here (on a fine day at least) include the Black Mountains of Wales (part of the Brecon Beacons National Park) to the northwest. In the middle distance are the hills of south Wales and Herefordshire (from left to right: Graig Syfyrddin, Garway Hill, Orcop Hill, and Aconbury Hill, near Hereford). Further right, in the near distance, are the hills (Chase Hill and Penyard Park) above Ross-on-Wye (hidden below), and beyond are the hills of the Woolhope Dome (note the TV mast above Much Marcle). In the distance to the northeast is the distinctive range of the Malvern Hills. To the far right, behind Euroclydon, is the flat wooded top of Wigpool Common, which will be visited towards the end of the walk. Geologically, much of this area (including both the Black Mountains and Herefordshire lowlands) consists of Devonian Old Red Sandstone rocks. The main exceptions are the Woolhope Dome and the Malvern Hills. The Woolhope Dome consists of older (Silurian) rocks, mainly limestones and shales of the Ludlow, Wenlock, and Llandovery Series. The strata dip consistently outwards to form a dome-like structure *(see 5 below for further explanation)*. The Malvern Hills consist of even older rocks (Malvernian) of Precambrian age: up to about 700 million years old and some of the oldest in Britain south of Scotland. Most of the rocks are of igneous origin (formed by crystallisation of molten rock or magma), although they have subsequently been metamorphosed by the effects of very high pressures and temperatures due to deep burial in the crust. They are mostly intrusive rocks, such as diorite and granite, but there are also volcanic rocks (basalt and rhyolite), which are somewhat younger (only about 560 million years old). To the west of the hills are Silurian sedimentary rocks (mainly shales and limestones), as well as a small area of Cambrian shales and sandstones. To the east are much younger Triassic marls and sandstones of the Worcester Basin. The Malvern Hills thus mark a major break between rocks of very different ages: they lie along the Malvern axis, a major fault line. This fault is a very ancient zone of crustal weakness that has undergone repeated reactivation, the last important one being the Permo–Triassic rifting which formed the Worcester Basin.

Hope Mansell Dome (5)

A dome is a geological structure in which the strata dip consistently outwards from a point, so that after erosion the oldest rocks are exposed in the centre, being surrounded by younger ones. This sort of structure is also known as an 'inlier'. The core of the Hope Mansell Dome lies east of the village near the bottom of the valley. This area consists of Brownstones, part of the Devonian Old Red Sandstone. The Brownstones are overlain on three sides (Howle Hill to the west, Ruardean Hill to the south (behind you) and Wigpool

Common to the east) by the Quartz Conglomerate and Tintern Sandstone (Upper Old Red Sandstone), the various units of the Carboniferous Limestone, and (but only to the south and east) the Pennant Group of the Coal Measures. Although these younger rocks form the high ground on three sides of the Hope Mansell valley, the rocks dip consistently outwards, so that the strata really do form the shape of a dome. They are thus analogous to, but in the opposite sense to, the Forest

of Dean basin, in which the youngest rocks (Coal Measures) in the centre are surrounded by Carboniferous Limestone and then Old Red Sandstone, with the rock strata dipping consistently inwards. The northern (far) end of the Hope Mansell valley, though, consists of the Old Red Sandstone rocks of Penyard Park, above Ross-on-Wye. Any overlying Carboniferous rocks there have now been eroded away.

Hope Mansell (6)

Hope Mansell is set in a very secluded green valley, being sheltered by hills on three sides. The only access is by narrow winding lanes, and the village houses are spread out along these. The village of Hope is mentioned in the Domesday Book (hope being derived from an old English word meaning valley), with the Mansel (single l) part of the name added when the Malosiel family held the manor in the 14th century. The parish church of St Michael has been much added to and altered over the centuries. The oldest

part is the north wall of the nave, which dates from the 12th century. The chancel and east window are 13th or early 14th century, the south doorway is 14th century, and the south porch was added in the 17th century. The sandstone font, a round bowl with moulded stem, is probably 13th century. The church was extensively restored in 1889, and the stained glass chancel windows date from this time. There are several attractive old houses in the village. These include Ye Old Cottage at Street Farm, a late 17th century sandstone rubble house with some timber framing and a slate roof, and Sutton House opposite. They are

a short distance beyond where the walk route turns right just past the church.

Lea Bailey Gold Mine (7)

Bailey Level was driven in 1906 by the Chastan Syndicate to work gold in the Quartz Conglomerate at the base of the Devonian Upper Old Red Sandstone. The theory was that the conglomerate resembled gold-bearing rocks of South Africa. It was reached about 300 ft from the entrance and was 25 ft thick. However, only about 6 grains of gold per ton were present, and the venture was an expensive failure, soon abandoned. Whether it was a case of wishful thinking or an outright scam is unclear. In 1921 the level was extended to more than 1800 ft by the Wigpool Coal and Iron Syndicate (later Co.) in order to exploit iron ore in the Crease Limestone. A narrow-gauge railway was laid along the trackbed of the Mitcheldean Road & Forest of Dean Junction Railway *(see 8)* to Mitcheldean Road Station on the GWR's Hereford, Ross & Gloucester line. However, this venture was also short lived; only 3000 tons of ore were won and operations had been abandoned by 1927. The narrow-gauge railway equipment lying around today was part of a more-recent scheme to re-open the level as a tourist attraction.

Mitcheldean Road & Forest of Dean Junction Railway (8)

The Mitcheldean Road & Forest of Dean Junction Railway Act of 1871 authorised the company to build a line from Mitcheldean Road station, on the Hereford, Ross

Bridge over the MR&FoDJR's trackbed.

and Gloucester Railway, to Whimsey on the Great Western Railway's Forest of Dean Branch. The new line was intended to carry South Wales traffic and stimulate iron-ore mining around Drybrook, and it had the support of the Crawshays and Alfred Goold, owner of the Lower Soudley ironworks. Construction began in 1874, but progress was slow, and the line was not completed until after it had been taken over by the Great Western Railway in 1880. However, the heavily-graded line, which included tunnels at Drybrook and Euroclydon, was never worked throughout, partly because of competition from the Severn and Wye Railway's line to Lydbrook which had opened in 1874. The southern section from Whimsey was opened as far as Speedwell Siding, near Nailbridge, for mineral traffic in 1885 and to Drybrook Halt for passengers (as an extension of services on the Forest of Dean Branch) in 1907. The track north of Drybrook was taken up in 1917, but was reinstated to Drybrook Quarry in 1928, and there have even been plans in recent years to relay the section from the quarry to connect with the Dean Forest Railway's line *(see Walk 2)* at Parkend. The only use the northern section ever got was in the 1920s, when the Wigpool Coal and Iron Syndicate attempted to work Lea Bailey Level for iron *(see 7)*. A narrow-gauge railway was laid along the old trackbed to Mitcheldean Road, but the venture was soon abandoned. Euroclydon Tunnel was used for storing ammunition during World War 2.

Yankee Cinema (9)

There was once an entrance to Wigpool Mine here, but the present excavation is an old quarry. American troops stationed here during World War 2 used it as a cinema, the screen being hung on the vertical wall at one end. The troops, an engineering battalion, left suddenly just before the D-day landings, leaving wooden seats and film cases (all long since rotted away) lying around. How many of these troops survived the war?

Wigpool Iron Mine (10, 12)

Iron has certainly been mined here for centuries, and may have supplied ore to the Roman iron-smelting settlement at Ariconium, which was only 2½ miles to the north. Wigpool Iron Mine comprised the Wigpool, Belt, Wigpool Belt, Injunction Belt, and Injunction Iron Mine gales. The first two of these were granted in 1846, and Injunction Iron Mine gale in 1850. By 1854 the gales were held by Messrs Allaway, who had interests in ironworks and

tinplate works in Lydney, Lydbrook and Cinderford. A shaft (No. 1 Pit) had been sunk by about 1858, when a 30-inch horizontal rotary engine was installed for both winding and pumping. Production of iron ore was sporadic in the 1860s, but had risen to 6815 tons by 1870. Financial problems resulted in the formation of a new company, the Lydney and Wigpool Iron Ore Co. Ltd, in 1871. Expansion of the mine soon took place, with the addition of the Wigpool Belt gale, and production reached 22106 tons in 1873. The No. 1 (or Deep) Pit was sunk to a depth of 530 ft in the Lower Dolomite (part of the Carboniferous Limestone Series), and the No. 2 Pit to 380 ft. Most ore was won from the Crease Limestone, but significant quantities also came from the underlying Lower Dolomite. About 150 000 tons were produced between 1861 and 1883, much of it being dispatched down a tramroad which ran, via Westbury Brook Iron Mine, to Whimsey on the Great Western Railway's Forest of Dean Branch. By 1883 the company was again in financial difficulties and went into liquidation in 1886, the plant being auctioned off the following year. Several attempts were made to re-open the mine between 1911 and 1923. It was bought by a Mr Witfield for £4000 in 1915 and some ore was raised, but the project was abandoned in 1918. Some further work was done by the Wigpool Coal and Iron Syndicate (later Co.) in 1921–7 from the Bailey Level, but only 3000 tons of ore were won before the company went into receivership. Today only the stone engine house (now a dwelling) survives above ground. There are several mine entrances (e.g., Steam Hole and Fox Hole) on Wigpool Common, as well as areas of scowles (ancient near-surface workings), including 'The Delves'.

Wig Pool (11)

This is a remnant of the acidic bog and heathland which once covered much of Wigpool Common. The pool existed as long ago as 1282, but was drained during conifer planting in 1955. However the drainage ditches were blocked in 1970, and the pool allowed to refill. There is still a variety of acid marshland plants, such as marsh pennywort, lesser spearwort, marsh speedwell, common marsh-bedstraw, floating sweet-grass, and various sedges. Drier areas support purple moor-grass, common bent, tufted hair-grass, rushes, and bilberry. Mallard, common frogs, and palmate and smooth newts breed here. The pool is now a nature reserve belonging to the Gloucestershire Wildlife Trust, and there are plans to reinstate areas of heathland as the conifers are harvested.

Wigpool Tramroad (13)

This was an extension of the Westbury Brook tramroad, which connected the iron mine of that name *(see Walk 10)* to Whimsey and the Forest of Dean Railway's tramroad to Bullo Pill on the Severn. This opened in about 1842 and probably used part of the formation of the Bishop's tramroad which served Newbridge Engine Colliery at Nailbridge. The extension to Wigpool was authorised in 1854, by which time the (by then) Forest of Dean Branch of the South Wales Railway had been converted to a broad-gauge line, so that the Westbury Brook tramroad now terminated at a transhipment wharf at Whimsey. The Wigpool tramroad diverged from the Westbury Brook line near Fairplay Cottages (near which there was also a short branch to Fairplay Iron Mine, *see Walk 10*) and the distance to Wigpool No. 2 Pit was just over two miles. It is not clear when the tramroad opened, but the first recorded production of iron ore was not until 1865. Closure of the mine came in 1886, and the tramroad had been removed by the turn of the century. There was also a tramroad from Wigpool No. 2 Pit to Mitcheldean Road Station yard, on the Hereford, Ross and Gloucester Railway (opened 1855; amalgamated with the Great Western Railway in 1862). This descended Bailey Hill by a rope-worked incline.

Enlarged extract from Ordnance Survey First Edition 1 inch to 1 mile map (Old Series) c. 1820

An attractive riverside village, former ports, early railway tunnels, and a spectacular viewpoint. The walk is mainly on field paths and forest tracks, with a steady climb to Blaize Bailey and descent back to Newnham; 13 stiles.

Riverside car park off A48 at northern end of Newnham: GR SO 694120. Alternative parking along the High Steeet. **Refreshments:** Railway and Ship Inns, tea shop and shops in Newnham; snack bar in the riverside car park at popular times. **Bus:** 73 (Gloucester–Chepstow) to Newnham.

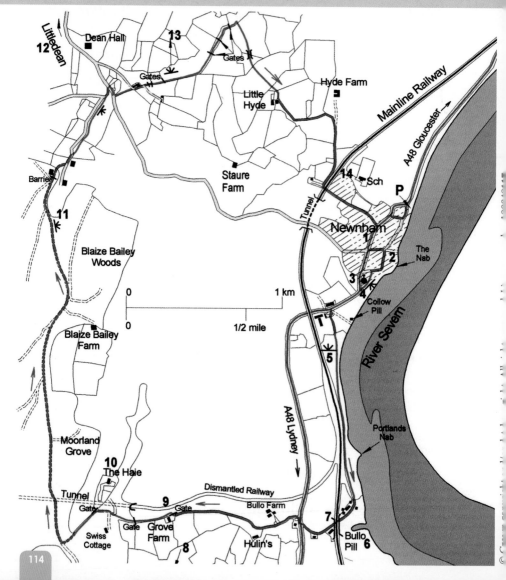

TURN LEFT out of the car park and follow Church Road past cottages, partly constructed of black slag blocks, Quay House, and the Drill Hall (former warehouses). Turn right opposite the latter into Beeches Road, then turn left into the High Street, passing the Clock Tower. Lined with old buildings, High Street is particularly attractive in March when the daffodils are in bloom *(1)*. Turn left into Severn Street, noting the slag blocks in the wall on the left. Turn right past Passage House at the bottom of the hill, the old ferry slipway being just ahead here *(2)*. Pass the former Brightlands School on the left, and, just after the road bends right, turn left through a metal gate ("Peace Garden") at the bottom of the churchyard. Follow the iron railings uphill above the river, passing to the left of the church *(3)*. There is an excellent view of the Severn and Cotswold Hills from here *(4)*. Continue onto a tarmac footpath which leads downhill onto the main road. Where the road bends right, by Underhill House, turn left and then right on a tarmac drive. Bear left by some buildings onto a grass path, go through a kissing gate, and continue straight ahead through a gate to the field beyond. Keep between the river and a railway line, climbing a small rise. Ahead can be seen Portlands Nab, and behind is Newnham Church, The Nab, and Collow Pill, where a marine engineering company usually has some interesting boats. A slight depression where the field narrows marks the site of an ill-fated attempt to build a tunnel under the river *(5)*.

Continue above the river and go through a kissing gate into trees, an area rich in wild flowers in spring. Pass another kissing gate and follow the path between a fence and hedge to another gate by a house. Keep ahead along a gravel road, which soon bends right. To the left is Bullo Pill *(6)* and ahead a railway viaduct, part of the former South Wales Railway *(7)*. Follow the lane under the archway and out onto the main road. Turn right for 20 yds, cross with care, and take the tarmac lane (signposted bridleway) by the telephone box. On the left is the red-brick Bullo House, built in the mid to late 19th century for the harbour master at Bullo Pill. The lane, which soon becomes a dirt track, passes Bullo Farm, Hulin's, and Grove Farm, approaching which a large house (Oaklands Park, *8*) can be seen through trees on the left. At Grove Farm, go through a wooden gate on the right, then turn left to follow a hedge and then a sunken track on your left. In the trees at the bottom of the cutting on your right is the trackbed of the former Forest of Dean Branch *(9)*, which leads to the Haie Hill Tunnel. The large pink house above is The Haie *(10)*. Continue with a fence on your left, ignoring a stile, to go through a wooden gate into woodland. The path goes uphill to a gravel track where you bear left. Where this track turns sharp left (to Swiss Cottage), continue ahead on a dirt track to a gate, just before which is a stile on the left. Cross this and bear right to follow a path, which may be rather overgrown in summer, just inside the edge of the woods. Cross another stile and continue along the path, which becomes a broader grassy track and descends to a T-junction.

Turn right and follow this track, which soon becomes gravel, uphill through a pine plantation. Bear slightly right at a track junction, and eventually come to a small clearing, where you bear left uphill to Blaize Bailey lookout *(11)*. Continue on the gravel track, bearing slightly right at a junction. Where the track bends left downhill, bear right past a barrier and a house onto a tarmac lane, where you turn left. After 70 yds climb a stile on the right by a metal gate and turn left to follow the hedge on your left. Cross a pair of stiles and then another by a gate to emerge back onto the lane. *This route gives more good views of the Severn Vale, with the early 17th century multi-gabled Staure Farmhouse down the hill towards Newnham. However, if the grass in the fields is too long you can remain on the lane instead.* Continue ahead on the lane for a short distance past 'The Bungalow' (on your right) to a junction. Bearing left here takes you into Littledean *(12)*, but turn sharp right downhill to continue the walk.

After 100 yds, turn left at a footpath sign, to head steeply downhill between hedges (not through the kissing gate) and over a stile. Cross another stile onto a tarmac lane, continue ahead past a house, and then, where the road bends right, take the bridleway (not the stile) ahead. Go between hedges through two gates into a field. Follow the hedge on your right, passing a gate/stile, after which the hedge and path bend left downhill past ancient oaks, with lovely views of May Hill *(13)* and Chestnuts Hill to the left. Look out ahead for a metal gate, which leads to a sunken track between hedges. Follow this, ignoring a stile on the right, through two more gates into a field. Follow the fence on your right for 70 yds and, just past a small hollow, cross a stile (not easy to see) and go through a hedge gap. Bear slightly right across the field ahead, keeping parallel to the right-hand edge, to a marker post and footbridge, which only come into view as you get close. Cross the bridge and a stile and then continue in the same direction to another stile. Bear slightly left across the next field, aiming to go past an isolated tree to a stile in the hedge a little to the left of a house. Climb this and go through a gap in the hedge (by a marker post) a short distance ahead. Bear right, going left of a house (Little Hyde) onto a gravel track and turning left past a shed. The track bends left and then right to join a tarmac lane, where you turn right. Follow the lane as it turns sharp left over the railway line, the site of Newnham Station *(14)* being on the left and Newnham Tunnel on the right. Continue along the road to the T-junction by the Clock Tower and turn left to return to the car park.

Newnham (1)

The history of Newnham is closely linked with the River Severn. In Roman times, three important roads converged on the site and there was a ford and possibly even port facilities. A small hamlet had grown up by Saxon times, and by the late medieval period Newnham had become an important port with trading links to Ireland, London, Bristol, and the Midlands. In 1171 Henry II sailed from the town with an army to invade Ireland. It was also was much visited by kings for hunting in the Forest of Dean. Newnham continued to grow until the late 18th century, when it had become one of the most important ports on the Severn, exporting goods such as timber, bark, hides, and, increasingly, coal. Ships were built here, including one of 600 tons in 1778. There were few other industries, although

Sir Edward Mansell erected a glass furnace in the early 17th century, said to be the first in the country to be fired by coal; this had closed by 1700. There were also tanneries and a chemical works (verdigris factory). Trade was lost to Bullo when a tramroad was opened in 1810, and opening of the Gloucester and Sharpness Canal in 1827 was a further setback. Newnham's history as a port thus came to an end and the town's fortunes declined, although there were still over 40 shops and trades (cobblers, tailors, etc.) active in 1902.

In spite of this, Newnham is today an attractive village with a reasonable (if depleted) range of facilities. The tree-lined High Street, with its clock tower, is particularly worth a visit in the spring, when the daffodils are in bloom. It is lined with fine buildings, many of them listed. Particularly noteworthy are Britannia House, Kingston House, Lamb House (formerly Lamb & Flag Inn), Olde Bank House, Olde King's Head, Old House, The Limes & White House, The Sanctuary (formerly the Upper George Inn), and Wilcox House (all 17th century or older), and Ashley House, Church House, and Unlawater

Cottages partly constructed of slag blocks.

(18th century). There are also many 19th century buildings, including Newnham House and The Club, originally the Town Hall, of about 1850. Some of these were originally inns, of which there were 18 at one time or another. Only two survive, the Railway and Ship Inns, the early 18th century Victoria Hotel (a former coaching inn) having recently closed. Cottages in Church Street and walls in Severn Street are partly constructed of black slag blocks. These are of copper slag, probably brought up-river as ballast from works at Swansea, rather than being from the Newnham glass works as some sources have claimed. The 17th century Passage House at the bottom of Severn Street was once the Bear Inn (and Passage Inn). By the river are the 17/18th century Quay House and the Quay Warehouses, the latter built in about 1755 by a local shipping entrepreneur, Robert Pyrke, partly using slag blocks and an

important relic of Newnham's period as a port. Brightlands was built in 1868 as the Severn Bank Hotel, but soon became a private house (Riverdale), then a school, and now flats.

Severn Ferry (2)

Newnham was probably first settled because the river is relatively easy to cross here. Indeed it is occasionally possible to walk across when both the tide and river flow are low, although not without expert local knowledge! A ferry was recorded here in 1238, although there is some evidence that its western end

Newnham Ferry in c.1908. *From an old postcard.*

Newnham Nab, with the church and boats at Collow Pill.

was originally ½ mile south near Portlands Nab. This site appears to have abandoned in about 1600, possibly because of erosion of the river bank. The ferry remained in use until after the Second World War — clearly the opening of the Severn Railway Bridge a few miles downstream in 1879 did not divert all the ferry traffic away. Small rowing boats were used for passengers, who had to be carried across the mud between the boat and the river bank. Larger boats were used for animals (horses, cattle, sheep, etc.) or carts. In June 2000 two Royal Marines hovercraft were used in a re-enactment of the Newnham to Arlingham ferry as part of the local millennium celebrations.

Newnham Church (3)

Newnham's Church of St Peter stands on high ground above the River Severn. The first church here was built in 1380 on land donated by Humphrey de Bohun near his castle, to replace an earlier church, which had been damaged by floods, lower in the town. The church was completely rebuilt by Waller and Son of Gloucester in 1874. It was almost completely destroyed by fire in 1881 and was again rebuilt by Waller. Of the 14th century church, only parts of the tower and north porch survive. However, a Norman font with twelve niches containing figures of the Apostles, and a fragment of a tympanum showing the Tree of Life can be seen. The original church was the scene of a battle in 1644 during the Civil War when it was captured from the Royalists by Colonel Massey, some damage being done when a gunpowder keg exploded.

View from churchyard (4)

The wonderful view from the churchyard takes in part of the Severn Vale, including the impressive meander (a complete U-bend) of the River Severn. Just opposite is the Passage Inn, near the ferry landing place; beyond this is Arlingham's church tower, and, in the distance, Stonehouse and Stroud. The cities of Gloucester, with the Cathedral tower prominent, and Cheltenham can be seen away on the left. The Cotswold Escarpment forms the skyline, including (from left to right) Cleeve Hill (beyond Gloucester), Haresfield Beacon, and Stinchcombe Hill (above

Dursley). Just downstream, towards Bullo, is the small headland of Portlands Nab, apparently the ferry terminus until about 1600. Portlands Nab was once much larger — until the mid-19th century a hundred people could dance upon it! Like the cliffs on this section of the river, it consists of Triassic Keuper Marl (part of the Mercia Mudstone Group). Newnham is a good place to watch the famous Severn Bore, a large natural wave formed as the incoming tide travels upstream into the narrowing river. The phenomenon depends on the unusually large tidal range (up to nearly 50 ft) in the Severn Estuary, said to be the second largest in the world, after the Bay of Fundy in Canada. The bore occurs at any time of spring tides, but is biggest near the spring (February–April) and autumn (August–October) equinoxes. The highest recorded bore (9¼ ft) was on 15 October 1966 near Minsterworth, but 4 ft is more typical. The bore becomes bigger as it moves upstream, and so will be higher there than at Newnham. Its speed averages around 10 mph. Bore size is affected by wind direction, pressure, and the amount of fresh water in the river: southwest winds, low pressure, and low water levels are favourable.

Severn Tunnel (5)

The Bullo Pill Railway's tramroad opened in about 1810, but it was apparent that business would be adversely affected by competition from the Severn and Wye Railway, whose outlet at Lydney Docks was much better placed to make use of the proposed Gloucester and Sharpness Canal (eventually opened in 1827). Transhipment of goods to trows, and the subsequent voyage upriver was both slow and risky. An alternative means of access to Gloucester and beyond was thus needed, and this resulted in the Severn Tunnel Co. being incorporated on 24 May 1810. The aim was to build a tunnel of 12x13 ft section beneath the river between the parishes of Newnham and Arlingham, suitable for use by railway wagons, carriages, and foot passengers. Construction was soon started by Robert Tipping and was well advanced when, in November 1812, water broke into the workings, which had to be abandoned. Thus ended a valiant attempt to build what would have been the first subaqueous tunnel in the world. In the event, it was Marc Brunel who achieved this when his Thames Tunnel was opened in 1843. The masonry-lined top of the shaft near Newnham was still visible in 1965, and it was only in the mid-2000s that it was finally obliterated.

Bullo Pill (6)

Bullo Pill was just a small tidal inlet used for boat building until the Bullo Pill Railway Co. *(see 9)* was formed in 1809 to develop it as a port for exporting Forest coal and stone. A large dock basin with tidal lock gates and an upper basin for water storage were constructed, and coal tips were eventually built on both the dock basin and river wharves, the latter then handling most of the traffic. The company's tramroad from Cinderford

Bridge and Churchway had opened in about 1810, and when this was converted to a broad-gauge railway 1854, a short branch into the docks from the South Wales Railway's main line was constructed to replace the tramroad connection. An engine shed and two signal boxes were built by the main line at Bullo Pill Junction, where both the Bullo Pill and Cinderford Branches diverged. By this time Bullo had grown into one of the most important ports in the area, which, at its height, was handling over 1000 tons of cargo per day. Jelf's marble works, Boucher's wagon works, and Newnham Rubber Mills were here at different times. However, Bullo's trade declined during the early 20th century, much having been lost to the better facilities at Lydney and Sharpness *(see Walk 4)*, and the last boat called in 1926, although the rail connection to the rubber works lasted until 1963. The lock gates collapsed and the basin began to silt up, but new gates were installed in 1991 with a view to developing the basin into a marina. Nothing has come of this as yet, although some private vessels are currently stored here.

South Wales Railway (7)

The main line of the South Wales Railway (SWR) ran from Grange Court Junction, north of Westbury, to Neyland in Pembrokeshire, via Cardiff and Swansea. It opened in stages between 1850 and 1856. The section between Grange Court and Chepstow East opened on 19 September 1851, and I.K. Brunel's tubular suspension bridge over the River Wye at Chepstow was completed in the following July. The SWR was amalgamated with the Great Western Railway on 1 August 1863. The SWR was built to broad gauge, but converted to standard gauge over a single weekend in 1872. Today it is the only surviving railway in the area (other than the preserved Dean Forest Railway), being part of the busy main line from Gloucester and the Midlands to South Wales. *(See Walk 4 for more details of the SWR.)*

Oaklands Park (8)

The original house at Oaklands Park was built in the early 19th century by Sir James Jelf, formerly a Gloucester banker and a partner in the nearby Bullo Pill Tramroad. In about 1850 the house, park, and adjoining land, including Oaklands farm, were bought by the ironmaster and coal owner Henry Crawshay, who built a large new house in Renaissance style. The original house survives as a low wing at the north end of the present house, and some adjacent outbuildings and the lodge on the main road are contemporary with it. Crawshay, who owned Lightmoor and Foxes Bridge Collieries, Buckshaft and Shakemantle iron mines, and Cinderford and Parkend ironworks, died in 1879 and his widow Liza owned the state until her death in 1895. It was sold in 1899 to William Gwynne-Evans of Fordham (Essex) and remained in the family until 1976. The house and park were then bought by the Camphill Village Trust, a charity for the care of adults with learning difficulties. The community comprises about a hundred people who live according to principles based on the ideas of Rudolph Steiner. They farm 150 acres, producing milk and wool and growing organic fruit and vegetables, as well as doing craft work. Given their respect for the natural world, and resistance to the exploitation and abuse of people and animals, it is not surprising that the community refused to allow the slaughter of their healthy stock during the foot-and-mouth cull of 2001. There is another similar community nearby: Grange Village, on the Newnham-Littledean road.

Forest of Dean Branch (9)

The Bullo Pill Railway Co. opened a horse tramroad from Bullo Pill to Cinderford Bridge and Churchway in about 1810. It was used to transport coal, iron ore, stone, and other goods down to the Severn. The Forest of Dean Railway Co. was formed in 1826, but this, in turn, was taken over by the South Wales Railway (SWR) in 1851. The tramroad was replaced by a broad-gauge locomotive railway to Churchway, which opened to goods traffic on 24 July

1854. The SWR became part of the Great Western Railway in 1863, and the line was converted to standard gauge in 1872. Passenger services between Newnham, on the SWR main line, and Steam Mills (soon extended to Drybrook) began on 3 August 1907, and a loop to Cinderford was opened in April 1908. Passenger services to Cinderford ceased on 1 November 1958, but goods traffic lasted until 1967 *(see also Walk 3)*. The major engineering feature on the Forest of Dean Railway was the 1064 yard long Haie Hill Tunnel,

Haie Hill Tunnel.

originally constructed in 1809 as part of the Bullo Pill Railway's tramroad and enlarged to accommodate broad-gauge trains in 1851–4. When built, it was one of the longest railway tunnels in the world. The other end is seen on *Walk 3*.

The Haie (10)

The Haie, long-term home of the Kerr family, was built in about 1840, but a large porte-cochere (with the Kerr family arms) and staircase hall were added to the north front in 1883. Captain Ralph Kerr CBE (born 1891) went down with his ship, the battle cruiser *HMS Hood* when it was sunk in the Denmark Strait by the German battleship *Bismarck* on 24th May 1941. He made no attempt to leave the sinking vessel, preferring to remain at his station alongside Vice-Admiral Lancelot Holland, and was posthumously Mentioned in Despatches. The deaths of 1415 crew members of the

The Haie. The trees in the foreground hide the cutting leading to Haie Hill Tunnel.

Hood constituted the Royal Navy's greatest single ship loss of the Second World War. The Haie Estate was sold soon after the war.

Blaize Bailey (11)

The Blaize Bailey viewpoint was constructed using stone from a disused railway bridge at Fetter Hill in the Forest. The name comes from the Blythe or Bleith family, who owned

Horseshoe bend in the Severn, with the Cotswolds beyond.

the estate centred on Blythes Court, now the Culver House, down towards Newnham, in the late 13th century. In about 1876 the estate was merged with the Kerr family's Haie Estate. The view from here is even wider ranging than that from Newnham, including the meandering River Severn, with Gloucester and the Cotswold Hills beyond. To the left is Bredon Hill, and you may also be able to make out the tower of Tewkesbury Abbey. Newnham is below, Broadoak is just upstream to the left, and Westbury, with its prominent church spire, beyond. Most of the church was built in about 1300, and it is unusual for its detached bell tower of about 1270; the first spire was added in the 14th century, but has rebuilt several times. Westbury Court Garden (first laid out in 1696–1705, now National Trust) is nearby.

This is also a good place to look at the geology; a look at the geological section and map in the "Brief History of Dean" chapter should help to make sense of the plethora of names. Blaize Bailey is situated on the eastern side of the Forest of Dean basin, on Lower Old Red Sandstone Brownstones (sandstones of Devonian age). These rocks dip steeply to the west here (away from the river), under the Carboniferous rocks which make up the central part of the Forest. Towards the river are older Devonian and Silurian rocks underlying the Brownstones: the marls (limey mudstone) and sandstones of the St Maughan's and Raglan Mudstone Groups. Below them are Silurian sandstones, limestones, and shales of the Ludlow, Wenlock, and Llandovery Series, but these are seen mainly north of Blaisdon. In contrast, the Vale of Gloucester and Cotswold Hills consist mainly of much younger Triassic and Jurassic rocks, which are separated from the Silurian–Devonian rocks by the Blaisdon Fault and other faults *(see Walk 11)*. These younger rocks are much less strongly folded and only gently dipping. Much of the lower ground on this side of the Severn north of Bullo (including the cliffs near Newnham) consists of Triassic Keuper Marl (Mercia Mudstone Group), mainly mudstones, with some marls and sandstones, deposited in inland lakes under desert conditions. At Garden Cliff (just upstream of Westbury), the Keuper Marl is overlain by Rhaetic (uppermost Triassic) and Liassic (Lower Jurassic) rocks. The Rhaetic beds (Penarth Group) represent a change to marine conditions, and are mostly black shales, but include layers of sandstone with abundant bivalve fossils. Of particular interest is the Ceratodus Bone Bed, a sandy limestone full of the fragmentary remains of fish (teeth, scales, and spines) and marine reptiles (bones and teeth). The low ground across the river is largely of Lower Lias mudstones (with some limestone layers); the same rocks are seen around Whitby in Yorkshire and Lyme Regis in Devon, world-famous localities which are a rich source of ammonites and other fossils. There are good exposures at Hock Cliff, just across the river south of Arlingham. Small ammonites and belemnites (the bullet-shaped internal shells of extinct cuttlefish-like animals) can be found there, as well as excellent specimens of the bivalve *Gryphaea* (the Devil's toenail). Overlying these are Middle and Upper Lias mudstones, marls, silts, and sands (Cotteswold Sands), which are exposed near the base of the Cotswold Escarpment and on Robinswood and Churchdown Hills near Gloucester. The youngest solid rocks in the area seen here are the Middle Jurassic oolitic limestones (Inferior and Great Oolite Series) of the Cotswold Hills. These are the famous cream-coloured limestones so characteristic of the area and seen in numerous dry-stone walls and buildings. Like the Liassic rocks, they are commonly highly fossiliferous, with brachiopods, bivalves, and echinoids (sea-urchins) being particularly common.

Lying on top of these solid rocks along the Severn Valley are the remnants of a series of Quaternary river terraces (sand and gravel), deposited when sea levels were higher than today at different times during interglacial periods. Evidence for at least six distinct terraces are known, the highest and oldest probably having formed several hundred thousand years ago. Much younger (<10 000 years) are the deposits of alluvium (mainly sand, clay, and peat) which cover large areas near the river. Interestingly, it was only at the end of the last Ice Age that the River Severn took up its present course. Before then it had flowed north, but its course was blocked by ice and it was forced to find an alternative outlet to the south. This occurred either by the overflow of a huge lake of glacial melt water, or by water flowing beneath the ice sheet under very high pressure. The result was the formation of the Severn Gorge near Ironbridge in Shropshire. This area is famous as the birthplace of the Industrial Revolution (although the Forest also had its role to play), but this was dependent on the availability of the necessary raw materials (limestone, ironstone, sandstone, coal, and clay) which had been exposed in the steep-sided gorge by the action of glacial melt water. The Industrial Revolution would undoubtedly have happened, but had it not been for this geological event, its main cradle might have been elsewhere.

Littledean (12)

Littledean stood at the centre of a network of tracks, notably the Roman road which led up from the ford and ferry at Newnham. It is one of the ancient villages of Dean, although the woodland was cleared early. By 1086 a motte and bailey castle, later known as the Old Castle of Dene, had been built in a commanding position on a hill to the east. Nearby outcrops of Carboniferous Limestone, with associated iron-ore deposits, provided the basis for quarrying and mining industries for centuries. However, the local Old Red Sandstone provided stone for most of the older buildings in the village. The Church of St Ethlebert was built in the late 12th century, but little remains of this Norman structure. The present nave and chancel are 13th, the tower is 14th, and the north aisle and Brayne Chapel are 15th century. The tower originally had a spire, but this was destroyed in a severe gale

Littledean Jail.

in 1894 and never rebuilt. There are some fine buildings in Church Street, including the early 18th century Frogmore and Church Farmhouse; Old Victoria Inn dates back to the 15th century. Dean Croft, in Broad Street, is 17th century. Brayne Court, behind the Littledean House Hotel, is partly 16th century, albeit with 17th century additions and much 19th century remodelling. It may well date back to the 1580s when Thomas Brayne created a deer park west of the village. Of the many inns in Littledean, only the Belfry (formerly the George), King's Head, and Littledean House are still open today. Northeast of the village is Littledean Gaol, designed by William Blackburn and one of four built in the county for Sir George Onesiphorus Paul in 1791. It incorporated a two-storey building, with a central block containing an office, committee room, chapel, infirmaries, and accommodation for keeper and turnkey, and east and west wings containing the cells. Around the building were four courtyards and the whole was surrounded by a perimeter wall with a gatehouse on the south side. From 1854 the building was used as a police station and remand prison and in 1874 the east wing was remodelled as a petty sessional court. During the Second World War the cells were used as a store by the County Record Office and Gloucester Cathedral. The police station was closed in 1972 and the building, which continued to house archives until 1979, was purchased by an insurance company in 1985. It is now an interesting museum.

The most historically important building in Littledean is undoubtedly Dean Hall, just south of the village on Dean Hill. Originally there was an open hall of Saxon type here, perhaps occupied by the first Lords of Dene (or by earlier Saxon thanes) and this was later converted to a Norman hall, comprising first floor and undercroft. Gradually extended over three centuries, the Norman hall had developed into a substantial medieval manor house by the time it was largely replaced with the present Jacobean house after 1612. In that year it was bought from the Brayne family by Charles Bridgeman, who completely rebuilt it. Two Royalist were killed here during a Civil war skirmish. The house passed to the Pyrke family in 1664 and they made further major alterations: a formal front in the late 17th century and a 'Jacobean' façade in 1852. In the cellar are substantial remains of the original Saxon or early Norman (possibly 10th or 11th century) hall, and there is good reason to suppose that a Roman settlement had previously occupied the site, as fragments of Roman masonry can be found in the surviving part of the Saxon dwelling. There is thus some justification for the claim that Dean Hall is "England's oldest inhabited house". More evidence of Roman occupation are the remains of a Roman temple near the house. Sited at a spring on the edge of the escarpment overlooking the river, it is thought that the temple was dedicated to the deity of the River Severn (Sabrina). Unfortunately, Dean Hall is no longer open to the public.

May Hill

May Hill (13)
The rounded top of May Hill, with its distinctive clump of trees, is a conspicuous feature from far and wide, being visible from the Malvern Hills, much of the

Cotswold Escarpment, the Black Mountains, and even the hills of mid-Wales. Although it is commonly said that the cluster of trees was planted in 1887 to mark Queen Victoria's Golden Jubilee, much earlier accounts refer to a plantation on the summit. The 1887 plantings presumably replaced some of the older trees which had died or been used as fuel in a beacon to guide ships navigating the River Severn. The origin of the name May Hill is uncertain. It has been suggested it was derived from *Magesoetan*, an Anglo-Saxon tribe which lived in the area, and that the syllable *mag* evolved to become *may*. However, it is widely believed that the name originated from the May Day games, when young people from the district would gather on top of the hill to have a mock battle. May Hill was once also known as Yartleton Hill, but it is unclear whether that was the original name. Geologically, May Hill consists of some of the oldest rocks in the area: Silurian sandstones, limestones, and shales, about 420–440 million years old. They form an 'inlier', in which the strata were folded into an anticline (or dome), the older rocks in the core then being exposed by erosion. The rocks of May Hill form a continuation of the Malvern Hills line of faulting and folding *(see Walk 11)*.

Newnham Station (14)

Opened in 1851 or 1852, Newnham Station on the South Wales Railway (*see 7 above*) had two platforms, connected by a footbridge, and a goods siding serving a large stone goods shed. The main station building was on the down platform and there was a signal box on the up side. A bay platform was later built to accommodate passenger services on the Forest of Dean Branch *(see 9)* to Steam Mills (soon extended to Drybrook), which began on 3 August 1907; Cinderford was served from April 1908. In 1953 there were three services a day to Cinderford (with more on Saturdays) and about 12 to and from Gloucester, the down trains continuing to Cardiff, Swansea, or Cinderford. Passenger services to Drybrook ended on 7 July 1930, and to Cinderford on 1 November 1958, and Newnham Station finally closed on 2 November 1964. No trace of the station remains today.

A former industrial centre, views of Welsh mountains from The Kymin, attractive woodland, and massive rock outcrops. A hilly walk on field paths and woodland tracks, with some steep ascents and descents, but superb views; 4 stiles.

START at the car park by the River Wye in Redbrook, just north of the playing field, on the A466 Chepstow–Monmouth road: GR SO 536099. **Refreshments:** pub (The Bell) and shop in Redbrook; pubs in Penallt (The Boat) and Staunton (White Horse). **Bus:** 69 (Chepstow–Monmouth) to Redbrook.

REDBROOK *(1)* WAS ONCE an industrial village, although few traces of this now remain. The car park is on the site of the goods yard adjacent to Redbrook Station on the former Wye Valley Railway *(2)*. Cross the main road by the car park entrance and bear left up the gravel lane in front of houses, indicated by an Offa's Dyke Path sign. (We will be following the Offa's Dyke Path for about 2 miles.) Note the old railway embankment in the garden across the main road on the left. The lane bends right, passing Brewery Terrace on the left and the remains of Wye Valley Mills on the right, before emerging onto a main road at a tramroad incline bridge *(3)*. Turn right and follow the road uphill with care, as there is no footpath. (The stream marks the boundary between England and Wales here, and the first part of the walk is actually in Wales.) After about 350 yds take a tarmac lane which forks left uphill in front of a house and is signposted to Monmouth. Just opposite here was the site of one of the early 17th century forges, with a large mill pond above.

Follow the lane (Duffield's Lane, an 18th century turnpike road) steadily uphill past Cobbs Tump, after which it bends left, passes Duffield's Farm, and becomes a stony track. Views of the Wye Valley and Penallt Church *(4)* on the opposite hillside open up on the left. Continue ahead onto a grass track beside a barn, just past which you go through a kissing gate on the right. Bear left to cross the lower part of the field below Upper Beaulieu Farm to a gate, and then keep right of the trees through

two more gates onto an enclosed path by a fence. This leads to another gate, after which you follow the left-hand side of the field to a metal kissing gate. The path then follows a wooden fence to another gate, which leads to a National Trust car park. Bear right across this towards the Naval Temple *(5)* in the trees ahead. Just beyond this is The Kymin *(6)*, and glorious views of Monmouth and the Black Mountains *(7)*. In the opposite direction (southeast) are good views of Newland Church and the Forest of Dean.

About 100 yds past The Kymin, turn right at a track junction. Bear left past a house to a kissing gate, which has a Wysis Way waymark. Head diagonally right across the field into trees, and follow a gravel track which curves left to a gate and stile. Cross this and follow a path downhill to a wooden kissing gate on the edge of woodland. Turn right onto the gravel track beyond the gate and follow this down to a main road. Carefully cross the road and take the footpath just to the left (still signed Wysis Way) which descends through woods to a gravel track, where you go right. The next part of the walk is through the attractive Highmeadow Woods *(8)*. Bear right at the next junction and follow the track, now more of a gravel road, as it bends left and then right, ignoring a waymarked path on the right. Turn left at a T-junction, following a yellow arrow, eventually passing a plaque on the left marking the Everard Oak, dedicated to John Everard, a former Deputy Surveyor.

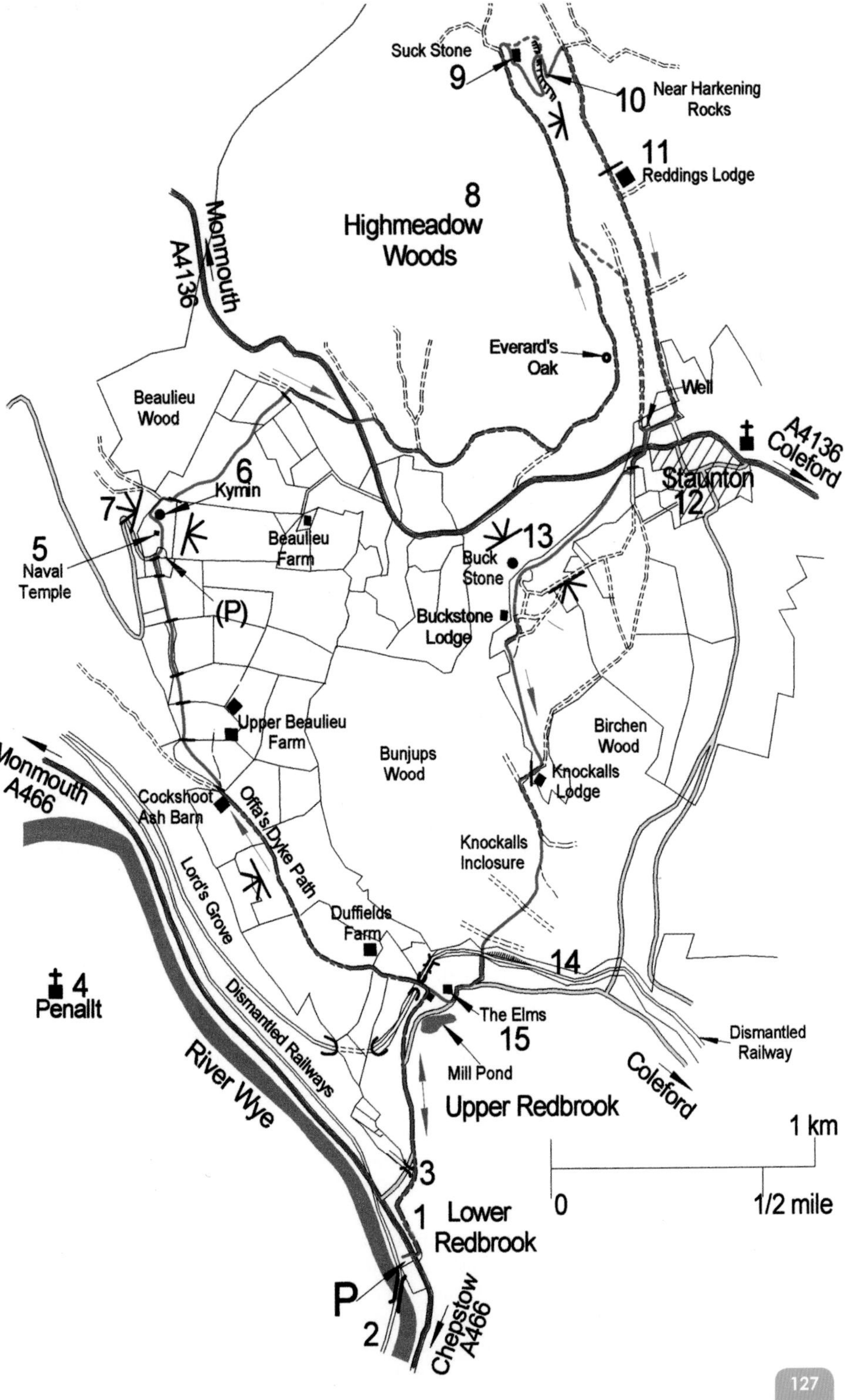

Suck Stone
9
10   Near Harkening Rocks

11
Reddings Lodge

8
Highmeadow Woods

Monmouth
A4136

Everard's Oak

Well

A4136
Coleford

Beaulieu Wood

6
Kymin

Staunton
12

7

5
Naval Temple

Beaulieu Farm

13
Buck Stone

(P)

Buckstone Lodge

Birchen Wood

Upper Beaulieu Farm

Bunjups Wood

Knockalls Lodge

Cockshoot Ash Barn

Offa's Dyke Path

Knockalls Inclosure

Monmouth
A466

Lord's Grove

Duffields Farm

14

4
Penallt

Dismantled Railways

The Elms
15

Mill Pond

Dismantled Railway

Coleford

River Wye

Upper Redbrook

1 km

P

3

0   1/2 mile

1   Lower Redbrook

2

Chepstow
A466

About 400 yds after the oak, look out for a stone marker with a yellow arrow which marks a path going sharply right uphill. This is a possible shortcut, albeit rather steep and often muddy. It comes out onto a broader path where you bear right and continue to St John's Well. Otherwise, continue on the gravel road to a cleared area with large rock outcrops uphill to the right. A wooden post just beyond the clearing marks a narrow path (Highmeadow Trail) which goes steeply up to the right. The waymarked path (yellow arrows) bends right to pass immediately below a huge fallen block, the Suck Stone *(9)*, then zig-zags upwards, passing below an outcrop of conglomerate rock to emerge onto the cliff top. Just ahead, right on the cliff edge, are Near Harkening Rocks *(10)*, which provide more good views of the Welsh hills, and would be a good place for lunch, or at least refreshments.

An obvious path leads directly away from the cliff edge through the trees to a dirt track. Turn right here and follow the track past a barrier, with Reddings Lodge *(11)* on the left, until you come to a small housing estate. Keep right onto a short tarmac road and at the end take the byway on the left of the house ahead. Just behind the house is St John the Baptist's Well, *past which the shortcut comes in on the right.* The path bends left to emerge at a main road in Staunton village *(12)*, which can be visited by turning left. However, the route continues up the lane opposite. After 100 yds, just beyond a gate, take the path (Highmeadow Trail) on the right, which heads uphill. Keeping the stone wall on your right, you eventually come to the Buck Stone *(13)*, from which there are good views of the Welsh and Herefordshire hills.

Keep ahead here, following a path signposted 'Redbrook Spur Trail', which we will follow most of the way back to Redbrook. This initially continues to follow the wall on your right, before curving slightly left and emerging from the trees near Buckstone Lodge. There are lovely views of Newland, St Briavels, and the forest from here. Just beyond the lodge, turn right along a tarmac road, then, immediately in front of the gate to the Buckstone Adventure Centre, take a waymarked path to the left. The grass path descends to the right of a house to a track junction, where you turn right to pass Knockalls Lodge and a barrier. Turn left at the T-junction and after about 200 yds, where the track bends left, take a waymarked downhill path on the right. Go right at a fork on the waymarked, but less obvious, path. Continue downhill, crossing over a gravel road, and then carefully down a steep section, which can be quite slippery in wet conditions. Cross another track and descend steeply to a stile. The cutting (left) and embankment (right) mark the trackbed of the Coleford Railway *(14)*. The path continues between wire fences, over two more stiles and steeply down to a road. Turn right past The Elms *(15)*, just beyond which is a signposted (to Kymin) rocky footpath going uphill to the right. Taking this avoids walking along a stretch of busy narrow road. Look out for a view of a well-preserved stone railway bridge on your right. You soon come out onto a stony track, where you turn left and descend back to the road. Bear right and return to the starting point via your outward route.

Redbrook (1)

Redbrook was once an important industrial centre due to the ample supply of water which powered mills in both the Red Brook (in Upper Redbrook) and Valley Brook (Lower Redbrook) valleys. From Swan Pool, on the former, down to the Wye, leats, dams, and reservoir ponds were built to supply water to several corn mills, blast furnaces, tinplate works, and copper works, although not all of these were working at the same time. King's Mill, a corn mill, was first recorded in 1434, rebuilt before 1793, and much extended in 1873 as Wye Valley Mills; the latter remained in use until 1925. Two charcoal blast furnaces were built in Upper Redbrook in about 1604, and one of these lasted until the early 19th century. Lower Redbrook Copper Works was founded by the Company of Copper Miners in England in about 1690, and an Upper Copper Works was established by John Coster of Bristol at about the same time. They used local charcoal and coal, with ore brought from Cornwall via Chepstow. For a while Redbrook was the largest producer in the country, but by 1735 it had become cheaper to smelt copper ore in the Swansea area using local coal, and the works closed. By the late 18th century, both sites were being used for tinplate manufacture. That at Upper Redbrook closed in 1818, but the works at Lower Redbrook survived until 1961, and was world famous for the

Lower Redbrook Tinplate Works in about 1850.

high-quality product it made. Today the manager's residence, dating from c.1700, survives as a private house, but there is now little evidence of the industrial past. The Upper Redbrook site was taken over by the Redbrook Brewery Co. in 1825, and this closed a century later. Brewery Terrace, built to house the workers, still exists. There was another brewery (Ansley's) further up the valley, lasting from before 1848 until demolition in the 1940s. Another local industry along both sides of the Wye Valley south of Redbrook was manufacture of millstones from Quartz Conglomerate rock *(see 9 below)* which was quarried here. Unfinished or broken millstones can still be found in the woods and on the river edges. Redbrook was also a port where the various products of local industries were shipped out, but this declined in importance once the Monmouth Tramroad was built. One of Redbrook's claims to fame is that it once had five pubs, three of which had four-letter names beginning in 'B', the Bell, the Boat, and the Bush. The first two survive, although the Boat is actually across the bridge in Wales (Penallt), but the last (Bush House) is now used by an osteopath. It is noteworthy for being partly constructed of slag blocks *(see Walk 12)*. St Saviour's Church was built in 1873 to a design by J.P. Seddon. Like many villages, Redbrook has lost most of its tradesmen and shopkeepers, but a village shop was recently re-opened. Today, it is on the routes of walkers on both the Offa's Dyke Path *(see Walk 14)* and Wye Valley Walk long-distance footpaths. The latter runs for 136 miles from Chepstow to the source of the Wye on the slopes of Plynlimon in mid-Wales.

Wye Valley Railway (2)

The Wye Valley Railway ran from Wye Valley Junction on the former South Wales Railway (by then part of the Great Western Railway) at Tutshill near Chepstow, to Wyesham Junction on the Coleford, Monmouth, Usk and Pontypool Railway near Monmouth, a distance of about 13 miles. The Act of Incorporation was passed on 10 August 1866, but construction, by Reed Bros & Co. of London, did not begin until May 1874. The line was opened on 1 November 1876, and was worked by the Great Western Railway from the start, although formal amalgamation with that company did not take place until 1 July 1905. Stations were provided initially at Tidenham, Tintern, St Briavels, and Redbrook-on-Wye, and halts were opened in 1927-32 at Netherhope, Brockweir, Llandogo, Whitebrook, and Penallt, as well as Wyesham on the old CMU&PR

View of Redbrook and the Wye, showing the Wye Valley Railway's viaduct.

section. There were four daily (except Sundays) passenger trains each way between Monmouth and Chepstow in 1910. Although very scenic, the Monmouth–Chepstow line was never very profitable, and closure to passenger services occurred on 5 January 1959, and to goods in January 1964. The southern part of the line then remained in use as a private siding to serve Tintern and Dayhouse quarries *(see Walk 14)*, the last train to the latter running in September 1992. Redbrook-on-Wye (known simply as Redbrook before 1935) Station opened with the line on 1 November 1876. The platform, stone station building, and signal box were on the down (eastern) side of the line. There was a goods yard, with a loop, sidings, goods shed, and both 5 ton and 30 cwt cranes, to the south of the platform. By 1925 the goods facilities were only used occasionally, although there was some traffic associated with the local tinplate works. The station was well known for its displays of flowers, and many prizes were won. The much-modified goods shed is now a private house. The old railway bridge across the Wye now provides a convenient footpath for customers of the Boat Inn, as well as users of the Wye Valley Walk long-distance footpath.

Tramroad Bridge (3)

The Redbrook Branch was part of the Monmouth Railway, a horse-drawn tramroad which ran from Broadwell to May Hill, near Monmouth, via Coleford, Newland, and Redbrook. This 3 ft 6 in. gauge line opened on 17 August 1812 and the Redbrook Branch appears to have gone into use about the same time. It was about ¾ mile long and incorporated a double-tracked, rope-worked, self-acting incline, which crossed the Redbrook–Newland road on a stone bridge. The branch was mainly used to suppy coal to the Upper Redbrook Tinplate Works, near the bottom of the incline, and the Lower Redbrook Tinplate Works, towards the end of the branch, but the Wye Valley Corn Mill and Redbrook Brewery were also served. There was a short spur to a wharf, owned by the company, on the River Wye, and the line extended another 400 yds to some waterside steps. The newly-formed Coleford, Monmouth, Usk, and Pontypool Railway agreed to purchase the Monmouth Railway in 1853, although this was never formalised and little was done to improve the tramroad. There was little traffic on the Monmouth Railway by 1872, by which time the Redbrook Branch had probably been abandoned. Much of the trackbed of the main tramroad was utilised by the standard-gauge Coleford Railway, which opened on 1 September 1883 *(see 13, and Walk 9)*.

Penallt Church (4)

Penallt Church (of unknown dedication) is about a mile north of the village centre, and there is only a handful of houses and farms nearby. It is set in a lovely position overlooking the Wye Valley. The church probably dates back to the 12th century (north wall of the nave), although the chancel is 14th century and the south aisle and tower are mid-16th century. The tower has a saddleback roof. Inside, the wagon roof has some interesting carved bosses, and the pulpit is dated 1634.

Naval Temple. (5)

The Naval Temple was built by gentlemen of Monmouth and dedicated to Her Grace the Duchess of Beaufort, daughter of Admiral Boscawen, in August 1800 in memory of admirals who had distinguished themselves in past wars: 1759–1801 (Admirals Boscawen, Bridport, Cornwallis, Duncan, Gell, Hawke, Hood, Howe, Keith, Mitchell, Nelson, Parker, Rodney, Thompson, Vincent, and Warren). A statue of Britannia surmounts the temple.

The Kymin (6)

The Kymin tower was built in 1794 as a banqueting house for members of the Kymin Club, who met on Tuesdays. It was visited by Nelson in 1802. It is now owned by the National Trust, and is open to visitors at certain times. The name is thought to be derived from the Welsh 'Cae Maen', meaning 'stoney field'. This is where the walk leaves the Offa's Dyke Path, which descends left towards Monmouth, but we join the Wysis Way for nearly 2 miles to Near Harkening Rock. This 55-mile long-distance footpath  links the Wye Valley Walk and Offa's Dyke Path by the Wye at Monmouth to the Thames Path near Kemble. The name comes from Wye and Isis (or Thames).

Monmouth Viewpoint (7)

Monmouth is an attractive market town, situated at the confluence of the Rivers Monnow and Wye. Much of its history has been connected with the Wye, so it is unfortunate that rebuilding of the A40 trunk road in the 1960s has virtually cut off the town from the river. The town was the birthplace of Henry V, whose statue appears on Shire Hall (1724) in Agincourt Square, close to a statue of Charles S. Rolls, founder of Rolls-Royce and pioneer airman, who lived nearby. Monmouth's greatest treasure is the 13th century fortified bridge over the River Monnow. The present Norman castle dates from the mid-12th century, but it was badly damaged during the Civil War, and only the ruined Great Tower and Hall survive. Great Castle House dates from 1673. The

View of Monmouth and the Welsh Mountains (Blorenge, Sugar Loaf, etc.) from The Kymin.

parish Church of St Mary has a 14th century tower, but was largely rebuilt in the 1880s. However, St Thomas Becket Church, near the Monnow Bridge, dates back to Norman times. There are many fine Tudor and Geogian buildings in the town. The Nelson Museum commemorates the Admiral's connections with Monmouth. The large building on the hill is part of the Haberdashers' School, founded in 1614. Of the two railway bridges crossing the Wye, that on the left was on the Chepstow line, and that on the right was on the line to Ross-on-Wye. Monmouth Troy Station was just beyond the junction of these two lines, but after closure the station building was moved to Winchcombe on the preserved Gloucestershire Warwickshire Railway near Cheltenham. Just beyond Monmouth is King's Wood, and in the distance can be seen some of the Welsh hills (The Blorenge, Brecon Beacons, Sugar Loaf, Skirrid, and Black Mountains, terminating in Hay Bluff).

Highmeadow Woods (8)

Highmeadow Woods are perhaps one of the most attractive areas of woodland in the country, particularly during the bluebell season and in the autumn. They are mostly ancient semi-natural woodland (oak, ash, beech, lime, etc.), but have been historically managed through coppicing and timber growing. Coppicing was once carried out on an industrial scale in many parts of the Forest to feed the iron works and lime kilns, but now continues only in wildlife reserves and some Forestry Commission woodlands. From the 1960s modern forestry was largely based on plantations of softwood species (larch, spruce, Douglas fir, etc.), which were eventually clear-felled and the ground replanted. Hence, much of the Forest is now a mosaic of mature deciduous trees and younger conifers, divided by forest roads and rides. However, the distinct contrast between traditional management and modern forestry is now being broken down, with considerable efforts being made to create management systems based on native tree species. Foresters in the Wye Valley and Forest of Dean have been at the forefront of these pioneering techniques, and are working towards a multi-purpose form of forestry.

Suck Stone (9)

Quartz Conglomerate, together with the overlying (i.e., younger) Tintern Sandstone Group, makes up the Upper Old Red Sandstone, of Devonian age, in this area. It forms a line of crags, 20 to 25 ft high beween little Doward and Staunton. The rock layers dip to the ENE, i.e., into the hillside, as can be seen in the overhanging crags above. A number of large blocks have fallen down the hillside, of which the largest is the Suck Stone. Although reported to weigh well over 10 000 tons, we estimate that it is actually no more than a quarter of this. A close look at the conglomerate ('puddingstone', also known locally as 'jackstone') shows that it contains conspicuous pebbles of quartz in a sandy matrix. You might also be able to see cross-bedding, where small-scale sandy layers are truncated by others which dip at a different angle. These features were produced as the sand was deposited under water with varying current directions, probably in a river bed during floods in the generally arid landscape. The overlying sandstones were also probably deposited in ancient river systems. Similar, but much larger-scale, features were formed in desert sand dunes, where the sand was wind-blown (as shown by the well-rounded shapes of the grains).

Near Harkening Rocks (10)

The Quartz Conglomerate rocks at the top of the hill are more resistant than both the over- and underlying sandstones, and hence form an obvious escarpment. The rocks beneath the conglomerate — sandstones (termed Brownstones) of the Lower Old Red Sandstone — have been eroded away to allow blocks of the former to tumble downhill. They are separated from the Quartz Conglomerate by an unconformity, which means that there was a long period of erosion before the conglomerate was deposited. In other words, there is a time gap in the rock sequence here. The name Near Harkening Rocks is said to be due to the fact that the gamekeepers and bailiffs could sit below the crags and listen out for poachers of deer or fish. Far Harkening Rocks are about ½ mile to the north, just above the Wye. The view from here takes in the Welsh hills, including the Blorenge, Skirrid, Sugar Loaf, Black Mountains, and even, on a particularly clear day, the Brecon Beacons. The Kymin hill can be seen to the left, and Hayes Coppice, just beyond the A40, to the right.

The Suck Stone

Cross-bedding in Quartz Conglomerate.

View from Near Harkening Rocks on a misty autumn day.

Reddings Lodge (11)

After excessive timber felling by Sir John Wynter in the mid-17th century, the Dean Forest (Reafforestation) Act of 1668 allowed the enclosure of 11 000 acres, divided into six Walks, each with a lodge, which housed a keeper *(see Walk 5)*. However, further problems, including neglect, theft of timber, and illegal grazing of animals, continued throughout the 18th century. Admiral Nelson visited the Forest in 1802 and his report of 1803 led to a new Enclosure Act in 1808. This allowed construction of 24 new lodges, and several more were built later in the 19th century. Reddings Lodge probably dates from around 1820 and seems to have been little altered since then. Also passed on this walk are Buckstone Lodge (built in 1897, possibly to replace Knockalls Lodge) and the early 19th century Knockalls Lodge. Other Forest lodges are seen on *Walks 5 and 7*.

Staunton (12)

Staunton, "the place of the stones", was the ancient name given by the Anglo-Saxons. There are several ancient stones in the area, including the Longstone, by the A4136 about ½ mile southeast of the village, a standing stone which probably dates back to the Bronze Age. All Saints Church is one of the oldest bordering the Forest of Dean, dating in part from the 12th century, although much of the building is 13th to 15th century. Inside the church is a corkscrew staircase leading to an unusual c.1500 stone pulpit, as well as a font which is believed to be a hollowed-out Roman altar. Some medieval glass survives in a tiny upper window in the chancel east wall. In the churchyard is the grave of David Mushet (1772–1847), metallurgist of Coleford, whose experiments revolutionised the steel industry *(see Walk 7)*. By the churchyard is an almshouse given to the village by Benedict Hall in the 17th century. Nearby is a 14th century stone cross, Church Farmhouse (late 16th –17th century), with its adjoining 17th and 18th century barns, and a stone-walled animal pound. The original White Horse Inn of 1813 was rebuilt later in the 19th century to accommodate the turnpike road. It advertises itself as "the last in England".

Buck Stone (13)

Yet more outcrops of Quartz Conglomerate are seen here. The Buck Stone once bucked or rocked, but it was rolled down the hill by vandals (clearly not just a modern phenomenon) in 1885. It was repositioned, but is now fixed in place. More evidence for the use of conglomerate to make millstones can be found in the woods near here. The view includes the Black Mountains (Waun Fach, Hay Bluff), Graig Syfyrddin, Garway Hill, Orcop Hill, and Aconbury Hill (near Hereford). Just beyond Monmouth is Buckholt Wood.

Coleford Railway (14)

The 10-mile Coleford Railway was opened on 1 September 1883, replacing an earlier tramroad *(see 3)*. It was worked by the Great Western Railway from the start, and was amalgamated with that company on 1 July 1884. The line climbed some 500 ft between Monmouth and Coleford and had some sharp curves, so it was a difficult one to work. Stations were provided at Newland and Coleford. Traffic was never very plentiful, and the line closed as from 1 January 1917 *(see Walk 9 for more details)*.

The Elms (15)

This is a large house with a walled garden, dating back to at least the early 19th century. There are good views of the railway embankment, bridge, and tunnel entrance behind.

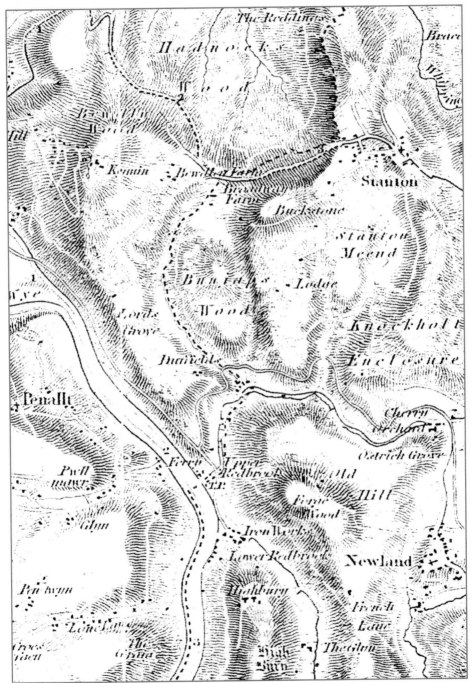

Enlarged extract from Ordnance Survey First Edition 1 inch to 1 mile map (Old Series) c. 1820

Views of both the Wye and Severn, Hewelsfield Church, Tintern Abbey view, and Offa's Dyke. A hilly walk along a variety of field and woodland paths, tracks, and lanes; 10 stiles.

Tidenham Chase car park (signposted for Offa's Dyke) on B4228 Chepstow to Coleford road, about 3 miles north of Tutshill: GR ST 558992. **Refreshments**: none on walk route, but pub and café (in village shop) in Brockweir.

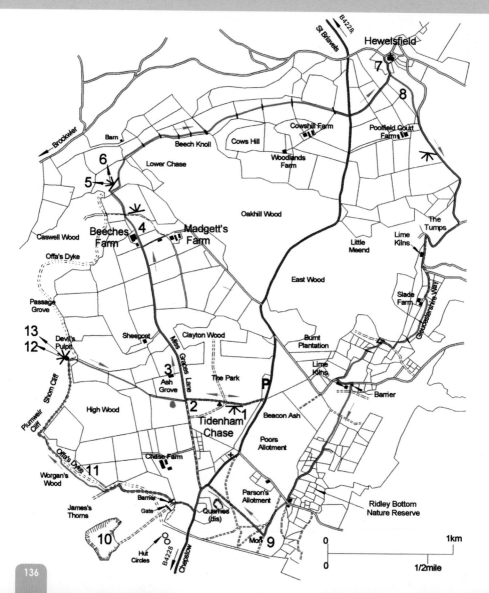

START BY WALKING AWAY from the main road, past a barrier and along a gravel track. There are good views to the left across the heathland of Tidenham Chase *(1)* to the Severn and beyond. After about 300 yards, at a junction, take the track immediately to the right of a survey pillar (712 ft) and go through a kissing gate. Continue past numerous boulders of Drybrook Sandstone through another kissing gate onto a concrete lane. In a dip to the left, immediately before the lane, is a manhole cover – the entrance to an extensive cave system *(2)*. Turn right along the lane (Miss Graces Lane, named after sisters of W.G. Grace, the famous cricketer, who lived in Chase House in the early 20th century). Note the old limekilns *(3)* in the woods on the left, some 250 yds along the lane. Where the concrete lane turns left, keep ahead on a dirt track, eventually passing to the right of Beeches Farm. In the caravan site to your right are some undulations, which are all that remain of a former settlement near the present Madgetts Farm *(4)*.

Bear left at the end of the farm buildings and go right of a waymarked post. Continue across a field, bearing slightly left as you start to descend to reach a stile in the bottom left-hand corner. Cross the right-hand stile and follow the left-hand edge of the next field to cross another stile. Turn right onto the Offa's Dyke Path *(see 11)*. Go left after 100 yds at a marker post and descend diagonally across a field (which can be very slippery in wet conditions) to the bottom right-hand corner. There are good views from here of the River Wye and Brockweir *(5)* to the left, and St Briavels and Hewelsfield Commons *(6)* in front. Cross a stile and bear right to follow the upper edge of the next field, just below woodland, leaving the Offa's Dyke Path here. Continue below the woods through four separate gates and then an adjacent pair, before continuing uphill to yet another gate at the end of the woodland ahead. Cross the middle of the next field to a gate in the far hedge and then maintain the same direction to another gate a little above the far left-hand field corner. Keep right of some large trees in the next field to a gate in the field corner, which leads to an enclosed track. This comes out onto a main road. Cross this with care and take 'Church Lane' ahead. Just before a house on the right is a stile and a public footpath sign where the route continues. However, it is worth going a further 100 yds along the lane first to see Hewelsfield Church *(7)*.

Return to the stile, and follow the path across the field between a large tree and a tree-lined depression (a sinkhole, *8*). Bear slightly right beyond the latter to a stile in the far right-hand corner of the field. Turn right on the tarmac lane, from which there are good views of Alvington, Woolaston, the River Severn, Oldbury Power Station *(see Walk 4)*, the Severn Bridges *(Walk 2)*, and the Cotswold Hills. Follow the lane until it descends to a sharp left-hand bend, where you turn right onto a stony track (part of the Gloucestershire Way (GW), a 100-mile long-distance footpath from Chepstow to Tewkesbury). The track bends right and reaches a junction, where you turn sharp left and descend past old lime kilns (the Lower Dolomite crops out here) to a tarmac lane. After 30 yds, fork right onto another stony track (signed GW and Slade Farm). Pass through a metal kissing gate on the left just before the farm, and continue along the field below the farm buildings, through a metal gate, and then bearing right in the valley bottom to go through another gate. Continue to a gateway in the fence ahead, but do not go through. Instead, follow the hedge uphill to the left to a kissing gate. Turn right on the dirt track for 120 yds, then turn left through a waymarked metal gate (the left one of three), following a path through trees to a stile. Follow the right-hand field edge beyond, then, where this bends right, continue in the same direction to the right-hand of two gateways. Now keep a fence on your left, coming to a kissing gate on the edge of woodland. A narrow waymarked path through the trees leads to a kissing gate and then a tarmac lane.

Turn left for 200 yds, then sharp right at a GW sign, to go past a wooden barrier and onto another woodland path. There are more ruined lime kilns on the right, nearby quarries having worked the Drybrook Limestone. Cross over a track (going through barriers on each side) and continue out of the woods to another dirt track. Turn left and almost immediately right through a metal gate and follow the left-hand edge of a field onto a footpath through the trees ahead. The path soon emerges onto a tarmac lane, which is followed ahead, ignoring side tracks, past Ridley Bottom Nature Reserve, to a T-junction. Continue ahead through a kissing gate onto a footpath. Bear slightly left at a junction onto a wider track, then left at a fork, which leads to Queen Victoria's Jubilee Monument *(9)*. Turn right in front of the monument, leaving the Gloucestershire Way here, and follow the generally muddy track straight out onto a main road. Turn left, passing Miss Graces Lane on the right. *For a shortcut, follow this lane to just beyond point 2 and turn right back to the car park.* Turn right after about 250 yds onto a tarmac lane just beyond a house.

Follow the lane to a gate, just before which you bear right past a barrier onto a gravel track, another section of the Offa's Dyke Path. (The gated road leads to the disused Tintern Quarry *(10)*, but this is presently closed to the public so please do not enter.) The track passes outcrops of limestone on a right-hand bend, then bends left before reaching a waymarked footpath where you turn right. The path climbs steeply at first, curves left, and then doglegs up onto Offa's Dyke *(11)* itself. It follows the Dyke for about ¾ mile, initially with glimpses of the Bristol Channel back to the left. The path bends sharply right above Plumweir Cliff and continues to the Devil's Pulpit, a rock pillar, where you are rewarded by a superb view of the Wye Valley, with Tintern Abbey *(12)* and the Wireworks Bridge *(13)* prominent. Continue along the path, which bends right here, and after about 100 yds go through a kissing gate on the right. Follow the left-hand field edge to a stile, bear half right across the next field to a stile, and then maintain the same direction to a stile by a gate. Bear left to follow the field edge to another stile and onto a concrete lane. Turn left for 10 yds and then right to reverse your outward path past the survey pillar back to the car park.

Exmoor ponies on Tidenham Chase.

Tidenham Chase (1)

Its name suggests that Tidenham Chase was once a hunting preserve, but for centuries the tenants of Tidenham Manor had rights of common there (and elsewhere) and were allowed to gather firewood and take timber for repairing their houses. However, enclosure proceeded steadily in the south of the parish during the 17th and 18th centuries, and by 1810 Tidenham Chase was virtually confined to the high northern plateau and covered about 1000 acres. Enclosure was finally completed in 1815, not without opposition. An area of 107 acres (Poor's Allotment, across the main road from the car park) was awarded in trust for the poor of the parishes of Lancaut and Tidenham. Most of this was to be used as animal pasture, but 30 acres were for a potato garden for those occupying property with a rateable value of £10 or less. At the time of the enclosure this category included 26 parishioners, each of whom was allowed to put a horse, a cow, and six sheep on the pasture. Most of this area has remained as rough grazing land, covered with bracken and gorse and a reminder of the former appearance of much of Tidenham Chase. Other allotments went to the various tithe owners, by far the largest being 104 acres (Parson's Allotment) awarded to the vicar.

Large sections of the Chase, including Parson's Allotment, are now forestry plantations, both conifers and broad-leaved trees. Most of the remainder is farmland (predominantly pasture). Tidenham Chase is underlain by rocks of the Carboniferous Limestone Series, mostly the Lower Drybrook Sandstone and Drybrook Limestone. Areas of the former include The Park (where you are now) and most of Poor's Allotment (now a Site of Special Scientific Interest, SSSI), which support important acid grassland and lowland heath habitats. Together they are the largest heathland site in Gloucestershire. Notable bird species include the nightjar, stonechat, hobby, woodcock, yellowhammer, linnet, snipe, and reed bunting. Characteristic plant species here include common bent, sheep's fescue, creeping fescue, western gorse, ling, bell heather, cross-leaved heath, bilberry, sheep's sorrel, and heath bed-straw. Vegetation associated with calcareous soils over Drybrook Limestone is dominated by fescue species with a wide range of herbs including rock rose, thyme, stemless thistle, salad burnet, and bird's-foot trefoil. Associated semi-natural woodland habitat in the eastern part of the site is unusual in having dominant oak and holly, together with yew, field maple, and whitebeam. Attempts are being made to restore these habitats, with control of bracken being an ongoing task. They are managed by spring and summer grazing by rare breeds, such as Hebridean sheep and Gloucester and White Park cattle, and Exmoor ponies have recently been introduced.

Miss Graces Lane Cave (2)

Appearances can be deceptive, because this unimpressive manhole leads to an extensive cave system. The Royal Forest of Dean Caving Club began digging a shaft in the depression in 1994, but it was not until December 1997 that the shaft, which was being lined with concrete, broke through into Autumn Frenzy Chamber at a depth of about 93 ft. After nearly two more years of digging from here, a rift nearly 100 ft below the entrance chamber was reached. A complex series of passages and rifts (called Winter Storm) on four different levels was eventually reached after still more digging. Since then further digging has allowed access into many more passages and chambers (Spring Fever and Canyon Series), and the total known horizontal cave length is now 2.5 miles, second in the Forest only to Slaughter Stream Cave, near Symonds Yat (*see Walk 1*). Not so long ago the Forest was thought to be devoid of major cave systems, but the efforts of cavers have shown this to be wrong. Cavers have recently begun to excavate another sink hole near the B4228 road south of Hewelsfield. Probably the most exciting underground discovery in the area was that of Otter Hole, below Chepstow Racecourse, in the mid-1970s. This contains some of the country's finest cave formations, but exploration is not for the faint hearted! The cave entrance is in the bank of the Wye and only accessible near low tide, when the entrance series is not flooded. Moreover, the caver has to negotiate some particularly sticky mud and a couple of boulder chokes before the formations begin. For these reasons, entry is restricted to experienced cavers belonging to bona fide caving clubs.

Limekilns (3)

There are several old quarries on this part of Tidenham Chase, although most of them are in the Lower Drybrook Sandstone. The presence of limekilns here suggests that the underlying Whitehead Limestone was also being worked, as it is only just below the sandstone at this location *(see also Walk 9)*. Two other sets of lime kilns can be seen on this walk.

Madgett (4)

A cluster of small rectangular enclosures is visible as very slight earthworks. Not much seems to have be published on the site, but it thought to have been the location of a medieval settlement known as Madgett or Modiete. Its proximity to Offa's Dyke may be significant. Miss Graces Lane (originally Madgett Road) is thought to be part of a prehistoric track which linked the Severn near Stroat with the Wye at Brockweir. There is also an ancient hollow way near the site of the ferry from Tintern which leads up the hillside towards Offa's Dyke and Madgett. The monks of Tintern Abbey established a grange, which included a chapel, at Modesgate in the 12th century. A little way down the hill near the bottom of the field you cross a more substantial earthwork, which extends westwards to the Dyke, which is only about 200 yds away in the woods on your left.

The trow *Goodhope* at Brockweir in 1904.
Brockweir Local History Group/Hallam Collection.

Brockweir (5)

Tradition has it that in 584 King Meuric of Gwent defeated the Saxons under Caewlin at the Battle of Tintern Ford near Brockweir. He was joined by his father, Tewdrig (Theoderic), who left his monk's cell to aid his son and was killed in the battle. The River Wye has been used for transport for millennia, and although it was once a grange of Tintern Abbey, Brockweir developed largely to serve this traffic. It became an important boat-building centre and port for sailing vessels, which worked to the Bristol Channel ports and elsewhere. Being near the tidal limit of the River Wye, it was also a place where goods were transferred between sea-going and smaller up-river craft. The famous trow (rhymes with 'crow') was a flat-bottomed sailing barge used on both the Severn and the Wye. There were various types, but the shallow draft was essential for craft working upriver as far as Hereford or even, when the river was high enough, to places like Hay and up the River Lugg to Leominster. The craft were man-hauled over the various rapids and weirs, although horses had been introduced by the early 19th century. The weirs had been constructed in medieval times to catch salmon, but hindered free passage up and down the river. It was not until 1662 that the Wye Navigation Act attempted to resolve these problems, and develop the river's potential. Cargoes included coal, iron, timber, and stone; Herefordshire cider and other articles were exported. Bark for tanning, which was mainly taken down river to Chepstow, was a major industry. Vast quantities of timber were used to make ships, barrels and other articles, and charcoal. For example, construction of a 150 ton ship required 3000 wagonloads of timber. The woodlands were carefully managed to produce mature trees for keels and masts, and by coppicing and harvesting wood for charcoal on an 8–12 year cycle. The village had a thriving ship building, fitting-out, and repair industry. 13 ships were launched at Brockweir in 1824, and the barque *Constantine* (509 tons and 121 feet long) was the last large boat built, in 1847. However, once the Wye Valley Railway was opened in 1876 *(see Walk 13)*, the up-river trade went into a terminal decline. Another distinctive river

Brockweir wharf and bridge today.

craft was the Wye coracle, or truckle, used extensively for salmon netting and angling until the 1900s. Made of interwoven willow twigs covered in horse-hide, or, later, pitched canvas, these one-man vessels were similar to those used by the Celts in pre-Roman times.

In the early 19th century Brockweir was said to be one of the most lawless places in the country, with about 16 public houses to cater for the stevedores who loaded and unloaded vessels at the quayside. At that time there was no church and "The Lord's Day was kept as a day of unhallowed revelling and desecrated by cock-fighting, gambling and quarrelling". In 1831 a Tintern doctor, worried about the spiritual state of the villagers as well as their physical health, wrote about the situation to the Moravian Minister in Bristol. The result was that the Moravian Church was built, reportedly on the site of the cock-pit, in 1833. It continues in use to this day. Brockweir village is situated on the English side of the Wye, whereas the Monmouth–Chepstow toll road (opened in 1828, now the A466) and Wye Valley Railway (opened in 1876, closed in 1964) were on the opposite bank and accessible only by ferry. Hence, in 1893 a petition ('memorial'), signed by 236 local villagers seeking permission and finance for a bridge, was presented to the Gloucestershire and Monmouthshire County Councils. However, there were many financial and legal problems, including claims for compensation from the ferryman (Edwin Dibden) and the Great Western Railway, and disputes with property owners in Brockweir (which accounts for the odd alignment of the bridge at the village end) to be overcome before work began in August 1905. The bridge was constructed in Chepstow by Edward Finch & Co. and the spans were floated up the river on barges. It has three lattice-girder spans supported by two pairs of cylindrical iron columns and masonry abutments. By July 1906 locals were using the bridge, although it was not yet complete! During World War 2, the bridge had a narrow escape when a Wellington bomber, returning from a mission over France, crashed just upstream after its crew had safely baled out. Today Brockweir is an attractive riverside village, with just one pub (the Brockweir Country Inn, probably 16th century) and a new eco-friendly shop (½ mile up the road towards Hewelsfield). Other interesting buildings include the 16th century Manor House (which stands facing the bridge), the 16th/17th century Glen-Wye (formerly an inn, part of which had to be demolished when the bridge was built), the 15th/16th century Malt House (although parts may date to the 1300s), Phoenix House (also possibly 14th century in part), and Spring Cottage (1700 or earlier). The Malt House is thought to have been part of the Tintern Abbey grange, and was only used as a malt house from about 1750 until 1876. The stone quay is still visible, and in front of Quay House is the screw from *La Belle Marie*, Brockweir's best-known trading vessel, which carried goods to and from Bristol. Flora Klickman (1867–1958), authoress and editor of *The Girls Own Paper*, wrote many stories about her cottage (Sylvan View) in Brockweir. Her most famous, *The Flower Patch among the Hills*, was published in 1916 and her last, *Weeding the Flower Patch*, in 1948. She is buried in the Moravian Churchyard.

St Briavels and Hewelsfield Commons (6)

These were originally part of the woodland of the Hudnalls, which belonged to the Royal Manor of St Briavels, and hence was extraparochial, until 1842, when most was incorporated into St Briavels Parish, the rest going to Hewelsfield *(see Walk 6)*. In medieval times, most of the flatter land of the present Commons (which is now a misnomer, since they are no longer used as such) seems to have been relatively open woodland, with grassy clearings used as pasture. Much of this was settled and enclosed by squatters between about 1750 and 1810, leaving only the steeper slopes above the Wye as woodland. If the squatter was able to keep the chimney of his new cottage smoking from sunset to sunrise, his claim was thought to become legitimate. Land clearance would have been hard work in view of the many large boulders lying around, and the result was a landscape of small fields, isolated cottages, and small patches of woodland, separated by narrow winding lanes and footpaths, with numerous hedgerows and thick stone walls, incorporating many older trees. Indeed the Common must have one of the densest networks of drystone walls, which served both as boundaries and 'stone dumps', in the country. In the mid-19th century about half the Common was under crops and half grassland (pasture), although the proportion under crops has gradually declined. In more recent times many wealthier people have moved in, enlarging houses and building new ones. The area now consists mainly of pastures, horse paddocks, and the remaining small-holdings. In 2001 local residents set up the Parish Grassland Project to raise interest in the landscape and help restore their fields as flower-rich grassland. The area already supports a wide variety of grasses, herbs, rushes, flowers, and fungi (some of them rare). There are also many species of mammals (including deer, lesser horseshoe bats, and badgers), birds (including buzzards, kestrels, sparrowhawks, and goshawks), snakes, frogs, toads, newts, and invertebrates (butterflies, moths, etc.). There is a good view of this unusual landscape from here, with St Briavels Common opposite and Hewelsfield Common on the hillside further to the right. The highest point is at Hart Hill, 817 ft above sea level. In contrast to the Carboniferous Limestone of Tidenham Chase, the Commons are underlain by Old Red Sandstone rocks, which has led to more intensive cultivation over the centuries. However, much of the area was originally covered by abundant blocks of sandstone and, in particular, quartz conglomerate, so that clearing fields would have been an onerous task.

Hewelsfield Church (7)

Hewelsfield comprises a small group of dwellings around the imposing Church of St Mary Magdalene. This is situated within a circular churchyard (with a yew tree said to be 1300 years old). The long tiled roof extends from the ridge of the Norman (12th century) nave, over the north aisle and the southern porch and vestry to within a few feet of the ground. The squat tower, with pyramid roof and 6 bells, chancel, porch, and north transept date from the 13th century, and the north vestry was added in the 16th. There is a hermit's room, priest's door, and primitive sundial. The 13th century font has an octagonal scalloped bowl on a round pedestal. The house on the opposite side of the churchyard from the lych gate has a date stone of 1706. Throughout the

19th century it was the Parrot Inn. Hewelsfield Court was owned by the Gough family until it was rebuilt in the late 18th or early 19th century; two nearby stone barns date from the 17th and 18th centuries.

Sinkhole (8)

A sinkhole is a generally more-or-less circular, funnel-shaped depression in limestone areas, which is formed either by solution of the limestone at the surface, or by the collapse of underlying caves. Most are dry, but some have a stream disappearing underground, when they are called swallow holes. This sinkhole is in Lower Limestone Shale, the lowest part of the Carboniferous Limestone Series, and has unfortunately been used as a rubbish dump. Sinkholes do not appear to be particularly common in the limestone around here, although there are a couple of small ones in Hewelsfield churchyard! Some limestone plateaux, like Mynydd Llangattock near Crickhowell in South Wales, are a mass of sinkholes. Such features, together with caves and underground drainage, are characteristic of the topography developed on limestone (termed 'karst'), which is due to the relatively high solubility of limestone in water (particularly if it is slightly acidic).

Queen Victoria's Jubilee Stone (9)

We are back on Tidenham Chase here, in the area known as Parson's Allotment, as it was awarded to the vicar when the Chase was enclosed in 1815 *(see 1 above)*. It is now a mixed plantation managed by the Forestry Commission. The tall and narrow stone (inscribed VR 1837–97) was hauled up from the bank of the Severn and erected to commemorate Queen Victoria's Jubilee of 1897. At one time there was a row of much older stones, which extended from Stroat to Madgetts, possibly defining an ancient boundary. Only a few remain and their age is unknown, although they may have marked an ancient route from the Severn to the Wye at Brockweir. The Broadstone is a large standing stone near the Severn, about 2 miles southeast of here, which probably dates from the Neolithic (Late Stone Age) or Bronze Age. There are other standings stones at Staunton (the Longstone) and below Huntsham Hill, near Symonds Yat (the Queen Stone), and there used to be another Longstone near St Briavels. Excavation of a Bronze Age round barrow on Tidenham Chase has yielded a copper knife or dagger and a bronze awl. Together with other sites nearby, marked as "Hut Circles" on OS maps, they indicate that the area was being settled at this time.

Tintern Quarry (10)

Tintern Quarry worked the massive Drybrook Limestone and the overlying Crease and Whitehead Limestones, part of the Carboniferous Limestone Series. Quarrying appears to have begun here around 1930, mainly for road metal or aggregate. A siding connection with the Great Western Railway's Wye Valley line was brought into use in 1931, but after the line closed in 1964, the section from Wye Valley Junction, near Chepstow, was operated as a private siding. The quarry was owned by W.G. Turrif Ltd, and the last train ran in December 1981.

Offa's Dyke (11)

Offa's Dyke is thought to have been built by Offa, the Saxon King of Mercia from 757–96. His kingdom covered the area between the Trent and Mersey rivers in the north and the Thames Valley in the south, and from the Welsh border in the west to the Fens in the east. At the height of his power, he also controlled Kent, East Anglia, and Lindsey (Lincoln), and had alliances with Northumbria and Wessex, sealed by the marriage of two of his daughters to their Kings, Ethelred and Beorhtric, respectively. Hence, Offa was the first man to call himself "King of the English" and to mint national coins: silver pennies and gold dinars. Although he had some success in fighting the Welsh, Offa was unable to conquer them, and it was probably in the 780s that he negotiated a border between the Welsh and the English and began construction of the Dyke. This was therefore most likely to have been designed as a boundary marker, rather than a defensive structure. It may also have been designed to impress potential enemies with Offa's power: the amount of labour needed to build it is proof that Mercia possessed a high degree of cohesion. Offa's Dyke is a linear earthwork which roughly follows the Welsh–English border, from Sedbury Cliffs, on the Severn Estuary, to Treuddyn, near Mold in North Wales. However, there are large gaps, particularly between Monmouth and Kington, and, of the total distance of about 140 miles, only about 80 miles are actual earthwork. This consists of a ditch and rampart, mostly constructed with the ditch on the Welsh-facing side, and appears to have been carefully aligned to present an open view into Wales. As originally constructed, it must have been about 70–80 ft wide and as much as 25 ft from the ditch bottom to the bank top. It has been suggested that this southern section above the Lower Wye Valley is not part of Offa's Dyke at all, but the evidence is far from compelling and there is little doubt that it is more-or-less contemporary with the main (64 mile long) section further north. Wat's Dyke, which lies just east of Offa's and extends from near Oswestry almost to the North Wales coast, is probably only a little younger, probably dating from the 820s during the reigns of Coenwulf and Ceolwulf. The section of Offa's Dyke between here and the Devil's Pulpit is particularly impressive, with its commanding position overlooking the Wye. The Offa's Dyke Path (of which this is a part) was opened in the summer of 1971 and links Sedbury, on the Severn Estuary, with Prestatyn, on the coast of North Wales. In its 177-mile length, the path passes through eight different counties and crosses the border between England and Wales over 20 times. It includes parts of the Brecon Beacons National Park and three Areas of Outstanding Natural Beauty — the Wye Valley, the Shropshire Hills, and the Clwydian Hills.

Tintern Abbey (12)

The Cistercian Abbey of Tintern is one of the greatest monastic ruins in Wales. It was only the second Cistercian foundation in Britain and the first in Wales, and was founded on 9 May 1131 by Walter de Clare, Lord of Chepstow. It soon prospered, thanks to endowments of land in Gwent and Gloucestershire, and by 1139 had sufficient numbers to set up a colony in Kingswood, Glos. In 1189 William Marshal became Lord of Chepstow and patron of Tintern, and in 1201–3 the Abbey of Tintern Parva (Little Tintern) was established on his lands in Ireland. During the 13th century the abbey was more or less completely rebuilt, starting in about 1220 with the cloisters and the domestic ranges around them. Roger Bigod III, Lord of Chepstow from1270–1306, took a keen interest in the abbey, and is remembered as the builder of the abbey church, completed in about 1301. This is still Tintern's crowning glory, albeit roofless and without window glass or internal divisions. By the late 13th century the monks at Tintern were farming well over 3000 acres of arable land on the Welsh side

of the Wye and kept some 3264 sheep on their pasture lands. The lands of the Abbey were divided into agricultural units or granges. In 1326 King Edward II visited Tintern and spent two nights there. After the Black Death swept the country in 1348–9 it became impossible to attract new recruits for the lay brotherhood. Changes to the way the granges were tenanted out, rather than worked by lay brothers, show the difficulties Tintern was experiencing. The Dissolution of the Monasteries under Henry VIII in 1536–40 brought monastic life in England and Wales to an abrupt end. Tintern Abbey was surrendered to the Earl of Worcester in 1536, the roofs were stripped of lead, and the abbey fell into decay. The ruins became one of the highlights of the Wye Tour in the late 18th and 19th centuries *(see Walk 1)*. Tintern remains popular with tourists, and the ruins, now under the protection of CADW, are open to the public. Did a piece of lead sheet found near the Devil's Pulpit by one of the authors come from Tintern Abbey?

With its monastic history at an end, Tintern soon became an industrial centre, hard as this may be to envisage today. The river provided transport for the raw materials and finished

Tintern Abbey from the Devil's Pulpit.

Forge at Tintern.

products of iron production, and its tributaries provided water power for mills and furnaces. The first brass made in Britain was founded at Tintern in 1566. Wire-making quickly followed, and employed some 100 men in Tintern alone. More than 5000 people throughout the county were making goods from the wire: hooks, eyes, needles, wire combs, farthingales (frameworks to support ladies' skirts), bird cages, etc. For the next 300 years the wire works and forges along the Angiddy valley dominated the village and surrounding communities, and the managers even paid for preachers and schoolmasters. Angiddy Ironworks, the ruins of which can still be seen today, operated from the early 17th to the early 19th century. There was another at Coed Ithel, near the banks of the Wye towards Llandogo, and Whitebrook, two miles north of Llandogo, was famous for paper milling, as well as wire making. Most of the industries had closed by the end of the 19th century *(see 13)*, and the Wye Valley Railway came and went in less than a century *(see Walk 13)*. Today, Tintern has a number of hotels, guest houses, pubs, cafes, and shops. Abbey Mill was originally a corn mill, then a woollen mill, and now houses craft shops and a restaurant. The Anchor Hotel was originally the abbey cider mill, and a ferry once operated from there. Other pubs are the Cherry Tree, Moon and Sixpence, Rose and Crown, and Royal George.

Wireworks Bridge (13)

The proposed route of the Wye Valley Railway from Chepstow to Monmouth *(see Walk 13)* by-passed the village of Tintern, which is on the opposite (western) bank of the River Wye. Hence, an agreement was signed on 22 November 1872 between the Wye Valley Railway Co. and the Duke of Beaufort (the landowner) that the former would construct a branch (the Wireworks Branch or Tintern Railway) across the river to serve the Abbey Wireworks. Work commenced on 5 June 1874, the contractors being Messrs Reed Bros. & Co. of London, and the branch was completed by August 1875, 14 months before the main WVR line. It was just over half a mile long and included the Wireworks Bridge over the Wye. This has three truss-girder spans of 66 ft, with masonry piers and abutments, the latter pierced by flood arches. The length between abutments is about 213 ft. The bridge was designed by S.H. Yockney of Westminster and constructed by the Isca Foundry Co. of Newport. Unfortunately, the Abbey Wireworks closed in August 1875, and the branch was dormant until the Abbey Wire and Tinplate Co. re-opened in the early 1880s, only to close for good by 1901. The branch was then used by Messrs J. Jones & Son, who owned a sawmill and turnery at Tintern, to carry goods in horse-drawn wagons. The line never made money for the WVR, which was not even allowed to charge tolls for its use. By 1935, the track had become unusable, and it was lifted in 1941. Ownership eventually passed to the Gwent and Gloucestershire County Councils, and the bridge and trackbed now provides public access from Tintern to the woods on the Gloucestershire side.

Further Reading

It is impossible to give all the sources, both printed and on-line, that were used when writing this book, so only some of the most important will be listed here. The volumes on the Severn and Wye Railway and Forest of Dean Branch by Ian Pope and others are veritable mines (pun intended) of information, not only on the railways, but also on the industries they served.

- Currie, C.R.J., Herbert, N.M. (editors), Baggs, A.P. and Jurica, A.R.J.,1996. A History of the County of Gloucester, volume 5: Bledisloe Hundred, St.Briavels Hundred, the Forest of Dean. Victoria County History.

- Elrington, C.R., Herbert, N.M., Pugh, R.B. (editors), Morgan, K. and Smith, B.S., 1972. A History of the County of Gloucester, volume 10: Westbury and Whitstone Hundreds. Victoria County History.

- Hart, C., 1971. The Industrial History of Dean. David & Charles, Newton Abbot.

- Oldham, T., n.d. The Mines of the Forest of Dean and Surrounding Areas. Privately published.

- Paar, H.W., 1971. The Great Western Railway in Dean. David & Charles, Newton Abbot.

- Paar, H.W., 1973. The Severn & Wye Railway. David & Charles, Newton Abbot.

- Pope, I., How, B. and Karau, P., 1983. The Severn & Wye Railway, volume 1. Wild Swan Publications, Didcot, Oxon. Also volumes 2 (1985) and 3 (1988).

- Pope, I. and Karau, P., 1992. The Forest of Dean Branch, volume 1. Wild Swan Publications, Didcot, Oxon. Also volume 2 (1997).

- Walters, B., 1992. The Archaeology and History of Ancient Dean and the Wye Valley. Thornhill Press, Cheltenham.

In addition, various issue of *The New Regard*, the journal of the Forest of Dean Local History Society, were consulted. Details of this high-quality publication may be found on their website: www.forestofdeanhistory.org.uk. A set of three 'Mines Trails' walk leaflets, which give details of some of the collieries in the Forest and are in a similar style to this book, may be downloaded free-of-charge from this website. An additional leaflet, the 'Bicslade Tramroad Trail', has just been published. A 'Roll of Honour' CD, which gives details of known mining and quarrying fatalities in the Forest of Dean, as well as an index of Freeminers, can be ordered from the same source. The 'Images of England' website (www.imagesofengland.org.uk) contains details of all listed buildings in the area, and, indeed, the whole country.

Historic Attractions open to the Public

The opening times given are only intended as a guide. Please check before travelling.

- **Abbey Mill, Tintern** - Daily - 01291 689228 - www.abbeymill.com

- **Chepstow Castle** - Daily - 01291 624065 - www.cadw.wales.gov.uk

- **Chepstow Museum** - Daily - 01291 625981- www.visitwyevalley.com

- **Clearwell Caves** - Daily, Mid-February to end-October, and December - 01594 832535 - www.clearwellcaves.com

- **Dean Forest Railway** - Norchard shop and museum, daily; operating days between March and October, plus December (check for details) - 01594 843423/845840 - www.deanforestrailway.co.uk

- **Dean Heritage Centre, Soudley** - Daily - 01594 822170 - www. deanheritagemuseum.com

- **Great Western Railway Museum, Coleford** - Saturday afternoons - 01594 833569 - www.colefordgwr.150m.com

- **Hopewell Colliery, on B4226 Coleford–Speech House Road** - Daily, Easter to October - 01594 810706

- **The Kymin Round House** - Saturday–Monday, end-March to end-October; grounds, all year - 01600 719241 - www.nationaltrust.org.uk

- **Littledean Jail** - Thursday–Sunday, plus Bank Holidays, April to end-October - 01594 826659 - www.littledeanjail.com

- **Lydney Park Spring Gardens (including Roman temple)** - Restricted opening, April to June - 01594 842844

- **Nelson Museum, Monmouth** - Daily - 01600 710630 - www.visitwyevalley.com

- **The Old Station, Tintern** - Daily, Easter to end-October - 01291 689566 - www. visitwyevalley.com

- **Puzzle Wood (ancient iron mines), near Coleford** - Daily, Easter to end-September - 01594 833187 - www.puzzlewood.net

- **Tintern Abbey** - Daily - 01291 689251 - www.cadw.wales.gov.uk

- **Westbury Court Garden** - Wednesday–Sunday, March to end-October; daily, July and August - 01452 760461 - www.nationaltrust.org.uk

Useful Contacts

- **James Bevan Coaches** (routes 717 & 727) - 01594 842859 - www.jamesbevancoaches.com

- **Stagecoach** (other routes) - Traveline 0871 2002233 - www.stagecoachbus.com

- **Glocestershire County Council Bus Service Information** - 01452 425543 - www.gloucestershire.gov.uk/buses

- **National Rail Enquiries** - 0845 7484950 - www.nationalrail.co.uk

- To report a problem with a public right of way, please contact:
  Public Rights of Way Team
  Environment Directorate, Gloucestershire County Council,
  Shire Hall, Gloucester, Glos. GL1 2TH
  01452 425577
  e-mail: prow@gloucestershire.gov.uk
  www.gloucestershire.gov.uk

Other titles from Fineleaf

The Old Roads of South Herefordshire
By Heather Hurley
ISBN 978-0-9534437-4-1

Personalities of the Forest of Dean
By Henry G Nicholls, first published 1863
ISBN 978-0-9534437-2-7

Excursion from the Source of the Wye
By Mark Willett, first published 1810
ISBN 978-0-9534437-0-3

Treatise on Cyder-Making
By Hugh Stafford, first published 1753
ISBN 978-0-9557577-1-6

May Hill
Paintings and drawings by Valerie McLean
ISBN 978-0-9534437-8-9

Geology Explained in the Forest of Dean and Wye Valley
By William Dreghorn
ISBN 978-0-9534437-1-0

Geology Explained in the Severn Vale and Cotswolds
By William Dreghorn
ISBN 978-0-9534437-5-8

Geology Explained in South Wales
By T R Owen
ISBN 978-0-9534437-6-5

Geology Explained in the Lake District
By Robert Prosser
ISBN 978-0-9534437-7-2

Further landscape and art titles in preparation

Fineleaf Editions, 2009
www.fineleaf.co.uk